Spanning the Theory–Practice Divide in Library and Information Science

Bill Crowley

THE SCARECROW PRESS, INC.
Lanham, Maryland • Toronto • Oxford
2005

SCARECROW PRESS, INC.

Published in the United States of America
by Scarecrow Press, Inc.
A wholly owned subsidiary of
The Rowman & Littlefield Publishing Group, Inc.
4501 Forbes Boulevard, Suite 200, Lanham, Maryland 20706
www.scarecrowpress.com

PO Box 317
Oxford
OX2 9RU, UK

British Library Cataloguing in Publication Information Available

Library of Congress Cataloging-in-Publication Data

Crowley, William A., 1949–
  Spanning the theory–practice divide in library and information science /
Bill Crowley.
       p. cm.
  Includes bibliographical references and index.
  ISBN 0-8108-5165-2 (pbk. : alk. paper)
  1. Information science. 2. Library science. 3. Learning and scholarship.
I. Title.
  Z665.C786 2005
  020—dc22   2004014050

⊗™ The paper used in this publication meets the minimum requirements of
American National Standard for Information Sciences—Permanence of Paper
for Printed Library Materials, ANSI/NISO Z39.48-1992
Manufactured in the United States of America.

Contents

Preface

Mine is an optimistic book, written in the belief that the world works, even when troubled by pressing concerns demanding both attention and amelioration. I also believe that it is possible for human beings to develop theories to make the world work better, primarily through improving our ability to collaborate in identifying and solving problems. Here, I agree with the Canadian philosopher C. G. Prado that "progress in inquiry is possible in the sense that we get things more and more right as we elaborate and test hypotheses and descriptions."[1] As will become clear, I believe that such progress in theory building requires both an awareness of context and an acknowledgment of human limitations.

Throughout its pages, *Spanning the Theory–Practice Divide in Library and Information Science* seeks to engage the reader in the fascinating process of deriving theories from experience and using such theories in appropriate contexts. Readers already familiar with the topography of theory development will recognize that this approach is pragmatic in the broadest sense of the term. It is also an alternative to those aspects of postmodern theory that assert the impossibility of bridging such potential chasms as culture, language, gender, and class in order to define and solve common problems.[2]

My difficulties with such extreme variants of postmodernism aside, it would be irresponsible of me to underestimate such real, if negotiable, roadblocks as differences in language, custom, and culture. Communications problems are notorious even within the context of a single university where divergence in faculty perspectives and use of jargon often inhibit the exchange of ideas across disciplines.[3] However, the life histories of virtually all readers of this work are likely to be filled with memories of people communicating effectively. On a larger scale, it would be impossible to maintain local communities, nation-states, or international trade arrangements without the repeatedly demonstrated ability of individuals and cultures to communicate across their dissimilarities. As Steven Roger Fischer reminds us, productive exchanges across major national and geographic borders were often made possible through the development of "interlanguages," most notably such useful tongues as *lingua franca*, the medium through which Arab and European traders and other travelers often conversed in the Middle Ages, and Swahili, which served an equivalent role for nineteenth-century eastern Africa. More recently, we have seen the rise of International Standard English. This language, which is evolving independently of British, Australian, and American language rules, is becoming essential to a great deal of international trade and cross-cultural exchanges. It also demonstrates how understandings can be developed when spurred on by sufficient incentives.[4]

As a twenty-first-century work, *Spanning the Theory–Practice Divide* borrows freely, and with credit, from the historical or contemporary ideas of theorists, consultants, and practitioners in a number of disciplines and professions. Philosophically, it reflects my commitment to building upon insights offered by William James, John Dewey, Jane Addams, and more recent exponents of the value of pragmatism as a research philosophy. For reasons that will be explored in the appropriate chapters, I have termed this approach "cultural pragmatism." The differences that will be discussed between an emerging *cultural pragmatism* and variants of *classical pragmatism* should not to be taken as attacks on the philosophy's founding giants. They simply reflect the results of a hundred years of change, including changes in theory development. Such transformations have provided the successors of James, Dewey, and Addams with additional experience for generating and testing understandings of how the world actually works. For pragmatists, this is a clear plus, since deriving and testing ideas from and through the analysis of experience has nearly always been the essential component of pragmatic theory building.

At their best, pragmatists have learned to appreciate the humility of William James, that American intellectual giant of the late nineteenth

and twentieth centuries, who urged tolerance and charity for all involved in the scholarly enterprise.[5] In his search of the historical record,
James found repeated testimony regarding the "contradictory array of
opinions" for which "objective evidence and absolute certitude [have]
been claimed."[6] In other words, human lives are much too complex for
any one individual or research philosophy to claim sole ownership of
the "right" answers or even possession of the only research approaches
guaranteed to provide them.

Since the heyday of classical pragmatism, a period lasting from
shortly after 1900 to somewhere around World War II, researchers have
learned to analyze numerous sources of experience, not merely experience described by such adjectives as "American," "male," and "Protestant."[7] In addition to benefiting from a multicultural and cross-gender
spectrum of American research in theoretical information studies and
practical librarianship, I have drawn upon insights available in Canadian, European, and other English-language sources, most particularly
the higher education and social science literatures.[8]

In truth, modifying language to accommodate evolving understandings seems to be fully in accord with further advice from James. In his
posthumously published work, *Some Problems in Philosophy: A Beginning of an Introduction to Philosophy*, James advised us to "use concepts when they help, and drop them when they hinder understanding."[9]
As will be seen, I tend to follow James's advice to the theoretical letter.

Spanning the Theory–Practice Divide is a monograph with three fundamental purposes. First, it offers the reader an opportunity to develop
an understanding of why theory, in particular theory developed by university and college faculty, is too little used in the world outside of the
campus. Second, through analyzing the impact of recent technological,
social, economic, and political developments, it explores why it is in the
interest of faculty members, consultants, practitioners—and the general
public—to change the current situation. Third, drawing on a broad spectrum of research and theoretical insights, as well as my own experiences
as practitioner, consultant, and educator, it provides suggestions for
making academic research and theory more useful in nonacademic environments. In doing so, it also addresses a primary roadblock to
change—why theory that has little or no perceived relevance in off-
campus environments can be absolutely essential to advancing careers
in university contexts.

This book also deals with a reality that most theorists either disparage or, more likely, avoid discussing. It is a religiously influenced reality that would have undoubtedly challenged John Dewey's core belief in human progress while confirming William James's more insightful understanding of certain long-standing verities of human nature. Theory developers in the twenty-first century continue to operate in an environment, however globalized, where religious traditions provide fundamentally important explanations of how the world works to billions of people. What President Leon Botstein of Bard College termed the "early twentieth-century dream of a world of increasing secularization and the decline of the religious" has simply not come about.[10]

Whatever their attitudes toward religious explanations, twenty-first-century theory builders in materially advanced cultures, particularly those in the professions, humanities, and social sciences, now face a critical choice. As with many of their predecessors in the past century, researchers can continue to factor out the effects of religious understandings, in effect eliminating difficult-to-analyze "faith" factors, from the process of hypothesis formulation or model development. Such avoidance has a clear appeal. It serves to minimize intellectual discomfort for those theorists lacking a philosophical standpoint that has some level of interaction with those whose worldviews contain elements of divine revelation. But the price paid for such artificial intellectual comfort is likely to be the same as it was in the past—the production of less-than-useful theory.

The second alternative, to this writer the much more productive approach, is for secular scholars to recognize that the continuing relevance of religious experience makes it a source—one source among many—of the raw material for the development of effective theory. Admittedly, to assign religious traditions an intellectual status comparable to that of feminism, Marxism, postmodernism, or pragmatism for generating potentially useful and testable ideas is a stance that has the potential to offend the unshakably religious and the unfalteringly secular alike. Nevertheless, the price may be worth paying if it provides theorists with an expanded repertoire of useful concepts—ideas always subject to further testing through experience—for understanding the world. It is also an approach that is highly context relevant and will not be universally supported. Treating religious assertions as subject to testing and analysis is not likely to be encouraged in cultures where divine revelation is recognized as an unassailable source for answers to worldly problems. Yet, in advanced Western or other societies, a new flexibility toward religious analyses and answers is likely to be a positive. Where religions, philosophies, or ideologies still influence human actions, it only makes sense for scholars to surface and evaluate their precepts and assumptions to determine just how accurately they reflect the workings of the "real" world.

For cultural pragmatists, the existence of religious definitions of the world is simply another reality to be addressed in the ongoing effort to make campus-based and other theories useful in solving off-campus problems. The basis for this pragmatic confidence is actually quite simple. There are societies, including the American, where no tradition has the unchallenged power to enforce its understanding of the world. In such circumstances, reasonable people, with or without a religious component in their lives, are more likely to be open to accepting analyzed human experience as a useful guide to identifying problems and crafting their solutions. As will be explored, the key to such positive activity remains the development, acceptance, and use of a shared interlanguage embodying common understandings for defining problems and developing their potential solutions. As a step in advancing such communication, the author has developed an extended *glossary* to provide the reader with his understandings of the meaning of crucial concepts, particularly those concepts whose meanings are subject to debate among theorists.

This is a book without villains. There are long-standing and understandable reasons for the present mismatch between the imperatives of research and the needs of practice. Indeed, the causes of this divide are imbedded in the very process that brought higher education to its contemporary prominence. Consequently, although the divide can never be closed, it may in time be bridged.

Since I will be asserting a number of approaches for bridging the practitioner–theorist divide, it makes sense to provide readers with relevant information on my professional and theoretical background. Readers who are practitioners may value the fact that I have twenty-three years of "real world" experience in New York, Alabama, Indiana, and Ohio, including work as a reference librarian, public relations representative, consultant, multitype cooperative administrator, and state government division head (deputy state librarian). Fellow academics may have a particular understanding for the 1993 midcareer epiphany that led me to enroll as a full-time student at Ohio University in Athens, earn a PhD in higher education in two years, and spend a third year as a researcher for the university's president emeritus. My degrees also include an MA in English from Ohio State University with a thesis in occupational folklore, an MS in library service from Columbia University, and a BA in history from Hunter College of the City University of New York. While such eclecticism is a bit of an academic sin, it really is a plus for an interdisciplinary work such as this that no two degrees are in the same field or from the same institution.

I have published or copublished in journals with historic library affiliations and in others with a stronger affiliation with the less defined domain of information studies, as well as in the higher education literature. In the process, I have addressed such topics as the process of developing local government information policies, the present and future status of the academic librarian in Canadian and American universities, the growth of higher education in Namibia, American legislative activism, and the competition between "library" and "information" in graduate education. For many years I was active in professional associations, including service as chair of the State Library Agency Section of the American Library Association's Association of Specialized and Cooperative Library Agencies. In 1996 I joined the faculty of Dominican University's Graduate School of Library and Information Science. Dominican University is a twenty-acre jewel in River Forest, Illinois, my colleagues are first-rate, and our students insist that classroom theorizing be at least minimally relevant to their professional lives.

There are a number of primary audiences for *Spanning the Theory–Practice Divide*. A critical part of the potential readership consists of faculty, consultants, practitioners, and students in the diverse and multiplying fields concerned with information, knowledge management, librarianship, and school library media. This is the division of modern culture where I have spent the greater part of my adult life and with whose problems I am most familiar. Yet, these are fields where the conflicts among and between faculty theorists and off-campus practitioners are so intense that there exists no mutually acceptable language for their discussion. There are disagreements among the many "information" worlds defined by faculty theorists and substantial portions of the "library" environments cherished by many practitioners. Whenever

I teach Introduction to Library and Information Science, I am confronted by the reality that I am helping to educate librarians, information specialists, knowledge managers, school library media specialists, competitive data analysts, web masters, and others whose working lives are not easily described by a single term. Of late, even the phrase "information studies" has acquired a certain dated air. Nonetheless, with the realization that librarians, attorneys, physicians, and other professionals retain their primary identities when discussing the information component of their work, "information studies" will be used when something close to a generic term has to be employed to identify a common concern for data, information, knowledge, and (perhaps) wisdom.

This work's analysis of the ongoing conflict between theorists and practitioners should be appealing to another important component of this work's potential readership. Here I refer to practitioners, educators, consultants, and students in the field of higher education. This is the same area where Ohio University awarded me a PhD. It is also the field whose theoretical lenses helped provide me with the necessary analytical distance for considering issues in the overlapping intellectual domains shared by so many with a concern for information and knowledge.

The field of higher education has an acknowledged responsibility, albeit one occasionally challenged by sociology and other disciplines, to study academic environments. However, the academic world's many and differing contexts contain yet further components of the potential audience for this book—scholars, consultants, and students in other programs of professional education supported by the modern university. Since I have freely borrowed from the literatures of such fields and disciplines while writing *Spanning the Theory–Practice Divide*, I view it as only proper to offer to return the favor.

The final audience for this work, no less important, consists of the proverbial "educated readers." In their capacities as taxpayers or members of the broader university and civil societies, such readers ought to be concerned with the relevance of the "products" of higher education to the broader context of national life.

Although readers will find citations to the literatures of various other countries in this book, it is overwhelmingly grounded in the broad, multicultural context and subcontexts that characterize the United States in the early part of the twenty-first century. As already noted, I am a cultural pragmatist. For that label to mean anything at all, it must stand for the belief that scholarship is often more or less context dependent even as it strives for relevance in larger environments. Briefly stated, the problem definitions, analyses, arguments, and solutions advanced in *Spanning the Theory–Practice Divide* are most applicable to the national and subnational contexts of the United States. Nevertheless, they are likely to retain considerable validity in circumstances, such as those found in Canada and much of Europe, where contemporary variants of historic "town–gown" tensions most resemble those in American environments.

The publication of this book follows a rewrite of almost monumental proportions. This effort was fundamentally advanced by the extensive and perceptive assistance provided by the anonymous reviewers, even when such aid was conveyed with a pungency that might have distressed the charitable William James. A particularly strong debt is owed to editor Sue Easun. In addition to her extensive duties as acquisitions editor of Scarecrow Press, Sue volunteered to help craft this book, knowing that it addresses a number of difficult questions and is inevitably going to discomfort many educators and practitioners alike.

In circumstances calling for extensive change, a sense of humor tends to be a most welcome asset. Consultants, whether employed full-time or working on a part-time basis, learn to cultivate this quality after observing how even the most insightful observations and recommendations can be ignored or buried by clients. I would not be surprised if a number of these worldly-wise individuals took a special joy in reading *Spanning the Theory–Practice Divide*. This reaction will be particularly likely if they scrutinize the book with the history of private and public sector consulting in the back of their minds. Such experience repeatedly demonstrates a fascinating paradox—people can legitimately be open to considering a range of dramatic change yet inevitably adopt only those recommendations that preserve or advance some version of things as they currently exist. It's not deceit or self-delusion at work; it's only the operation of human nature.

Still, every so often, things do change and for the better. It is the hope of such change that lies at the foundation of this book.

NOTES

1. C. G. Prado in *The Limits of Pragmatism* (Atlantic Highlands, NJ: Humanities Press International, 1987), 89. I also endorse Prado's commonsense questions: "Why should we think that an epistemology, an account of knowl-

edge, must be universally applicable? Why should we think that an account of knowledge in science, for example, must serve us as well—must be the same account—as one in history or ethics?" (vii).

2. See, for example, the analyses in Paul Diesing, *How Does Social Science Work? Reflections on Practice* (Pittsburgh: University of Pittsburgh Press, 1991); Jean-Francois Lyotard, *The Postmodern Condition: A Report on Knowledge,* trans. Geoff Bennington and Brian Massumi (Minneapolis: University of Minnesota Press, 1979); Alasdair MacIntyre, *Whose Justice? Which Rationality?* (Notre Dame, IN: University of Notre Dame Press, 1988); and Pauline Marie Rosenau, *Post-Modernism and the Social Sciences: Insights, Inroads, and Intrusions* (Princeton, NJ: Princeton University Press, 1992).

3. Tony Becher, *Academic Tribes and Territories: Intellectual Enquiry and the Cultures of Disciplines* (Buckingham, UK: Society for Research into Higher Education/Open University Press, 1989).

4. Steven Roger Fischer, *A History of Language* (London: Reaktion, 1999), 126, 132, 136, 178–79, 217–18.

5. See Gerald E. Myers, *William James: His Life and Thought* (New Haven, CT: Yale University Press, 1986), for a first-rate consideration of the life of James as both a man and a theorist.

6. William James, "The Will to Believe," in *The Writings of William James: A Comprehensive Edition,* ed. John J. McDermott (Chicago: University of Chicago Press, 1977), 726.

7. See, for example, the concerns raised in Mary B. Mahowald's "What Classical American Philosophers Missed: Jane Addams, Critical Pragmatism, and Cultural Feminism," *Journal of Value Inquiry* 31, no. 1 (March 1997): 39–54.

8. See, for example, Becher's *Academic Tribes and Territories*; Cynthia Hardy's *The Politics of Collegiality: Retrenchment Strategies in Canadian Universities* (Montreal: McGill-Queen's University Press, 1996); Edwin G. West's *Higher Education in Canada: An Analysis* (Vancouver, BC: Fraser Institute, 1988); and many of the fine papers in *Skill and Education: Reflection and Experience,* edited by Bo Goranzon and Magnus Florin (London: Springer-Verlag, 1992).

9. William James, *Some Problems of Philosophy: A Beginning of an Introduction to Philosophy* (1911; reprint, Cambridge: Harvard University Press, 1979), 98–97; quoted in Bruce Wilshire, "The Breathtaking Intimacy of the Material World: William James's Last Thoughts," in *The Cambridge Companion to William James,* ed. Ruth Anna Putnam (Cambridge: Cambridge University Press, 1997), 113.

10. Leon Botstein, "Some Thoughts on Curriculum and Change," in *Rethinking Liberal Education,* ed. Nicholas H. Farnham and Adam Yarmolinsky (New York: Oxford University Press, 1996), 56.

Acknowledgments

I presented a number of the concepts developed in chapter 4, in a preliminary form, at the 1999 annual conference of the Association for Library and Information Science Education (ALISE). This presentation was subsequently published as "Building Useful Theory: Tacit Knowledge, Practitioner Reports, and the Culture of LIS Inquiry" in the fall 1999 conference issue (volume 40, number 4) of the *Journal of Education for Library and Information Science*.

The extended book development process wouldn't have been possible without the hard work and continuing commitment of Norman Horrocks and Sue Easun. Their dedication, as well as the expertise of the anonymous reviewers, turned initial ideas into a completed volume. Additional appreciation is expressed to Kellie Hagan for her fine production editing.

Finally, this book is dedicated to my wife, Theresa Van Gundy Crowley, a truly remarkable human being whose intelligence, integrity, commitment, and patience form an ongoing inspiration.

Chapter One

Theorizing for Diverging Contexts

Why Research Results and Theory Development Are So Little Used Outside the Campus

SCENARIO: "THE PEOPLE IN THE AUDIENCE ONLY HAVE MASTER'S DEGREES"

Why another book on theory? The easiest way to address this question is to describe what followed when a longtime friend walked into my office. Beth (not her real name) has a PhD from a distinguished university, years of relevant experience in the "real" world, and a solid reputation in her part of the United States. When this incident occurred, Beth's PhD studies were barely completed and she had just returned from presenting the results of her research—actually a copresentation, delivered with the professor who had been her academic advisor—at a national conference of working professionals. Normally, speaking engagements of this sort can be significant in developing a professional career. Consultants and academics alike learn quickly that well-received talks are valuable for enhancing professional visibility. For consultants, national conferences often provide a more-than-reasonable speaker's fee, and the publicity and exposure may enhance the odds of winning future contracts from decision makers sitting in the audience. Academics more often than not speak free of charge. In their early years they believe, with reason, that a presentation can lead to, or derive from, publications that will help them achieve promotion and tenure. Later on, a judicious mixture of presentation and publication is a necessity when a professor wants to maintain influence in matters affecting her or his field of expertise.

1

But Beth shared no such tale of triumph. Too upset to sit, she walked around the office venting frustration that started at the conference and deepened on the plane ride home. The practitioners in the hall had formed a difficult audience. Among those who stayed for the whole session, there were a significant number who dismissed Beth and her copresenter's research as being "just another academic effort" and "out of touch with the real world." Having failed miserably in front of a few audiences myself, I was nodding in painful empathy. Then she surprised me by repeating the conclusion of her academic copresenter. "We can never expect them to understand our work," the professor emphasized. "You have to remember, most of the people in the audience only have master's degrees."

One gauge of the raw intensity of Beth's frustration was the fact that she shared this story with me, a master's degreed practitioner then years away from starting my own doctoral studies. Belatedly, she recognized the insult embedded in her words and reddened. Since the affront was unintentional, I smiled and accepted her claim that she didn't share her copresenter's views.

It's been a while since this incident, and my own understanding of its meaning has evolved. Looking at the incident from a faculty perspective, I want to stress my belief that it was highly unlikely that Beth's copresenter intended to slander the 450,000-plus individuals who earn master's degrees in any given year, or the millions more whose MA, MBA, MSW, MLIS, MIS, MS, or comparable master's degrees have helped launch effective professional careers.[1] More likely, she was trying to articulate, albeit less than diplomatically, a fundamental truth. *Even within a single "national" culture, university faculty members and nonacademic professionals in the world outside the campus exist within divergent subcultures.* As such, their careers are often guided by very different rules. The result is a structural and contextual chasm that must be bridged by any academician seeking to make her or his teaching, research, and consulting "practitioner relevant." To recall a perceptive assessment by the sociologist Harvey Molotch, the worlds of professors are often restricted by the very nature of higher education. Faculty, he wrote, "do not hang around commodity trading floors, or holy roller churches, or exclusive golf clubs." Instead, they busy their time attending committee meetings, worrying about teaching loads, and participating in a peer review system that attempts to fit proposed articles and books within academic standard and, on rare occasions, may be found writing essays bemoaning the irrelevance of their ideas outside of higher education environments. In Molotch's words, professors are so involved in their academic contexts that they lack time "for walking through the world."[2] The result of this separation from the "real world" is a recurring paradox: faculty develop theories rewarded by fellow academics but rejected by practitioners whose off-campus lives such theories claim to explain.

WHAT IS "USEFUL"?

The negative reception of Beth's academic presentation by its practitioner audience is not entirely unexpected. Practitioners and consultants, most of whom operate outside of a university context, often see no reason to embrace research that their own experience judges irrelevant. Sue Ellen Christian, a public health reporter with the *Chicago Tribune*, underscores this point:

> Once science leaves the narrow construct of the laboratory and hits the streets, it runs through a complex filter of culture and society, and is forever changed. When released into homes and villages, science is scrutinized against the yardstick of common sense, not the measure of peer review. It is weighed against current mores and personal history and the experiences of relatives and friends. It is shaped by the science that has come before it, and by the politics of distrust.[3]

At the same time, concerns over the university world's ability to "connect" with its larger society have intensified. The positive lure of an Internet economy, as well as an increasing mismatch between the subjects of doctoral degrees and the academic job market, annually send many would-be faculty out of higher education and into corporate, government, and nonprofit agency positions.[4] Whatever the resulting benefits, the culture shock can be disconcerting for those who have sacrificed much to earn a PhD, only to exit the university world with such advice as "Do not use the title *Doctor* unless it is appropriate for the job you are seeking, and even then, use it sparingly" or "You can head off employer stereotypes [about PhD holders] by anticipating them."[5]

Beth's negative encounter characterizes a long-standing dispute over whether or not faculty research can and should be judged on its relevance to practitioner concerns. Patrick T. Terenzini's 1995 presidential address to the Association for the Study of Higher Education was devoted to an examination of the "gulf between higher education research and the worlds of policy and practice."[6] My own field, increasingly referred to by faculty as some variant of *information studies*—to the irritation of a number of off-campus *library* practitioners—possesses a substantial body of literature that illustrates an enduring concern over this clash between the academic environment and off-campus world.[7] In the field of *social work*, Norman A. Polansky's classic consideration of the irrelevance of much of its literature argues that the dominance of faculty-produced publications in professional journals works *against* the best interests of a "practitioner field" because of the following:

- Faculty are driven by the need to "publish or perish." As a result, concern for job security, not relevance to the worlds of practice, is often the force behind theory development.
- If theory for a professional field is going to be relevant, it needs to be developed by those who are "directly engaged with clients."
- After practitioners gain a certain level of expertise, they are in the best position to develop theory since the "main source of believable *new* ideas is one's clientele, not reading."
- Distance from actual practice gives faculty an unfortunate "illusion of certainty."
- Institutions of higher education are better envisioned more as "repositories of knowledge in professions . . . than creators of it."[8]

What is particularly fascinating about Polansky's assertions regarding the need for more theoretical contributions by practitioners to the professional literature—presumably displacing articles and books produced by faculty—is that he wrote them as a regent's professor emeritus with the University of Georgia.

The field of law has been a battleground over the disassociation of faculty research and publication from the everyday needs of legal practice.[9] One measure of the split between the world of "the academy" (academic shorthand for "higher education") and the many worlds of practice is the proposal by Meir Dan-Cohen that legal scholars should, in effect, pay no attention to legal practitioners and "simply talk to one another" over issues of substance. In Dan-Cohen's proposed scholarly world, legal practitioners should not expect scholars to communicate directly with them. Instead, practitioners should accept the role of an audience for a theatrical production of sorts where the legal scholars, as actors on an intellectual stage, ignore the audience and concentrate on "creating and inhabiting the make-believe world within which their fictional discourse is conducted."[10]

Taken to their logical conclusion, Dan-Cohen's arguments suggest that academic legal scholars should be concerned only with each other. Admittedly, the practitioners sitting in the metaphorical "audience" still have to be entertained. But such entertainment is clearly secondary, a by-product of faculty-to-faculty theoretical interaction. Within Dan-Cohen's extended metaphor, the possibility that others involved with legal issues—such as judges or other decision makers—might find something of interest in the journals that publish faculty exchanges is, more or less, an unexpected bonus.

The academic field of business administration or management science is regularly criticized for being irrelevant to many of the communities that hire its graduates, even as MBA degrees from elite institutions continue to function as "golden passports" for would-be corporate executives.[11] However, the *contemporary problem* of business school irrelevance to practice, ironically, seems to be a direct result of implementing a solution to a *prior problem*—business schools being viewed as too vocationally oriented and out of step with the university world. The solution to this earlier problem, as described by researcher Sydney Ann Halpern, involved hiring faculty with PhDs from other disciplines in order to bring business school research more in line with scholarship in disciplines with more-rigorous research traditions.[12] Decades ago, sociologist Robert K. Merton described such unlooked-for outcomes as the "unanticipated consequences of purposive social action" and stressed that such developments may even change the values that led to the search for a solution to the original problem.[13]

In the 1950s, business schools may have prided themselves on their close relationships with business practitioners. Today, the full-time faculty members of such schools are more likely to adhere to productivity norms that are shared not with business practitioners but with academic colleagues in the university's other fields and disciplines. In *Gravy Training: Inside the Business of Business Schools*, journalists Stuart Crainer and Des Dearlove explore a range of problems that result when business faculty adhere too closely to a university reward system that privileges research that is irrelevant to "real-life" concerns.[14] To this end, the authors quote Frank Morgan of North Carolina's Kenan-Flagler business school, who stresses that a "successful career at a business school" requires "at 95 percent or more, a publication record that isn't relevant to the practicing manager and doesn't advance knowledge very far."[15] Such publications are usually ignored by practitioners and may be incomprehensible to academics in other fields. However, they are usually the key to securing the prized academic goal of tenure, particularly in research university environments.

The irony that theory totally removed from the world of everyday affairs can be remarkably "useful" to its developer reflects both the fragmentation of the academic world and its inability—or unwillingness—to engage with the practical concerns of the larger society. Yet the matter is even more complex. As noted, academics often do not understand other academics, even within the same discipline. In preparing for his 1987 Ryerson Lecture at the University of Chicago, literary theorist Wayne C. Booth spent several months interviewing other professors across his campus, trying to discover how much they could understand about one another's work. His measure of such comprehension was a simple question. Booth asked his colleagues, all of whom had achieved some level of success at a world-class university, "Could you, given a week's warning, read an article or book in a given field and then enter into a serious dialogue with the author at a level of understanding the author would take as roughly comparable to his or her own?"[16] The responses provided by Booth's university colleagues were overwhelmingly negative. They include:

- the claim by one philosopher that no one else at the university could understand his work
- an admission by a "world-famous" mathematician that he "cannot follow the proofs offered by most mathematicians"
- a revelation by the editor of a biology journal that he understands only about half of the articles he publishes

According to Booth, such lack of understanding produces a context where, "when one eavesdrops on a group of experts in a given field, talking about experts in other fields, one hears a lot of contemptuous dismissal."[17]

In a context where publications are critically important to promotion and tenure, yet may not be understood by colleagues even within one's own university or department, university promotion and tenure committees are frequently reduced to counting raw numbers of publications instead of evaluating their intrinsic worth.[18] When the theories of colleagues are so often incomprehensible to fellow academics, is it any wonder that off-campus practitioners seldom use those same theories for guidance in their professional lives?

WHAT IS "USEFUL" THEORY?

Yet, this book was not written to bemoan the academic past or present. Rather it seeks to promote the development of useful theory for the future benefit of faculty, consultants, and practitioners. *Useful theories, whether they are termed "theories," "hypotheses," "models," "slogans," or "aphorisms," are mental constructions that reflect, to some degree, "how things work" in real-world contexts.* From the point of view of cultural pragmatism, practitioners are correct not to accept any theoretical claim about how the world operates at face value. Instead, pragmatic theorists urge that theories be judged on how well they answer some variant of the question "Does using this theory or model in this context improve effectiveness in defining and solving relevant problems?" Public library practitioners, for example, may be receptive to faculty theories or consulting recommendations that enhance effectiveness in planning when the contemporary work patterns of adults appear to affect access by their children to library programs. Knowledge management practitioners may be similarly receptive to faculty-generated theories regarding how they might address the impact of variant national cultures on staff willingness to use centralized information sources in a globalized environment. Theories in these and other areas are likely to be seen as worth testing if they offer a realistic possibility of solving service problems in community or worldwide environments.

For cultural pragmatists, theory development is an ongoing process, and the true test of any theory is always analyzed experience. Ideally, such experience is part of an ongoing planning, implementation, and evaluation process, as well as being based on a shared interlanguage or mutually acceptable repertoire of common understandings about the world. Pragmatists are comfortable with testing their theories and the theories of others in a variety of contexts. Such theories are modified as necessary and ought to be discarded when other concepts prove more effective. Over time, even with the occasional tendency of theory developers to defend their creations regardless of the opposing evidence, the process of theory development is expected to progress and produce concepts that come as close as humanly possible to describing how portions of the world actually function. The best theory predicts; it does not merely describe.

Ironically, Dan-Cohen's "legal theory on the stage" scenario, where practitioners are seen as having little to do as theories are argued among academic researchers, is of enormous help to those who would craft solutions. A problem that is not defined is often a problem that cannot be solved. By advocating that the faculty–practitioner intellectual divide be intensified, Dan-Cohen forcefully highlights the extent of the problem. In the end, however, his argument in favor of abandoning efforts to bridge the gulf between researcher theories and practitioner realities is a self-defeating approach. It bodes little good and much ill for the university world's relationship to its supporting culture. When Dan-Cohen argues against theory relevance, he also repudiates the broad, evolving compact under which American culture agrees to maintain its higher education institutions. In the process, he also provides a superb case in point for those who argue against the societal value of spending always-limited resources to support what appear to be self-absorbed faculty researchers.

Faculty research irrelevance exists because it is sustained by university cultures. Even what the off-campus world might see as the most "impractical" work of scholarship becomes immensely relevant for the researcher involved if it serves to advance a faculty member's reputation, earn promotion and tenure, or lead to the offer of a position with the university of her or his dreams. Available time in higher education environments is more limited than nonacademics might imagine. Teaching, advising, and committee work often leave little opportunity for research, particularly if an academic seeks anything near a normal family life. As a result, when facing career milestones, an aspiring faculty member may choose to concentrate on producing a body of published work designed primarily to catch the positive attention of publication-counting peers.

In *Gravy Training*'s well-analyzed attack on business schools, Crainer and Dearlove termed the reliance on publications as the basis for rewarding faculty as "grand paper clip counting exercises that stand up to demands for academic rigor but fail to add one iota to the real sum of human knowledge."[19] "Fail to add one iota" hyperbole aside, these investigative reporters extensively document that the present reward system forces business school professors to produce research that is of little value off campus.

The defects in Crainer and Dearlove's otherwise useful analysis result from the authors' failure to put the problems of business schools into adequate historical context. As a result, they fail to appreciate that current problems of irrelevance are the consequences of earlier efforts at reform. In the 1950s, business schools were viewed as being too vocationally oriented and lacking in intellectual rigor. The solution to that problem was to seek academic respectability through such approaches as rewarding scholarship and employing PhDs from other disciplines who possessed a strong research orientation. Business schools achieved academic respectability through successfully embracing university standards that value research technique over off-campus utility. To now condemn success in adhering to academic norms reflects a lack of appreciation for context and, worse, is likely to be unproductive of needed change. A more positive approach, for business schools as well as a wide spectrum of other professional programs, is to encourage universities, colleges, schools, and departments to modify the reward structures of higher education to encourage both academic rigor and off-campus relevance.

Arguably, faculty members in the developed nations are more or less free to research virtually any topic in their fields or disciplines that attracts their interest. While this freedom of inquiry has a number of practical limits, in that the results of inquiries must meet the same academic norms for publication that foster real-world irrelevance, the stakes are even higher when someone else is asked to pay for the effort. Players in the game of academic funding often have their own priorities. The public, whose taxes and tuition payments support so much of the academic enterprise, prefers professors to be teaching. Thus, powerful chairs of state senate appropriations committees fall prey to endorsing popular sentiment when they argue that "universities should start increasing course loads for professors to free up money for additional full-time teaching slots and should redirect resources from research to teaching."[20]

The demands on government treasuries or family investment portfolios inevitably exceed the dollars available to meet demands. It is thus understandable that legislators and taxpayers, whose own effectiveness may be judged through biannual election cycles, annual tax bills, or quarterly profit and loss statements, may want measurable results from faculty research in roughly equivalent time spans. This approach naturally favors applied fields such as computer science or biochemistry that generate products with a more readily discernable impact on daily lives. Areas such as the humanities, social sciences, and many professions— where proving cause and effect between what is taught and what is effective on a daily basis in off-campus environments can be much more difficult—are likely to suffer through such measurement. Even when faculty success cannot readily be gauged by new treatments for disease, next-generation software upgrades, or emerging technologies to reduce pollution, the idea of accountability for the expenditure of government or tuition dollars still has great appeal to the larger society. At a time where Booth's findings at the University of Chicago regarding the incomprehensibility of faculty research even to colleagues could be replicated throughout higher education, faculty are increasingly likely to be pressured to produce something "tangible." The obvious response to such demands is for scholars to forgo research and theory development without a market impact in favor of teaching courses and offering degrees that "equip" students for employment.

This is a world increasingly characterized by *globalization*, a process that harnesses the dynamics of multinational corporations to new telecommunications infrastructures. It is an environment where nonacademic decision makers are likely to prefer funding research programs and scholarly projects explainable to taxpayers as worthwhile investments for enhancing economic productivity and creating jobs. According to Sheila Slaughter and Larry L. Leslie, who analyzed the national higher education and research policies of Australia, Canada, the United Kingdom, and the United States, fields close to the market, such as biotechnology, computers, and electronics, gain financial support, even as areas such as languages, arts, and education fall behind in obtaining resources from university and government sources.[21]

Such negative government policies regarding entire fields and disciplines where faculty research and teach have their echoes in the corporate, for-profit sector. Paco Underhill, author of *Why We Buy: The Sci-*

ence of Shopping and a self-described "urban geographer and retail an-thropologist," is the founder of Envirosell, "a research and consulting firm that advises a blue-chip collection of Fortune 100 companies."[22] In describing why his firm moved away from hiring graduate environ-mental psychology students, Underhill stressed that these employees had "come to the job burdened with textbook theories they wanted to apply." For a source of personnel less blinded by speculative lenses, En-virosell turned to writers, artists, and actors who have "no theories to uphold or demolish."[23] It should be stressed that Underhill's preferred labor source—"writers, artists, and actors"—consists of those who "do." He made no mention whatsoever of hiring would-be literary crit-ics, art historians, or others who create and use theory in an effort to place "doing" in a larger cultural context.

Given that the irrelevance of much faculty theory and research is now a truism, the public and its elected or appointed decision makers feel free to ignore even relevant faculty findings in making decisions crucial to American society. In an article entitled "In the Nation's Battle against Drug Abuse, Scholars Have More Insight Than Influence," D. W. Miller stressed, "Although scholars have learned a lot about effective therapies for drug dependency, their findings often do not influence the providers who treat drug addiction in this country, or the policy makers who de-cide how to wage the battle against drug abuse."[24]

Decades ago, Robert K. Merton—in an essay entitled "Role of the In-tellectual in a Bureaucracy"—offered a still-viable explanation for the reluctance of the larger society to embrace many university findings. For Merton, "intellectuals" were often outsiders in bureaucratic envi-ronments where effective change has to be generated from within. That such structures have an inherent bias against change is only an addi-tional complication.[25] It is a contention of this book that the lessons found in Merton's essay will need to be applied to higher education it-self. The development of useful or effective theory in university envi-ronments will require changing faculty-supported—and largely faculty-controlled—rewards systems. It will also require examining the logic behind such systems and why they maintain their appeal to researchers, even as they are increasingly seen as problematical by the larger culture. This is particularly the case in those fields and disciplines without a di-rect connection to student or societal success in globalized market en-vironments.

In the nation's major research universities, faculty members are often rewarded on the basis of standards that privilege the quantity of published works over their quality. The usefulness of theory in off-campus environments is far less important for many researchers than the reality that published theory, however irrelevant, can be submitted for counting by on-campus promotion and tenure committees. The resulting situation is broadly negative, since it "shortchanges teaching and service as well as research."[26]

This lack of relevance of research and theory outside the academy is a persistent concern for those who believe that demonstrating the practical usefulness of higher education's theories in the larger world would provide a stronger claim on American society's support. Unfortunately, attempts to examine the relevance of the current system of theory development have produced negative results. Such was the case in *Why Sociology Does Not Apply: A Study of the Use of Sociology in Public Policy*, where Robert A. Scott and Arnold R. Shore found the discipline of sociology to be one where researchers deliver "results that address theoretical issues of likely interest to their professional colleagues, but which seem to carry no discernable or practically useful implications for policy."[27]

Similarly, faculty research and theory development on a broader scale were found wanting in *Research Policies for the Social and Behavioral Sciences*.[28] Prepared by the nonpartisan Congressional Research Service of the Library of Congress, the report brought new understandings of the gulf between social science research and policy making:

> It may be that some expectations for using behavioral and social science research directly in policymaking do not recognize the many obstacles both to the production of policy-relevant knowledge and also to its application in complex processes of bureaucratic and political decisionmaking. Some of these obstacles that affect researchers are discussed in this report. They include: producing counterintuitive findings, producing research which is irrelevant to policymaking, political naivete regarding bureaucratic functioning and the vagaries of political decisionmaking, conflicts stemming from the need to respond to the academic reward system which may differ from the rewards of policy-advising, inadequate knowledge and inappropriate quantification, and fraud and deception.[29]

All in all, this laundry list of research irrelevance produced by the Congressional Research Service seems almost overwhelming. It bespeaks an intellectual divide composed of "obstacles," "naivete," and "conflicts" that brings to mind more the intense misunderstandings of the average high school cafeteria than the opportunities for information sharing that ought to be prevalent in a nation characterized by greatly expanded opportunities for higher education.

GAME PLAYING, PROBLEM SOLVING, AND SEVERAL COMMON FALLACIES

If understood as a game, exchanges limited to theorists can be intellectually stimulating. Real problems tend to result only when university faculty, forgetting that they are academic practitioners writing for other academic practitioners, embrace what might be termed the *fallacy of the academic lens*, that is, *the erroneous assumption that a faculty member who follows academic norms for "good" research will inevitably produce findings useful to practitioners in the worlds outside of the university.*

The sources of this fallacy are not all negative. At times, it can and should be seen a theoretical version of "wishful thinking." Faculty concentrating on "academic" research in order to advance a career may find it reassuring to believe, however inaccurately, that all or much of the labor involved with research and writing will transcend personal self-interest to serve a larger "good." Unfortunately, the continued unwillingness of both professionals and the general public to use much faculty research demonstrates why this hope is more often a fallacy.

Not surprisingly, the fallacy of the academic lens has its parallel in what might be termed the *fallacy of public expectations*. Occasionally embraced by funding sources and practitioners "outside" of higher education contexts, the fallacy of public expectations holds *that only the unjustifiable intransigence of university and college faculty prevents the production of useful research.* What is "useful," in the terms of this fallacy, tends to be defined by those outside of the university in terms of their own self-interest. Businesses see "useful" in terms of their own products. Governors and state legislators may tend to define usefulness in terms of what contributes to the economy of their states or districts.

Cultural pragmatism accepts the fundamental premise of *classical pragmatism* that consequences are the "necessary tests of the validity of propositions."[30] With due allowance for the fact that some concepts are more difficult to test than others, this normally means that an assertion is true "in theory" to the degree that it produces results in the "real world," however defined. In addition, cultural pragmatism holds that through whatever means a theory is developed, its application is always context dependent, even though some contexts are or can be made larger than others. Here, it is well to keep in mind John Dewey's warning "that neglect of context is the greatest single disaster which philosophic thinking [theorizing] can incur" and equally appropriate to understand that contextual relevance in theory development is increasingly difficult to sustain in larger and more complex environments.[31] More recently, Patrick Wilson provided the reminder, "Like the clothes one wears, the food one eats, the accent and vocabulary of one's speech, so also the things one is informed about and the questions on which one has views are influenced by social location."[32] The often conflicting demands of the "social locations" from which faculty researchers generate theory (the academic environment)—and the multiple contexts in which consultants and practitioners are urged to use such faculty theory (the rest of the world)—can reflect very different realities. These differences are such that proactive means have to be devised and implemented to bridge the resulting intellectual and contextual "gaps."

"Better" theory contributes to *effectiveness*, generally through facilitating *prediction*, which in turn involves specifying a "context," such as a culture, nation, neighborhood, profession, or institution within which whatever is envisioned by the theory developer will or will not take place.

CONSTRUCTING AND COMMUNICATING USEFUL THEORY

In the complex and varying arenas that constitute human cultures, "good" theory advances *understanding*. But theory is just one source of understanding among many. Outside the university, competitors to faculty-generated theory, such as models fashioned from common sense, religious beliefs, explicit knowledge learned in school, and tacit knowledge discovered on the job, all vie to provide explanations of what is happening in the world. The uses of "classic" theory or the historically privileged insights of disciplinary giants, the proverbial "dead Germans," will be discussed further in chapter 3.[33]

However, remembering that "good," "better," and "contextual" criteria must be applied to even classical theory makes it easier to bring renowned insights into play when discussing contemporary concerns. In such use, the age or even the reputation of intellectual formulations is far less important than their present workability. Take, for example, one of the early nineteenth-century achievements of John Stuart Mill. Arguably, Mill's well-known "appraisals" of volumes 1 and 2 of Alexis de Tocqueville's *Democracy in America* retain their value as significant contributions to understanding nineteenth-century American mores while assisting in the analysis of their twenty-first-century counterparts.[34] These "appraisals" also provide the reader with a third and subtler intellectual bonus: they confound arguments regarding *incommensurability*, the perceived inability of humans to communicate effectively with one another due to a lack of common standards for meaning and other shared foundations.

When his nineteenth-century English phrasing is updated, a number of Mill's concepts remain remarkably pertinent for those who would develop useful theory for American audiences. Fundamental to the effectiveness of such theory is what he emphasizes as American resistance to intellectual subservience. A contemporary elaboration of Mill's thought, recast in the form of maxims, would counsel faculty, consultants, practitioners, and all others seeking to develop theory for the "real" American world to do the following:

Recognize that "commonsense" perceptions often determine the acceptability of theory. Personal and group experiences constitute a powerful cultural lens for judging the validity of any theory in the American context.

Emphasize theory effectiveness, not how theory may enhance understanding. With numerous sources of understanding available, the demonstration of results is much more persuasive to American audiences.

Accept the limited recognition accorded to academic authority. Theory developed by those with advanced degrees and impressive institutional affiliations is handicapped in competing with theory crafted by those who can demonstrate relevant experience. This is particularly so if such experience has resulted in financial success or in the achievement of other culturally supported aims.

Use common speech, not academic jargon, for communication.
   Where necessary, work with practitioners to develop an interlanguage for bridging the variant understandings within the university
   and the nonacademic world.[35]
**Accept the fact that religion and values play strong roles in American
   life.** Although society in the United States has evolved from Christian
   through Judeo-Christian to Judeo-Christian-Islamic-Buddhist, and so
   on, the possible influence of religious beliefs and values on both private and public decisions should never be underestimated.[36]

To scholars and practitioners familiar with American culture, there is
little that is "new" in these truisms. That many university researchers
nevertheless ignore them, or their equivalents, should not be seen as an
accusation of widespread and deliberate deceit or even as an indictment
alleging willful ignorance. Rather, it is a frustrating situation that flows
from the condition of being an "academic practitioner."
   The resistance to applying academic theory to wider contexts continues even as faculty, through national systems of mass higher education,
regularly proselytize on the value of their ideas in real and virtual classrooms of captive student audiences. However, in an essay entitled "Social Science as Public Opinion," sociologist Edward Shils notes only a
limited success with such efforts, since the theories of social science
could never replace the critical role of "direct experience as the basis for
assessing concrete situations."[37]
   Shils's assertions do not augur well for public reception of the intellectual products of much of the university. Increased access to higher
education has exposed many more Americans to the tenets of the social
sciences—and by implication, other university-based disciplines. Yet,
the roles played by the life experiences of these individuals in helping
to restructure, amend, and distort these academic formulations only underscores the lack of match that often exists between faculty theories
and off-campus environments.[38]

CROSSING BORDERS

The professions that shape so much of contemporary American society,
including the academic professions, still allow individuals to "practice"
in multiple contexts. For example, full-time faculty members—who are

by definition "practitioners" in higher education contexts—have always consulted in the wider world. Similarly, nonacademic practitioners have often taught in universities on an adjunct or part-time basis. In many cases, full-time knowledge managers, attorneys, librarians, and social workers teach part-time and use vacation days to operate a consulting business. By their very nature, many medical school appointments carry with them the expectation of practice in university hospitals, at times supplemented by a professor's willingness to volunteer in community clinics. It is not unknown for professors of law to maintain a private practice or, less profitably, to take an active role in law clinics affiliated with their schools.

Faculty-developed theory is frequently useless for field practitioners because it is often created to meet the expectations of higher education. The chances for applying such theory with success off campus are minimal unless such use meets the rules for judging effectiveness that govern the new environment. From the point of view of transferring theory outside the university, Dan-Cohen's insights regarding law school faculty are applicable to comparable exchanges among faculty across the fields, disciplines, and professions, including business, higher education, information studies, and the various aspects of evolving librarianship. Faculty publications, electronic or hard copy, are largely self-referential works written by insiders for insiders and using insider language. In addressing the issue of usefulness, the question is whether the theory–practice gap should be intensified or diminished. Dan-Cohen's position appears to celebrate the very existence of the divide. But is such a celebration warranted?

Exploring the gulf between faculty theories and practitioner realities will require entering contested territory where the reader may be faced with the always difficult task of giving up "long-standing convictions in the face of contrary evidence."[39] Assertions that it is higher education's fault when theory generated for success in the university is not adopted elsewhere are unlikely to be received with universal acclaim. For those who labor to produce usable theory, it is difficult to come to terms with the reality that much of the nonuniversity world sees academic rules for theory development as being (1) broken and (2) inapplicable outside of higher education contexts.

Analyzing the causes leading to the separation of faculty-generated theory from the practical requirements of consultants and the realities of building-level practitioners is a bit like trying to fill in a crossword puzzle.

This is the metaphor advanced by Susan Haack as being more appropriate for modeling standards of empirical evidence than trying to establish benchmarks comparable to mathematical proofs.[40] In Haack's words, and in my own view, the search for answers is likely to involve variations on the category of "supportive-but-less-than-conclusive evidence."[41]

For theorists, the inability to know that that our theories actually do reflect reality, however defined, is not a preferred situation. Still, this lack of certainty and closure should be viewed not as a source for despondency but as a welcome challenge. For example, famed nineteenth-century theologian and academic leader John Henry Newman could and did accept the possibility—in nontheological matters—that "in a particular instance, it might easily happen, that what is only second best is best practically, because what is actually best is out of the question."[42]

Newman's counsel that *second best* may well be the *practical best* is enormously helpful when discussing the development of useful research and theory. Inherent in the very concept of practical best theory—*which I will henceforth refer to as "useful theory"*—is an ongoing reminder of both human limitations and the need for appropriate modesty in advancing abstract claims. At some point, the most effectively analyzed experience, even when coupled with the latest in computer-enhanced reasoning, will fail to generate accepted explanations or fall short in predicting new occurrences.

Humans, whether theorizing in faculty, consultant, or practitioner environments, often function with an uneasy balance in motivations. The first and most obvious reason for theorizing is the need to solve actual problems. A second reason, perhaps equally positive, is professional and personal ambition. Admittedly, such ambition can be seen in American culture as conflicting with a more idealized commitment to advancing the interests of humanity. In consequence, it has tended to be less admitted to in public forums as a driving motivation. However, in the same American culture, there is an honored place for those who do well for themselves as a *by-product* of benefiting the larger society. The folk saying that someone "did well while doing good" quite nicely captures this fine distinction.[43]

However motivations are defined, or defended, it is fairly well accepted that many theorists want to solve problems in ways that earn them recognition for achievement from colleagues and, ideally, acceptance as a leader in their intellectual field.[44] It is not unknown for theorists to dream of being spoken of or written about by colleagues or rivals in the same context as Charles Darwin, John Dewey, Marie Curie, or Albert Einstein. Unfortunately, the sustained originality required for the theoretical breakthroughs necessary for such recognition may not be supported by a rewards system marked by rigid tenure and promotion deadlines, a system that often privileges quantity over quality in publications that report research and/or expound on theory. The compelling need to publish thus encourages theorists to hypothesize beyond the evidence, to assert the applicability of cherished concepts even in contexts where their relevance is, at best, uncertain.[45]

In retrospect, it is highly likely that the story of my friend Beth and her academic mentor—whose account of research findings being rejected by practitioners was narrated at the beginning of this chapter—embodies a common failing of academic theoreticians. Practitioner-relevant research and theory development, when done "right," tends to be heavily resource intensive. Beth and her faculty mentor lacked the dollars and time necessary to insure that their findings were applicable over a substantial part of the numerous local contexts represented by the members of their audience. In generalizing beyond what their evidence could support, they took a calculated risk and found themselves contradicted by the professional experience of their audience members. The result, as already discussed, was far from a happy experience for all involved.

The adoption of a pragmatic or other research philosophy as a foundation for research can play a useful role in minimizing such nonproductive encounters. For example, had Beth and her mentor followed pragmatic norms, they might not have yielded to the temptation to theorize beyond the evidence. They might even have presented their findings in a manner that would have invited the sharing of contrary experiences from their audience. Almost by self-definition, cultural or other pragmatists are likely to be less exposed to the temptation to overgeneralize. Theoretical modesty—the awareness of the critical importance of context—is embedded in their own intellectual history. Decades ago, John Dewey labeled ignoring contextual limitations as the *fallacy of unlimited extension or universalization* and observed: "When context is taken into account, it is seen that every generalization occurs under limiting conditions set by the contextual situation. When this fact is passed over or thrown out of court, a principle valid under specifiable conditions is perforce extended without limit."[46]

If cultural pragmatism is rooted in the theoretical modesty symbolized by the phrase "useful theory," just what sort of theory is represented? Briefly, it can be described by borrowing the first component of Alfred North Whitehead's twofold aim of science—"the production of theory which agrees with experience."[47] Under present understandings, such an observation necessarily argues for elaborating on the implications of such related questions as "Whose experience?" "In what context?" and "As understood by whom?"

With these caveats in place, it is possible to consider the present separation of the academic world from off-campus contexts. Arguably, this "town–gown" divorce was the result of a number of efforts to redefine the purpose of higher education that extended throughout much of the nineteenth and twentieth centuries. Among these struggles was the reverse crusade to eliminate religious, specifically Protestant, control of the nation's major universities and the triumph of the faculty research model over the alternatives ideals of teaching and service.[48]

Analysis of the research–teaching dichotomy also requires considerable attention to nuance since the nature of the divide has been immensely complicated by American culture's inability to decide what it really wants. This society demands successful research to cure disease and poverty, even as it argues that teaching the next generation of students must be *the* priority of the modern university. In seeking to bridge this divide, it is again useful to visit the competing fallacies that are in play.

As discussed above, scholars may be unconsciously or consciously operating under the fallacy of the academic lens, the erroneous assumption that a faculty member who follows academic norms for "good" research will inevitably produce findings useful to practitioners in the worlds outside of the university. For their part, members of the public may be embracing the counterpart fallacy of public expectations, which holds that only the unjustifiable intransigence of university and college faculty prevents the production of useful research. The logical extension of this fallacy is the public's view that recalcitrant faculty, faculty who do not produce anything "useful" in their research, ought to have their duties redefined. Such a redefinition usually entails redirecting faculty time from research into teaching, since increasing the teaching load offers more measurable components such as courses, grades, credits, and degrees.

THE SITUATION IN INFORMATION STUDIES AND
LIBRARY, INFORMATION, AND KNOWLEDGE PRACTICE

As with other fields and disciplines, there are numerous roadblocks to the development of "useful theory" for what many faculty theorists see as the vast and overarching field variously termed "information studies" or "information science." However, the situation here may actually be less amenable to the development of faculty theory useful to off-campus environments. In addition to the expected differences among theorists and practitioners that naturally flow from variations in working environments, the "information" field — if it is a single field — seems to be losing a common language for communication.

For most of the twentieth century, when knowledge was not electronically distributed but printed in books, journals, and reports, "information studies" was not a formally defined area of study, particularly in American and Canadian universities. Virtually by default, the academic area logically connected to information use and analysis was "librarianship" or "library science." In this more compact intellectual world, there often existed a common language for exchanges among many faculty members and numerous off-campus practitioners. In effect an interlanguage, this basis of exchange was created from understandings developed and passed on through shared, or at least related, professional experiences. Since such experience was valued as a teaching tool, it was expected that library school faculty members would work as practitioners before taking higher education positions. As a result, a valuable part of their class instruction consisted of passing on what they had learned in the "real world," supplemented by new knowledge gleaned through consulting, professional reading, attendance at conferences, and so on. Also contributing to the relative ease in faculty–practitioner communication was the reality that most "library schools" did not focus much on research and theory development but concentrated on the education of future professionals for academic, public, school, and special libraries (corporate, medical, law, and so forth).

In a number of cases, experienced practitioners turned "library" faculty taught with only the same master's degree credential earned by practitioners. Along with research and publication, a doctorate — although valued by the employing higher education institution — was seen as being of less importance to library schools than maintaining connections with the worlds of professional practice. This situation changed with the rise of "library" PhD programs in the latter half of the twentieth century. Since research toward a dissertation is an essential part of most doctoral study, "library schools" supporting such study generated a counter-dynamic that was more in accord with university expectations and less in touch with day-to-day practitioner issues. Through the process known as "academic drift," many "library" PhDs educated at elite institutions who secured faculty appointments in less-prestigious schools brought the research and publication imperatives of their doctoral programs to their new employers.[49] The result was a lessening of norms shared with off-campus practitioners and a greater sense of connection with PhDs in other departments of the university.

This distancing of library educators from practitioners could and did result in significant changes in faculty perspectives. As far back as 1933, Pierce Butler—a professor at the University of Chicago's Graduate Library School (the first "library" doctoral program)—described a fundamental division between theory and practice at a time when librarianship was attempting to grow into "library science."[50] Butler is scathing, if myopic, in his diagnosis of the reasons why practicing librarians do not use the results of faculty research. He declares that the librarian has a "unique immunity" to curiosity, stands alone in the "simplicity of his [or her] pragmatism," and satisfies any existing intellectual interest through rationalizing "each immediate technical process by itself."[51]

Even at this relatively early date, Butler's uncharitable, indeed misguided, analysis serves to underscore the nature of the chasm, particularly at the elite university level, separating the values prized by higher education and those upheld by many practitioners in the contemporary "competitive analysis," "library," "information," "knowledge management," and "school library media" professions. The chasm's growth through the twentieth century may have been the primary reason why the University of Chicago's Graduate Library School closed in January 1989. In one of the more perceptive analyses of this program termination, the Columbia University Review Committee for the School of Library Service attributed the cessation of library education at Chicago, at bottom, to "the divorce of the School's research activities from what the profession perceived as its needs for training."[52]

There is a timely, if perhaps inadvertent, irony in the fact that the members of the same Columbia University committee that so aptly summarized the reasons for the Chicago "failure" also provided critical arguments used by their university provost to secure board approval for the subsequent closing of Columbia University's own School of Library Service in June 1990. However, the primary reasons advanced for the Columbia termination were diametrically opposed to those cited for the closing at Chicago. According to "official" university documents and other sources, "library" education at Columbia was eliminated by the university administration on the basis of the university's fiscal priorities and the "low prestige and even negative reputation of library schools," as well as the fierce opposition of the tenured faculty to repeated demands that they

- sever long-standing ties to all library communities, excepting academic and special librarians, and reorient priorities to support the needs of the newly emerging information communities
- deemphasize professionally relevant education and practitioner connections to privilege "research, particularly in the areas of information science and the management of complex institutions"
- become, in the administration's view, a transformational school capable of leading an Ivy League institution into the promising, if yet to be determined, information future[53]

.

The shutdown of the Columbia University School of Library Service program, although relatively rapid once the decision was made, actually terminated a struggle between the university administration and the library service faculty extending through much of the 1980s. It was only after two separate committees studied the issue, and it became clear that the library school faculty would not cooperate in advancing the administration's research-oriented "information" agenda at the sacrifice of practitioners' "library" interests, that the provost and president ended effective debate and secured board approval to close the school.

The conflicts and ultimate closures at the University of Chicago and Columbia University are useful in illustrating how the values privileged by faculty in some elite institutions (expanding knowledge through research and publication) can differ from the standards prized by practitioners (relevant professional education). However, the Columbia example is particularly illustrative in that it highlights a fundamental conflict that is capable of tainting even "useful theory"—the real possibility that the research interests of many faculty now so diverge from the realities of many (but far from all) practitioners that the groups involved have lost a common language for communication.

On a multi-institutional basis, the gap between theorist and practitioner expectations is described by Charles R. McClure as follows:

> Library researchers would like to think that their studies have had an impact and cannot understand why library decision-makers ignore all that "good research" in the professional literature. And library decision-makers repeatedly dismiss that literature and ask researchers to deal with more meaningful topics and produce results with direct application for their library.[54]

McClure goes on to stress that "the ongoing issue, however, is to demonstrate, in fact, that research *does* [emphasis in original] improve overall library effectiveness." For him, the solution involves expanding the dialogue on solving the problem through the active involvement of "decision-makers, researchers, professional associations, schools of library/information science, and funding agencies."[55]

Although I endorse this emphasis on dialogue, I also believe that researchers and practitioners will simply talk past one another unless their communication is grounded in shared understandings. For practitioners, a start to such concurrence begins with accepting the reality that even faculty research deemed "useless" outside of the university can advance on-campus goals. As stressed by McClure, "irrelevant" research can have considerable valuable when it helps faculty achieve their goals of promotion and tenure or otherwise meets the demands of their university employer.[56]

For their part, university-based researchers must understand the cultural realities that describe how research must be shaped in order to be received by practitioners. Here, it is useful to revisit the five aphorisms offered as possible guides to advance the acceptability of academic research, which were derived earlier from John Stuart Mill's "appraisal" of volume 2 of Alexis de Tocqueville's *Democracy in America*. These aphorisms include the need for theorists to (1) recognize that "commonsense" perceptions often determine the acceptability of theory; (2) emphasize theory effectiveness, not how theory may enhance understanding; (3) accept the limited recognition accorded to academic authority; (4) use common speech, not academic jargon, for communication; and (5) accept the fact that religion and values play strong roles in American life.

If considered only after the fact, the realities summarized by these aphorisms cannot assist in theory relevance. As "mental recipes," they are designed to guide the development of theory, not merely to direct its subsequent dissemination. When research is completed and a theory is derived from or confirmed by the results, it is usually far too late to seek the advice of those who are expected to use the theory to solve problems in their own lives. This caution is fundamental. It is almost inevitably the case that the contexts within which theories are developed differ from the contexts in which theories are supposed to be applied. Unless researchers and practitioners are speaking the same "language" and share similar understandings, there exists little hope for bridging the perceptual gaps that separate the university and the nonacademic world.

As noted, the problem of crafting a shared language to support the development and use of theory among researchers, consultants, and practitioners may be uniquely difficult to solve within "information studies," a context where faculty interests are often perceived to differ widely from practitioner issues in "librarianship," "knowledge management," "school library media," or even "competitive data analysis." Much of this disconnection can be traced to a demonstrable variance in contexts and language. Within the university world, the direction of theoretical movement has been to subsume "library" under "information." In 1964, Don R. Swanson of the University of Chicago could claim that "information science" was an "integral part of library science." Marcia J. Bates of the University of California, Los Angeles, would assert precisely the reverse in 1999.[57]

Notwithstanding academic realities, among practitioner communities the subsuming of "library" under "information" has not been universally accepted.[58] John N. Berry III, editor in chief of *Library Journal*, a publication that is particularly influential among various "library" communities, writes for many library practitioners, some known personally by this author, when he editorializes, "We owe no allegiance to this upstart, academically challenged discipline of 'information.'"[59]

Readers with a background in, or familiarity with, the history of higher education are doubtlessly aware that faculty theorists, consultants, and off-campus practitioners are on shaky intellectual ground when insisting that a given unit be termed a "library," "library and information science," "information," or "knowledge management" department, school, or college. There has always been an element of fashion and a felt need to project relevance in the ongoing renaming of academic programs. In the universities of the Middle Ages, for example, everything but law, medicine, and theology tended to be subsumed under philosophy. Over centuries, the growth in new knowledge led to increased faculty specialization and new disciplinary languages in various academic environments. To adapt and extend a phrase of Roger Blumberg's, such academic divergences frequently represented "expedient partitions of academic culture."[60] By definition, "expedient partitions" can and do change when those who support them find it advantageous to do so.

The evidence is clear: in the information—knowledge—library and media fields we currently lack accepted methods for developing, expressing, and testing theoretical understandings among the divergent contexts occupied by faculty, consultants, and practitioners. Central to this present work is a proposed process for bridging theoretical divides through the negotiation of interlanguages to facilitate collaboration among such groups. With such an aim, it must be acknowledged in advance that my use of "information studies" in this work as a descriptor for the complex and ever-evolving spectrum of business, information, knowledge, library, media, and scientific professions that deal with "information" in myriad research and practitioner environments threatens to provide the reader with an example of what *not* to do. Some practitioners in "library" and "knowledge" environments view the term "information studies" as too limiting to reflect their full professional interests. It may well be the case that theorists seeking to involve practitioners in defining and solving emerging questions in such environments, under certain circumstances, may need to minimize "information" language and embrace "knowledge" or "library" languages in order to make progress in defining and solving problems without alienating potential collaborators.

CHAPTER SUMMARY

Chapter 1 began with a recounting by Beth of how the results of faculty research and theory were dismissed by an audience of "real-world" practitioners as irrelevant to their working lives. In examining the causes of this disconnection, the chapter explored how university faculty members and nonacademic professionals in the world outside the campus exist within divergent subcultures. Each such culture, it was noted, has different standards for judging both relevance and success, standards that are seldom accepted in other domains.

The chapter also explored pragmatic lenses through which the public has historically judged the worth of academic research—standards that value the results of practitioner experience over rarefied concepts, and theory that is useful in actually solving problems over theory that provides another type of understanding among many. It described a practitioner world that limits deference to academic authority, emphasizes effectiveness in communication through shared languages, and even accords religious belief a role in facilitating public and private understandings and decisions. The general public's often-demonstrated preference for "useful theories," that is, theories, hypotheses, models, slogans, aphorisms, or other mental constructions that reflect, to some degree, "how things work" in real-world contexts, was also stressed. The critical test of theories—"Does using this theory or model in this context improve effectiveness in defining and solving relevant problems?"—was also examined.

Finally, the chapter examined the reception of theory produced by the academic field of "information studies" in the numerous practitioner information, knowledge, library, and media communities. In addition to examining the negative (if expected) reception accorded faculty-generated theory by practitioners in a number of fields and disciplines, the chapter explored the additional strains on theory development and reception that result when theorists and practitioners lack a common language for discussing mutual interests.

NOTES

1. The figure on master's degrees is taken from "Earned Degrees Conferred, 2000–2001," *Chronicle of Higher Education* 50, no. 1 (August 29, 2003): 19.

2. Harvey Molotch, "Going Out," *Sociological Forum* 9 (1994): 231.

3. Sue Ellen Christian, "When Culture, Medicine Don't Quite Cooperate," *Chicago Tribune*, May 7, 2000.

4. See, for example, the annual "almanac issues" of the *Chronicle of Higher Education*, for data on the approximately forty thousand earned doctorates awarded annually, and such essays as Michele Tepper's "Doctor Outsider," *Minnesota Review* 50–51 (Spring/Fall 1988): 257–62.

5. Howard Figler, "Succeeding in the Nonacademic Job Market," in English Showalter et al., *The MLA Guide to the Job Search: A Handbook for Departments and for PhDs and PhD Candidates in English and Foreign Languages* (New York: Modern Language Association of America, 1996), 83.

6. Patrick T. Terenzini, "Presidential Address: Rediscovering Roots: Public Policy and Higher Education Research," *Review of Higher Education* 20, no. 1 (1995), 7.

7. For arguments in favor of more practitioner-relevant research, see Daniel O'Connor and J. Philip Mulvaney's "LIS Faculty Research and Expectations of the Academic Culture versus the Needs of the Practitioner," *Journal of Education for Library and Information Science* 37 (Fall 1996): 306–16. A work challenging the usefulness of modern "positivist" approaches but rejecting conventional research relevance in favor of a critical theory approach to American society is Michael H. Harris's "The Dialectic of Defeat: Antimonies in Research in Library and Information Science," *Library Trends* 34 (Winter 1986): 515–31. Finally, a classic statement against "practitioner friendly" definitions of relevance remains L. Houser and Alvin M. Schrader's *The Search for a Scientific Profession: Library Science Education in the U.S. and Canada* (Metuchen, NJ: Scarecrow Press, 1978).

8. Norman A. Polansky, "There Is Nothing So Practical as a Good Theory," *Child Welfare* 65 (January/February 1986): 14.

9. Here, the interested reader might find much to ponder in the extended analyses contained in both Arthur Austin's *The Empire Strikes Back: Outsiders and the Struggle over Legal Education* (New York: New York University Press, 1998) and Anthony T. Kronman's *The Lost Lawyer: Failing Ideals of the Legal Profession* (Cambridge, MA: Belknap Press/Harvard University Press, 1993).

10. Meir Dan-Cohen, "Listeners and Eavesdroppers: Substantive Legal Theory and Its Audience," *University of Colorado Law Review* (1992), 569, 590, 591.

11. John Van Maanen has written a classic account of the value of the MBA degree from elite universities in "Golden Passports: Managerial Socialization and Graduate Education," *Review of Higher Education* 6 (Summer 1983): 435–55.

12. Sydney Ann Halpern, "Professional Schools in the American University," in *The Academic Profession: National, Disciplinary, and Institutional Settings*, ed. Burton R. Clark (Berkeley: University of California Press, 1987), 313–14.

13. Robert K. Merton, "The Unanticipated Consequences of Purposive Social Action," *American Sociological Review* 1 (1936): 894.

14. Stuart Crainer and Des Dearlove, *Gravy Training: Inside the Business of Business Schools* (San Francisco: Jossey-Bass, 1999), 39.

15. Frank Morgan, quoted in Crainer and Dearlove, *Gravy Training*, 255.

16. Wayne C. Booth, "The Idea of a University—as Seen by a Rhetorician," in *The Vocation of a Teacher: Rhetorical Occasions, 1967–1988* (Chicago: University of Chicago Press, 1988), 312.

17. Booth, "Idea," 313–14.

18. Ernest L. Boyer, *Scholarship Reconsidered: Priorities of the Professoriate* (Princeton, NJ: Carnegie Foundation for the Advancement of Teaching, 1990), 33.

19. Crainer and Dearlove, *Gravy Training*, 39.

20. The views of Steve Rauschenberger (R-Elgin), then chair of the Senate Appropriations Committee of Illinois, are reported by Meg McSherry Breslin in "Trend toward Temporary Faculty Worries U. of I.—Officials Fear School's Reputation Could Suffer," *Chicago Tribune*, April 9, 2000.

21. Sheila Slaughter and Larry L. Leslie, *Academic Capitalism: Politics, Policies, and the Entrepreneurial University* (Baltimore: Johns Hopkins University Press, 1997), 38, 61.

22. Paco Underhill, *Why We Buy: The Science of Shopping* (New York: Simon and Schuster, 1999), 256.

23. Underhill, *Why We Buy*, 13–14.

24. D. W. Miller, "In the Nation's Battle against Drug Abuse, Scholars Have More Insight Than Influence," *Chronicle of Higher Education* 46, no. 33 (April 21, 2000): A19.

25. Robert K. Merton, "Role of the Intellectual in Bureaucracy," in *Social Theory and Social Structure*, enl. ed. (New York: Free Press, 1968), 271.

26. Charles E. Glassick, Mary Taylor Huber, and Gene I. Maeroff, *Scholarship Assessed: Evaluation of the Professoriate* (San Francisco: Jossey-Bass, 1997), 20.

27. Robert A. Scott and Arnold R. Shore, *Why Sociology Does Not Apply: A Study of the Use of Sociology in Public Policy* (New York: Elsevier, 1979), ix.

28. House Committee on Science and Technology, Task Force on Science Policy, *Research Policies for the Social and Behavioral Sciences*, report prepared by the Library of Congress Congressional Research Service, 99th Cong., 2d sess., 1986, *Science Policy Study Background Report No. 6*.

29. House Committee on Science and Technology, *Research Policies*, 4.

30. John Dewey, *Logic: The Theory of Inquiry*, in *John Dewey: The Later Works, 1925–1953, vol. 12, 1938*, ed. Jo Ann Boydston (Carbondale: Southern Illinois University Press, 1986), 4.

31. John Dewey, "Context and Thought," in *John Dewey: The Later Works, 1925–1953, vol. 6, 1931–1932*, ed. Jo Ann Boydston (Carbondale: Southern Illinois University Press, 1985), 11.

32. Patrick Wilson, *Second-Hand Knowledge: An Inquiry into Cognitive Authority* (Westport, CT: Greenwood Press, 1983), 149.

33. See the discussion in Sydney J. Pierce, "Dead Germans and the Theory of Librarianship," *American Libraries*, September 1992, 641–43.

34. See John Stuart Mill, "Introduction: An Appraisal of Volume I of *Democracy in America*, Published in the London (and Westminster) Review in 1835 on the Occasion of the First Appearance of the English Translation," in Alexis de Tocqueville, *Democracy in America*, vol. 1 (New York: Schocken

30 Chapter One

Books, 1961), and "Introduction: An Appraisal of Volume II of *Democracy in America*, Published in the Edinburgh Review in 1840 on the Occasion of the First Appearance of the English Translation," in Alexis de Tocqueville, *Democracy in America*, vol. 2 (New York: Schocken Books, 1961).

35. Steven Roger Fischer, *A History of Language* (London: Reaktion, 1999), 178.

36. See Mill, "Introduction: An Appraisal of Volume II," particularly xxix.

37. Edward Shils, "Social Science as Public Opinion," in *The Calling of Sociology and Other Essays on the Pursuit of Learning* (Chicago: University of Chicago Press, 1980), 461.

38. Shils, "Social Science," 462.

39. Susan Haack, "Concern for Truth: What It Means, Why It Matters," *Annals of the New York Academy of Science* 775 (1996): 60.

40. Susan Haack, "Puzzling Out Science," *Academic Questions* 8, no. 2 (Spring 1995): 24.

41. Haack, "Puzzling Out Science."

42. John Henry Newman, *The Idea of a University*, ed. Frank N. Turner (New Haven, CT: Yale University Press, 1996), 20.

43. For an exploration of the positive functioning of such bourgeois values as "altruistic egoism" in the American context, see Robert B. Young, *No Neutral Ground: Standing By the Values We Prize in Higher Education* (San Francisco: Jossey-Bass, 1997), particularly 136–39.

44. A classic examination of the complex motivations for success among academic chemists is found in Karin D. Knorr, "Producing and Reproducing Knowledge: Descriptive or Constructive? Towards a Model of Research Production," *Social Science Information* 16, no. 6 (1977): 669–96. Of equal interest is dean of science Whitney J. Owen's argument in favor of piecemeal publication in order to make tenure within rigid academic rules, as recounted in her "In Defense of the Least Publishable Unit," *Chronicle of Higher Education* (February 13, 2004).

45. For a useful assessment of how the present system of "peer review" can undermine creativity in theory development and publication, see Benjamin D. Singer, "The Criterial Crisis of the Academic World," *Sociological Inquiry* 50 (1989): 127–43.

46. Dewey, "Context and Thought," 8.

47. Whitehead's second aim of science is "the explanation of commonsense concepts of nature, at least in their main outlines." See Alfred North Whitehead, *The Aims of Education and Other Essays* (New York: Free Press, 1929), 124.

48. These processes have not always been simple or productive of the intended results. For example, although recognizing that religious control of the mainstream of higher education "is all now in the past," political theorist Charles W. Anderson reasons that the banishment process may have gone too far. For Anderson, it makes "no sense at all" to exclude religious perspectives in teaching students

about finding "meaning in the universe." See Charles W. Anderson, *Prescribing the Life of the Mind: An Essay on the Purpose of the University, the Aims of Liberal Education, the Competence of Citizens, and the Cultivation of Practical Reason* (Madison: University of Wisconsin Press, 1993), 118–20.

49. For a discussion of "academic drift," see Burton R. Clark, *The Academic Life: Small Worlds, Different Worlds* (Princeton, NJ: Carnegie Foundation for the Advancement of Teaching, 1987), 143.

50. Pierce Butler, *An Introduction to Library Science* (Chicago: University of Chicago Press, 1933).

51. Butler, *Introduction*, xi–xii.

52. Roger S. Bagnall, *Report of the Review Committee for the School of Library Service* (New York: Columbia University, 1990), 5.

53. Bagnall, *Report*, 1–22 passim. Also, see Jonathan R. Cole, "Balancing Acts: Dilemmas of Choice Facing Research Universities," *Daedalus* 122, no. 4 (Fall 1993): 1–36; Jonathan R. Cole, *Report of the Provost on the School of Library Service at Columbia* (New York: Columbia University, 1990); and Catherine Thorpe, "School of Library Service to Close—Trustees: School to Be Phased Out in Two Years," *Columbia Summer Spectator*, June 6, 1990.

54. Charles R. McClure, "Increasing the Usefulness of Research for Library Managers: Propositions, Issues, and Strategies," *Library Trends* 38, no. 2 (Fall 1989): 281.

55. McClure, "Increasing," 292–93; emphasis in original.

56. McClure, "Increasing," 290.

57. See Don R. Swanson, introduction to *The Intellectual Foundations of Library Education: The Twenty-Ninth Annual Conference of the Graduate Library School, July 6–8, 1964*, ed. Don R. Swanson (Chicago: University of Chicago Press, 1965), 2–3; and Marcia J. Bates, "The Invisible Substrate of Information Science," *Journal of the American Society for Information Science* 50, no. 12 (October 1999): 1043–50.

58. See, for example, Dorothy M. Broderick, "Turning Library into a Dirty Word: A Rant," *Library Journal*, July 1997, 42–43; Michael Gorman, *Our Enduring Values: Librarianship in the Twenty-First Century* (Chicago: American Library Association, 2002), in particular the strong attack on "information science" on pages 67–72; and Wayne A. Wiegand, "Misreading LIS Education," *Library Journal*, June 15, 1997, 36–38.

59. John N. Berry III, "We Must Have *Library* Education," *Library Journal*, February 15, 1998, 82.

60. Roger B. Blumberg, "Ex Libris," *The Sciences* 35 (September/October 1995): 16.

Chapter Two

Developing a Research Philosophy

SCENARIO: THE VIEWS OF
A SWEDISH MASTER CABINETMAKER

Some of the more significant explorations of the roles of tacit knowledge in working lives are now under way outside North America. Books edited or coedited by Bo Goranzon of the Swedish Institute for Worklife Research, for example, are of particular value in the development of useful theory. One such publication, *Skill, Technology, and Enlightenment: On Practical Philosophy*, contains the declaration of master cabinetmaker Thomas Tempte, "I assure you: there is no dialogue between theory and practice!"[1] This negative evaluation is from a practitioner who strongly desires such exchanges. Earlier, in his remarks to a 1993 Stockholm conference, Tempte observed:

> A dialog between theory and practice creates energy. A monologue or one-sided imbibing of one of them creates stagnation. Perhaps I am naïve, but I believe in the power of this dialogue to create understanding. I have found that it works. I have been asked many times to give lectures, or to teach with compendium and slides. But that is exactly what I do not have to offer. Come and visit me instead at my workshop, look around my woodyard and storeroom. Or come out with me in the forest and I'll show you the trees that can be felled for different purposes. At this point, interest usually wanes, a sure sign that the practitioner's knowledge is of no great value. Of course there are many explanations for this—but, there it is. To me it would be unthinkable to leave my profession as yet and travel

around, talking. TALKING about it. One day perhaps, when age has taken its toll and I'm old and decrepit.[2]

Master Tempte seems to be asserting several things: First, there appear to be echoes of the old divide between "merely talking about it" and "actually doing it," or the aphorism "Those who can, do; those who can't, teach; those who can't teach, teach the teachers." It was hardly a compliment to the academics in his audience when Tempte suggested that he might talk about his work in a higher education environment when he was too old to actually do it. In addition, he may have demonstrated the workings of the fallacy of public expectations in attributing negative attitudes toward practitioners to faculty who request that he visit their classrooms instead of bringing their students to his workplace or, perhaps, even analyzing his creative process through the on-site study and extended one-to-one discussions often used to capture tacit knowledge. As discussed in chapter 1, the fallacy of public expectations holds that only the unjustifiable intransigence of university and college faculty prevents the production of useful research. In this fallacy, those outside the university define the conditions for determining what is or is not "useful."

The problems inherent in the fallacy of public expectations are many. Here, I will note that the fallacy is often based on an erroneous understanding of the duties required of university faculty. In the workaholic American environment, where a forty-hour week is often on the low side, the public may define the "problem" of faculty "jobs" as consisting only of hours spent with students in a classroom or lab. When framed this way, faculty time on task seems to range from twenty-five or thirty hours to perhaps three or fewer hours per week. These figures could lead almost anyone outside of higher education to wonder if professors really are underworked and overpaid. However, if university faculty were framing the analysis of the workload problem, the result would be quite different. When time spent on all faculty duties is analyzed, the total might be fifty or more hours per week—spent teaching, preparing to teach, researching, writing, mentoring newer faculty, recruiting students, advising new or continuing students, keeping up with the practitioner and faculty literatures, conducting committee work, evaluating university programs, and attending to other responsibilities.

HOW WE REALLY THINK

The previous chapter introduced the commonsense idea—now buttressed by research and theory—that people exist and think in an incredibly wide spectrum of contexts, each of which has its own rules for success. In their work *Induction: Processes of Inference, Learning, and Discovery,* John H. Holland, Keith J. Holyoak, Richard E. Nisbett, and Paul R. Thagard address the workings of context on the individual level. They note that new intellectual formulations, including theories offered by academic researchers, face strong challenges from existing, internalized models that already provide people with more or less effective notions of how their "worlds" actually work. For these authors, "people reliably distort the new rules in the direction of the old ones, or ignore them altogether except in the highly specific domains in which they were taught."[3] This reminder is offered as the basis for humility in teaching and theory development, since academics can reasonably expect their students to use what they teach, including their most prized theories, in real or virtual classrooms. They simply have no guarantee that these models will have any impact at all years after graduation.

Holland and his colleagues had the advantage of drawing on extended research from psychology, philosophy, artificial intelligence, biology, statistics, and other related fields. They concluded that individuals use *induction*, or "all inferential processes that expand knowledge in the face of uncertainty," to solve the "ill defined sorts of problems which abound in real life," in part, through the use of *condition-action* rules. These rules, which are *encoded* in our mental processes, have the form "IF such-and-such, THEN so-and-so." At the individual level, such rules are derived from both experiences and formal instruction. Rules are often associated in clusters and function more as suggestions than as commands. They are relatively slow to change and seem to be modified to the least extent necessary to address new situations. As rule clusters, they tend to be activated simultaneously to provide a provisional *model* of a given situation. They are in constant competition with one another to *predict* what will come next and what, if anything, ought to be done about it. Further, in the competition to become active, such rules "bid" for opportunities to "post their messages." The persuasiveness of a rule bid is "a function of its strength, the specificity of its conditions, and the support it receives from the messages that match it." Throughout, "analogy, particularly in the guise of metaphor, is a subtle, powerful, inductive process . . . which imports experience to less familiar domains from other domains, to provide plausible hypotheses and plans."[4]

The details of the mental "framework" offered by Holland and colleagues are too rich for a mere summary to do them justice. However, it is possible to take from the work a number of advisories, both explicit and tacit, that need to be kept in mind by anyone attempting to develop theory:

- Although "external agents" can suggest new rules, the minds of students, practitioners, and others are not blank slates on which teachers and theorists can inscribe such rules with the expectation that they will govern behavior. New rules offered by teachers and researchers will often be ignored because they are unable to "compete effectively with the old, well-established intuitive rules that are entrenched in the [individual's] default hierarchy."[5]
- Survival and success in our various cultures do not require great concern for "coherent views of the world" and "scientifically accurate theories." Most of the time people are merely trying to "generate accurate predictions for whatever portion of the world they are focusing on at the moment." Individuals can and do have conflicting beliefs at various levels of their rule "default hierarchy."[6]
- Our idealized values hold that people should be thought of as individuals and not in terms of group stereotypes. However, when we lack information about past behavior on the *individual level*, "the default values we have for people of that person's *kind* are the preferred, indeed often the only, basis for making a prediction about the person." Fortunately, even weak information on individuals will override information based on group stereotypes.[7]
- The view of learning as involving rules in competition "suggests that strong rules learned in childhood will not be forgotten or replaced by subsequent learning." Rather, people will continue to be guided by these early rules when, from an individual point of view, such early rules are: effective in describing the current situation (*match*), have a history of being useful (*strength*), provide the most complete description of the present situation (*specificity*), and are most in accord with other rules currently active in one's mind (*support*). In such circumstances the adage that "the child is the father to the man" is both complicated and affirmed. The rules learned as children will be found in all men and women, competing with rules acquired as adults in ongoing efforts to solve problems, understand cultures, or envision the world in general.[8]

For theorists, *Induction* makes for both cautionary and liberating reading. There is a strong dose of realism in the concept that every rule a person has ever learned has the potential to be in play, competing to guide action with other rules acquired through experience, formal and continuing education, reading, listening to those at speakers' podiums, and so on. Under such aggressive circumstances, a faculty theory should ensure a significant difference in results before it is offered to nonacademic practitioners. Here, it is well to recall Allan Janik's observation that the questions solved by theory must have significant implications for nonacademic environments; otherwise, "the whole business is a waste of time" from the practitioner's viewpoint.[9]

To be useful, such faculty theories should aim to (a) predict, (b) be in accord with experience, and (c) solve practical problems more effectively. These criteria provide faculty with a greater *understanding* of why past theories may not have been accepted outside the university. And they explain why it is difficult for even the most accurate theory to be adopted. *A new rule inevitably runs up against the natural tendency of humans to rely on rules already proven successful.* It is only when existing rules prove to be insufficient to forecast outcomes that the "imported" rules provided by faculty theory can realistically compete in providing predictions for the world.

WHO NEEDS A RESEARCH PHILOSOPHY?

Over the years, a number of theorists, all socialized in American, Canadian, or Western European national cultures but holding appointments in American higher education, have told this writer that they see little or no need for "a philosophy" in their research. When questioned on their reasons for not identifying with a philosophical school, these researchers stressed their general acceptance of Western cultural norms and the more specific standards governing research within their fields or disciplines.

An alternative way of "reading" these responses is to suggest is that the researchers are overlooking the reality that they do have a research philosophy, albeit an informal, personal philosophy that each acquired during the normal course of human development. The latter is a perspective on the world that Malcolm Williams and Tim May have termed "a learned classificatory system."[10] This ongoing if underdefined approach to identifying and solving life problems is fostered in humans through the complex process of living with others in social contexts. As a "life" philosophy, perhaps unspoken yet sometimes articulated, it functions to advance accuracy in predicting effectiveness in day-to-day affairs and to provide a more generalized guide for making life choices. More formally, it can determine the need for further research or "methodical investigations into a subject or problem."[11]

Such individualized compilations of rubrics for decision making, more formally known as "rules" and "rule clusters," can have significant effects in a variety of spectra. For example, the rule system operating in the mind of a corporate CEO, hospital administrator, school superintendent, mayor, attorney, physician, library director, school library media specialist, or knowledge manager can impact the lives of a broad spectrum of people. More specifically, an internalized "if-then" rule in a CEO's mind such as "*if* public demand decreases for our products or services, *then* lay off underutilized staff and make the remaining staff work harder" will have a far different impact then a rule asserting "*if* public demand decreases for our products or services, *then* redirect the efforts of underutilized staff to provide new products and services."

However, most explorations of research "philosophies" tend to link them to such "explicit" intellectual perspectives as Marxism, pragmatism, feminism, critical theory, or similarly codified metaparadigms or worldviews. Always subject to question from other worldviews, the claims to objectivity advanced by some of these perspectives have been further undermined in the last several decades. Postmodern critics see such philosophies and their associated methods of research as promoting specific value systems and assert, "No scientist can ever be extracted from his/her physical and social context. Every measurement changes reality in the attempt to record it. Every conceptualization is based on philosophical commitments."[12] In considering such objections to the secular, Enlightenment, and Western ideal of "objective" knowledge that has been privileged for at least a century, it is well to recall that other, competing definitions of knowledge have long existed. These include, for example, *ilm*—an Islamic concept of knowledge that "presumes an on-going interaction and integration of revelation and reason as necessary aspects of real knowledge."[13] As will be seen below, *ilm* bears a striking resemblance to the "idealistic metaphysics transcending the actualities of human experience" or God-centered philosophy of the mid-nineteenth-century American academic world.[14]

In the many arenas of practice, there are often conflicts between our formal theories and the ways we actually work. For example, Chris Argyris holds that individuals operate with two types of "theories of action." The first type is composed of "stated beliefs and values" and may be more praised than followed. The second model—the theory actually used—"can only be inferred from observing" actions and real behaviors."[15] The consequences flowing from Argyris's distinction between "what is said" and "what is actually done" are fundamentally important for research seeking to guide practice.

Robert B. Young has captured several aspects of the dilemma faced by researchers attempting to understand the values that may be "in play" in a given context. According to Young, people tend to rank their value preferences "one-by-one" but "seldom describe how their values really operate."[16] He continues:

> Any research about value preferences has another problem as well. It asks people about what they believe, so it is affected by the popularity and power of those beliefs. Survey respondents are likely to put down a mission statement rather than their real values priorities on the answer sheet. As a result, the researcher obtains information about explicit values instead of the implicit ones that guide the pencils [and the actions] of the respondents.[17]

But if individuals are only going to follow their internal rules anyway, of what use is a formal research philosophy? There are several practical answers to this question, as well as a fundamental rationale addressing the very reason for research itself. First, on the practical level, to the extent that a research philosophy incorporates the thinking of others, it provides an alternative source of possibilities. Granted, mature adults tend to choose research philosophies that "resonate" with our already established views. However, knowledge of differences "within the fold," on the level of exchanges among friendly competitors over coffee at conferences ("You *almost* have it right"), may offer even those most committed to their own theories something in the way of an "acceptable" comparative perspective. Second, a research philosophy can provide the intellectual stimulation of like-minded peers. In a researcher's formative years, such philosophies may also supply "cognitive authorities"—Patrick Wilson's term for intellectual leaders or mentors—whose answers to "settled" questions and opinions on disputed issues can serve both to socialize and to guide new theorists.[18] Third, certain paradigms are in fashion and favored by private and public funding sources, resulting in "enriched, relevant theory, plus social encouragement to continue" various lines of research.[19]

In short, there is practical value in a research philosophy for stimulating introspection, offering encouragement, and (perhaps) providing financial resources to support theory development. Notwithstanding, the issue is far from settled. It is possible to see research philosophies as erecting barriers to freedom in theory development on the grounds that a researcher's affiliation with others in a scholarly "invisible college," or the same researcher's acceptance of earmarked funding from sources advancing their own agendas, could be an unacceptable compromise with her or his academic integrity. Such fears are legitimate but can easily be overstated. In an open society, theorists, particularly tenured full professors, are seldom coerced into sacrificing intellectual freedom through voluntary associations with more or less like-minded researchers. Similarly, it is often considered "bad form" for administrators to require researchers to apply for certain government, foundation, or corporate funding if accepting funds from such sources involves what the researcher views as unacceptable intellectual compromises.

On a more fundamental level, a research philosophy can assist a theorist in gaining a perspective on the cultural or professional constraints that affect how he or she develops ideas and extends concepts. For example, critical theory is "deeply committed to examining how we construct everyday realities and to questioning many of our taken-for-granted assumptions," an approach that is also supported by feminism and pragmatism.[20] Scholars drawing from any or all of these philosophies—if they are responsive to the imperatives of their philosophical stances—are less likely, for example, to accept arguments that there is "only one right way" of defining and studying a problem.

Such openness to alternatives may well encourage a theorist to address the conundrum of "How to do it well" versus "Is it well to do?" in her or his research. The "How to do it well" variety of research begins by accepting a culture or profession's definition of a problem (the research question) and then undertaking the process of advancing possible solutions. One example of a "How to do it well" research approach from the author's own field occurs when scholars analyze a spectrum of plans and budgets to determine how public libraries might better allocate the meager 1 to 2 percent of tax revenues they have historically received from local governments to meet community library and information needs. The alternative theoretical pathway—the "Is it well to do?" approach—would be more likely to examine whose values and interests are diminished or enhanced (a) when public libraries are provided in the first place, (b) when their funding is so limited, or (c) when programs targeting certain parts of the service community receive priority in spending public dollars appropriated for library programs. The latter research agenda involves the consideration of hitherto "unexamined commitments" in order to understand how a given culture supports privileges and allocates power.[21]

Depending on the reader's own preference, the "Is it well to do?" research approach can be viewed as an intrinsic part of the commitment to the search for truth, an argument that has often been advanced to justify awarding tenure to university-based intellectuals. More controversially, at least on most university campuses, "Is it well to do?" is a question that is often advanced in the "prophetic voice" critiquing public policy—including the policy of public universities—from the perspective of traditional or religious metaphilosophies.[22]

The theoretical lenses provided by research philosophies such as critical theory, feminism, and pragmatism are particularly useful in directing theorists to examine the ways in which existing power and prestige arrangements maintain themselves. To help maximize the potential value of such approaches, university research programs supporting examinations of the foundations of a given national culture ought to include self-reflective analyses of the very systems that dominate and reward research and theory development in higher education. For those new to the academic world, it can be a shock to learn that certain "truths" can be privileged above others and that revealing strong differences with senior faculty can be detrimental to one's prospects for promotion and tenure. Even those with only minimal experience in academic life soon learn, often to their detriment, the truth of Stephen S. Weiner's reminder that "politics are dirtiest and most unseemly in precisely those institutions where people do not expect to see politics at play at all: the church and the university."[23]

Conventional academic systems, whether dominated by senior faculty or academic administrators, can and do limit dissent through marginalizing those theorists who might raise awkward questions about fundamental values. Under such circumstances, adherence to a research philosophy, preferably one supported by publications and annual conferences with ample opportunities for one-on-one discussions, can provide would-be theorists with the intellectual and emotional support necessary to undertake the sometimes unpopular process of looking beyond readily accepted, if inadequate, explanations. How use of a research philosophy can assist theorists in the amorphous area of "information studies" will be addressed below.

Discussions of research philosophies inevitably encounter the difficulties of providing more than a short and imperfect overview of how, in the last two centuries, a spectrum of intellectual competitors has influenced researchers, scholars, and other theory developers. Even if space could be made available to analyze the numerous theoretical publications residing on library shelves and, more recently, available in databases, the result would still be an incomplete account. By definition, the public record cannot reveal what scholars voluntarily or involuntarily withhold from print, either in hard copy or electronic formats.[24] As Jennifer Platt observes, "Even when one is studying the intellectual history of an academic discipline, there may be reason to believe that there are components of the oral subculture not adequately represented in what is published."[25]

An argument can and should be made that theorists ought to take their research philosophies seriously, but not so seriously that they forgo opportunities to learn even from their intellectual opponents. It is an unfortunate yet inescapable fact that simple human frailty, and what David Laurence describes as an "intellectual multiplicity . . . [that breeds] . . . an easy disdain" toward the work of one's intellectual adversaries, can be discerned in the record of theory development.[26] It is to be expected that theorists will often prefer reading those who agree with their intellectual stances. Overall, such "easy disdain"

> serves as a shears to cut away what one lacks the time or the temperament to know even superficially, much less sympathetically. The mere mention of a certain subject matter or the use of certain terms or titles is seized as sufficient reason to relieve ourselves of the burden of considering a piece of work for its individual intellectual qualities.[27]

When researchers forgo the opportunity to engage with the works of theoretical adversaries, they also relinquish the possibility of testing their own rules and models. Even if there is little or no possibility of conversion, a policy of intellectual isolation can cause one to lose the mental spurs necessary for strengthening one's own formulations.

Adherents to *cultural pragmatism* may have it a bit easier in dealing with intellectual opponents, even if the history of pragmatism does reveal times where its founders clearly displayed impatience with those refusing to concede the veracity of their arguments.[28] If true to their guiding principles, however, pragmatists are almost compelled to seek out speculative engagement and see the potential for theoretical usefulness in a wide spectrum of opinions.[29] Although pragmatists of all stripes believe that theory derived from analyzed experience tends to be more accurate, they are not averse to importing ideas from virtually any philosophy, provided that the borrowed concepts subsequently pass the pragmatic test of usefulness or workability.

In the complex and varying arenas that constitute human cultures, "good" theory advances understanding. But understanding derived from theory is just one source of awareness among many. Outside the university, competitors to faculty-generated theory, such as models fashioned from common sense, religious beliefs, explicit knowledge learned in school, and tacit knowledge discovered on the job, all vie to provide explanations of what is happening in the world.

At its simplest, theory can be defined as a supposition that explains, seeks to explain, or predicts something.[30] "Better" or "useful" theory contributes to effectiveness, generally through facilitating prediction. Such effective prediction nearly always requires specifying a context, such as a culture, nation, neighborhood, profession, or institution within which whatever is envisioned by the theory developer will or will not take place.

The uses of "classic" theory, or the historically privileged insights of disciplinary giants, the proverbial "dead Germans," will be discussed further in chapter 3.[31] However, remembering that "good," "better," and "contextual" criteria must be applied to even long-established theory makes it easier to bring renowned insights into play when discussing contemporary concerns. In such use, the age or even the reputation of intellectual formulations is far less important than their present workability. Several of the early nineteenth-century achievements of John Stuart Mill, already discussed in chapter 1, can form a useful case in point. Arguably, Mill's well-known "appraisals" of Alexis de Tocqueville's *Democracy in*

America have an additional bonus for twenty-first-century readers.[32] Through demonstrating the possibilities of cross-cultural and bilanguage communication of fundamentally important concepts, the essays challenge arguments asserting *incommensurability* or the perceived inability of humans to communicate effectively with one another due to a lack of common standards for meaning and other shared foundations. When an Englishman can capture the essence of two books of fundamentally important insights written by a Frenchman from his experiences in the new United States—and the understandings resonate many generations after their first appearance in print—something important has been communicated.

SELECTING A USEFUL RESEARCH PHILOSOPHY

Several of the currently influential North American and European research philosophies will be discussed, from the perspective of cultural pragmatism, in the next chapter. However, the emphasis in chapter 3 will not be to "convert" readers to the author's own philosophy. Admittedly, this approach is at variance with the usual admonition that readers should immediately adopt the author's perspective on the subject under consideration. The reason for this restraint is relatively simple: pragmatism and pragmatists can claim no monopoly on "the truth." In reality, cultural and other pragmatists, if consistent with their own fundamental understandings, recognize that intellectual opponents may develop theories that surpass existing pragmatic contributions in the ongoing project to advance knowledge and understanding. Pragmatists, however, do reserve the right to apply to the concepts of all other theorists the same test of analyzed experience—preferably in a multiplicity of contexts—that they apply to their own hypotheses, models, and rules.

The reminder that intellectual space must be accorded the products of nonpragmatic thinkers was active even in the philosophy's early years. For example, William James's own analysis of the history of philosophy and theory development led him to write—with an exclamation point—"For what a contrary array of opinions have objective evidence and absolute certitude been claimed!"[33]

James was not the only leading pragmatic philosopher to advocate humility in the ongoing search for answers to humanity's unsolved questions. According to John Herman Randall Jr.:

Developing a Research Philosophy 45

Respect for the experience of other men, this willingness to learn from them what they have found out, above all, to learn by working with them, is the very core of John Dewey the man, and it is the core of his philosophy as well. From the point of view of the assorted absolutists—chancellors, commissars, or cardinals—who already know all the answers, this has been Dewey's unforgivable sin. He hadn't found The Truth, and he actually thought that other men were as likely to discover more of it as he or you or I.[34]

Given the spectrum of theoretical alternatives to be discussed in chapter 3, it is useful to preview for readers a number of candidates for selection as a research philosophy. For purposes of discussion, separate advice on "philosophy selection" will be provided for the three inclusive communities of faculty, consultants, and practitioners. Short descriptions of these research philosophies are provided in the glossary.

Faculty theorists can and do publish for audiences in at least two contexts—the academic world and the culture outside the university. The more immediate audience for faculty, due to the realities of promotion, tenure, and influencing colleagues, is likely to consist of other academics. Here, it is particularly important to respond to the preferences of (a) professors and deans likely to vote on promotion and tenure requests, (b) committee members vetting speakers for conferences, and (c) reviewers who gate-keep for prestigious journals. Allowing for differences in context, "academic" research drawing on the resources of *postmodernism, critical theory, feminism,* and *psychoanalysis* may be well received. *Positivism,* particularly using quantitative approaches, still has a constructive influence where expected readers, particularly on promotion and tenure committees, are drawn from or inclined to emulate the hard sciences. However, it should be noted that the European intellectuals who frequently set the standards for theory development on a global level have increasingly found *pragmatism* to be useful—if only as an object of attack—in making their own reputations.[35]

For academic researchers seeking to secure government or other grants, except in certain of the social sciences, a research program based on *pragmatism, positivism,* and, as appropriate, *feminism* might prove productive. Out of political necessity, those who award grant funding in government agencies charged with addressing social or other problems still envision that research can produce "value-free" or "objective" findings as a basis for recommendations and actions.[36] In consequence, adherence to a research philosophy that privileges "results," that analyzes experience with an aim toward prediction, is likely to enhance the perceived relevance of a theorist's work to a noncampus culture that more or less operates with a version of the same philosophy. It should be recalled that American "land grant" universities have a long tradition of generating "practical" solutions to national, state, and local problems. It was this history that led higher education theorist Clark Kerr, in recent years, to assert that "a reinvigorated land grant model [providing relevant research and service] might yet save the German-model state research university" in times of enhanced demands and resource restrictions.[37]

Both consultants and off-campus practitioners wishing to publish in "academic" journals are advised to follow the same counsel provided to faculty. However, when researching to provide advice or to make decisions in "real-world" contexts, pragmatism, including cultural pragmatism and the informal pragmatism that is so often practiced without the formal name, is likely to be the approach that produces the most useful results.

As in all matters pragmatic, the advice provided in this section should be ignored if the reader's own circumstances determine that another approach will prove more effective.

THE SITUATION IN INFORMATION STUDIES

In chapter 1 the review of the extended debate leading to the closing of the Columbia University School of Library Service dealt with higher education realities in the midst of demands for transformation. The point is worth emphasizing that the multifaceted relationships among university programs of professional education and practitioners in the library, information, knowledge, and media professions, as well as the internal disagreements within the academic field coming to be known as information studies, immensely complicate the contexts for research and theory development. The issue is far from settled. Faculty "information"—more recently, "knowledge"—theorists yet see themselves as struggling to expand the study of information, informatics, knowledge production, or human intelligence beyond the physical and metaphorical boundaries of libraries and the demands of the sectors that traditionally have employed their program graduates. Conversely, "library" scholars envision themselves as waging rearguard battles to maintain the distinction between "librarianship" and "information science," in part because they deem the term "information science" to be largely unreflective of the library's educational and public service missions. Thus engaged, researchers may see themselves as having little or no time to devote to creating, borrowing, or elaborating on a research philosophy. This restraint, for whatever reason, can limit the understanding of causes to the more obvious and observable. As will be seen below, exploring the closing of Columbia University's School of Library Service through the use of a variety of theoretical lenses can illuminate the actions of less visible cultural and social forces and help trace their influence on important issues of professional and public policy.

Closing the School of Library Service

Margaret Stieg has offered a general perspective on the closing of "library schools" that is particularly useful, for example, when analyzing the elimination of the Columbia University School of Library Service. According to Stieg:

> Library education has valiantly tried to redesign itself to better suit the priorities of universities. At various times it has tried to become a science, to become more theoretical, and to recruit more men and scientists. Now it is trying to accomplish all of these at one time by becoming information science. But its efforts at adaptation have had only limited success. The profession it serves remains, and therefore it remains, stubbornly humanistic, service-oriented, and female in composition.[38]

Stieg's short analysis of the enduring strengths of the humanistic, service, and female characteristics of the traditional library profession—and their continuing demands on professional education—does not claim allegiance to a specific research philosophy. Instead, this account strongly emphasizes that the elimination of library programs at leading public and private universities (specifically mentioning Chicago and Columbia), resulted from such major yet observable factors as financial constraints, demise of collegial attitudes and adoption of management/materialistic values, redefinition of functions, lessened geographical ties, and fixation on national rankings.

On the surface, the rationale advanced by the Columbia University administration for eliminating the School of Library Service—that the refusal of its faculty to concentrate their efforts on the university's priorities of information research and the education of special librarians (information specialists) and their academic counterparts made the investment of further university resources a low priority—is covered by Stieg's summary of factors contributing to the closing of "library" programs. Columbia's demand that the school abandon public and school librarians, leaving their education to programs at less-prestigious institutions in the New York metropolitan area, makes sense if one accepts without question the values articulated in the university's official documents. The university did not want to continue investing in a school that educated underpaid and undervalued professionals for relatively low-status professions. What it sought was a program in information theory development, capable of guiding an Ivy League institution through the process of engaging with an emerging information age. According to information theorist Michael Koenig, who taught at Columbia, the tenured faculty in the program, as might be expected, resisted the university's information aims and regularly demonstrated a preference for hiring library scholars with intellectual perspectives similar to those of already-tenured faculty.[39] The school faculty, in the view of Columbia administrators, insisted on maintaining contacts with traditional library constituencies and resisted continuing admonitions to concentrate their efforts on advancing the university's information research and teaching priorities.

Although not specifically directed to the Columbia closing, there do exist in the literature a number of works that evaluate education for the information, library, knowledge, media, and other emerging professions from a variety of philosophical traditions. Writing from what could only be termed a *critical theory* perspective, Christine Pawley, in "Hegemony's Handmaid? The Library and Information Studies Curriculum from a Class Perspective," argues that "universities are changing to meet the demands of a capitalism more aggressive than at any time since before the Great Depression." In consequence, she observes, library and information studies education must operate in a context where "universities . . . have abandoned any pretence to independence" and "curriculum will be influenced by the dominant corporate class."[40]

Building on Pawley's *critical theory* perspective, a "profitable" exploration of the closing of Columbia's School of Library Service might see the official rationale for program elimination as almost irrelevant to the actual realities. For critical theorists, the closing was an expected reaction by academic managers who had become convinced that the continuing commitment of the school's faculty to the ideals of public service, as embodied in public and school libraries, made their program superfluous to a university more interested in building connections to the corporate, for-profit world. In the past, the often-competitive values of public-service idealism and free-enterprise entrepreneurship have been able to coexist in a number of American university environments. Consequently, for critical theorists, the hard-line stance taken by Columbia managers in closing a program that emphasized nonmarketplace values represents a significant tilt with troubling implications for American national culture.

From a *feminist* perspective, the closing of Columbia's School of Library Service might be seen as demonstrating that those library and information fields with higher percentages of males (academic librarianship, information science) are privileged in contemporary university environments over fields with a larger female majority (public and school librarianship). In this approach, since Columbia University is an institution that traditionally has been dominated by males, it is understandable that male perspectives and interests would be prioritized and that demands to further transform the school program in the direction of a male-friendly or information environment would be advanced. Such an analysis might well take into account what Hope A. Olson terms the "white, male, eurocentric, Christian, heterosexual, able-bodied, bourgeois mainstream [that] is not viewed as a special interest" suppressing alternative, particularly female, models of professional education.[41] To what extent, a feminist theorist might ask, can the closing of the School of Library Service be explored as the privileging by Columbia University of matters traditionally associated with the male gender over equally—if not more—valid concerns of the traditional, female "other"?

Building on a recent analysis provided by *cultural pragmatists* Bill Crowley and Deborah Ginsberg, it is possible to explore the closing of Columbia University's School of Library Service as demonstrating the absence of *intracultural reciprocity*, "the changing, context-specific perceptions of mutual worth by participants in geographical, organizational, social and other arenas, as well as the willingness of arena participants to act on the basis of such perceptions."[42] In the Columbia example, it was

clear at the time of its closing that the School of Library Service was valued by the university administration only to the extent that it might be rad-
ically transformed in a direction that changed its fundamental mission. For
cultural pragmatists, discussion of "winners and losers" in the immediate
academic environment would also require exploring the impact of the program termination on the long-range futures of the information, library,
knowledge, media, and other emerging professions, as well as the larger
culture that supports both their education and their employment.

Taking the concept of intracultural reciprocity beyond a Columbia
application, it is possible to understand critical, if unanticipated, consequences that can flow from transforming "library and information" into
"information," "communication," "knowledge," or other-named
schools. Such transformations may well have demonstrable benefits for
a number of stakeholders, for example, program faculty, corporate employers, and students with an interest in the for-profit sector. However,
it is possible that the privileging of "information" over "library" in programs accredited by the American Library Association (ALA) may be
contributing, albeit quite unintentionally, to a changing climate of perceptions that can and will threaten the professionalism of program graduates. Crowley and Ginsberg theorize, from the perspective of cultural
pragmatism, that the enormous growth in the number of potential competitors in the provision of information—ranks that include graduates of
community college information technology programs and holders of
four-year or graduate degrees in a variety of other fields—coupled with
the expansion of end-user electronic resources, has made it increasingly difficult for many librarians, information specialists, and knowledge managers to be acknowledged as organizational leaders in the
management of information on the basis of their master's degree from
ALA–accredited programs. In consequence, it may become the case
that graduates with degrees from ALA-endorsed programs will be
"subject to replacement by other information intermediaries who may
have lower educational credentials and, in a number of cases, cost less
. . . to employ."[43]

Culturally pragmatic theorizing about the unanticipated threats to the
careers of students educated in programs designed around the for-profit
"information" model of professional education—as opposed to a "library," not-for-profit model that includes education for youth services,
film programming, readers advisory services, and so on—is supported

by recent data summarized by Mary Corcoran, Lynn Dagar, and Anthea Stratigos. Drawing on a recent Outsell, Inc., "benchmark report on the corporate information professionals and their current and emerging roles," these consultants stress that "information professionals are working within an industry that is moving toward the commodity stage." They also remind their readers that information suppliers in a commodity-businesses model often compete on the basis of price and that the "standard procedure for commodity businesses is to lower their operational costs as the price point is driven down."[44] In other words, corporate information and knowledge managers, analysts, and other suppliers who may possess graduate degrees from ALA-accredited programs now face both the external threat of having jobs outsourced and the internal threat of having them filled by less costly personnel educated in community college or other undergraduate programs.

Whatever the reader's view of the circumstances surrounding the closing of Columbia University's School of Library Service—or her or his perceptions of the seemingly inevitable transformation of schools of library and information studies into schools of information—it is clear that drawing on research philosophies such as critical theory, feminism, or cultural pragmatism can provide additional perspectives for a fuller understanding of the implications of the program termination or transformation. At a time where the very nature of "facts" is increasingly seen as open to multiple definitions, it is simply becoming less acceptable to limit analysis to the operation of "surface variables" while forgoing the more depth-providing view that can be supplied by the lenses of one or more research philosophies.

CHAPTER SUMMARY

Chapter 2 has sought to provide the reader with a greater understanding of the way people actually solve problems. In the process, it has explored the highly personal system of internal *if-then rules* through which individuals identify and solve problems, a process through which past solutions are applied, modified, or discarded. This sequence, it was stressed, represents a pattern that is lifelong in duration and highly conservative, in that new approaches to solving problems have to prove their success before being adopted.

The implications for public acceptance of a faculty-developed theory of such a rule-bound system of problem identification and solution were also considered in the chapter. So too was the value of a researcher's adhering to a research philosophy, both as a means of expanding her or his own willingness to consider rules offered by others and as a source for assistance and support in the ongoing duty of theorists to explore issues beyond the level of the immediate and the obvious. In this context, in preparation for chapter 3's consideration of the revival of pragmatism and the continuing strength of other philosophical approaches, the chapter applied understandings offered by critical theory, feminism, and cultural pragmatism in order to provide a more in-depth understanding of the forces leading to the closing of Columbia University's School of Library Service.

NOTES

1. Thomas Tempte, "The Practical Intellect and Master-Apprenticeship: Some Reflections on Cross-Contacts between Theory and Practice," trans. Angela E. Andegren, in *Skill, Technology, and Enlightenment: On Practical Philosophy*, ed. Bo Goranzon (London: Springer-Verlag, 1995), 17.

2. Tempte, "Practical Intellect," 16.

3. John H. Holland, Keith J. Holyoak, Richard E. Nisbett, and Paul R. Thagard, *Induction: Processes of Inference, Learning, and Discovery* (Cambridge, MA: MIT Press, 1987), 206.

4. Holland et al., *Induction*, 1, 11, 14, 16, 29, 71, 95.

5. Holland et al., *Induction*, 96.

6. Holland et al., *Induction*, 38.

7. Holland et al., *Induction*, 214, 221.

8. Holland et al., *Induction*, 49, 354.

9. Allan Janik, "Why Is Wittgenstein Important?" in *Skill and Education: Reflection and Experience*, ed. Bo Goranzon and Magnus Florin (London: Springer-Verlag, 1992), 35.

10. Malcolm Williams and Tim May, *Introduction to the Philosophy of Social Research* (London: University College London Press, 1996), 17.

11. Williams and May, *Introduction*, 7.

12. Gulbenkian Commission on the Restructuring of the Social Sciences, *Opening the Social Sciences: Report of the Gulbenkian Commission on the Restructuring of the Social Sciences* (Stanford, CA: Stanford University Press, 1996), 75.

13. Munawar Ahmad Anees and Merryl Wyn Davies, "Islamic Science: Current Thinking and Future Directions," in *The Revenge of Athena: Science, Exploitation, and the Third World*, ed. Ziauddin Sardar (London: Mansell, 1988), 255.

14. Abraham Kaplan, *The New World of Philosophy* (New York: Random House, 1961), 14.

15. Chris Argyris, "Tacit Knowledge and Management," in *Tacit Knowledge in Professional Practice: Researcher and Practitioner Perspectives*, ed. Robert J. Sternberg and Joseph A. Horvath (Mahwah, NJ: Lawrence Erlbaum Associates, 1999), 126.

16. Robert B. Young, *No Neutral Ground: Standing By the Values We Prize in Higher Education* (San Francisco: Jossey-Bass, 1997), 122.

17. Young, *No Neutral Ground*.

18. Patrick Wilson, *Second-Hand Knowledge: An Inquiry into Cognitive Authority* (Westport, CT: Greenwood, 1983), 18.

19. Paul Diesing, *How Does Social Science Work? Reflections on Practice* (Pittsburgh: University of Pittsburgh Press, 1991), 361.

20. Pushkala Prasad and Paula J. Caproni, "Critical Theory in the Management Classroom: Engaging Power, Ideology, and Praxis," *Journal of Management Education* 21, no. 3 (August 1997): 286. For a useful analysis of the meeting points between feminism and pragmatism, see Jane Duran, "The Intersection of Pragmatism and Feminism," *Hypatia* 8, no. 2 (Spring 1993): 159–71.

21. Murray Hausknecht, "At First Glance: The Role of the Intellectual," *Dissent* 33, no. 2 (Spring 1986): 131.

22. Richard E. Wentz, "The Merits of Professors Emeriti," *Chronicle of Higher Education* 48, no. 13 (December 14, 2001): B5.

23. Stephen S. Weiner, "Shipyards in the Desert," *Review of Higher Education* 10, no. 2 (Winter 1986): 159.

24. Richard J. Light, Judith D. Singer, and John B. Willett, *By Design: Planning Research on Higher Education* (Cambridge, MA: Harvard University Press, 1990), 30.

25. Jennifer Platt, "Evidence and Proof in Documentary Research 1: Some Specific Problems of Documentary Research," *Sociological Review* 29, no. 1 (1981): 39.

26. David Laurence, "From the Editor," *ADE Bulletin*, no. 107 (Spring 1994): 1. The Association of Departments of English, a subsidiary of the Modern Language Association, publishes the *ADE Bulletin*.

27. Laurence, "From the Editor," 1–2.

28. John Dewey, for example, seemingly wanted to deal only with a religious experience that had been reconstructed according to his own ideas. See Milton R. Konvitz, introduction to *John Dewey: The Later Works, 1925–1953, vol. 9, 1933–1934*, ed. Jo Ann Boydston (Carbondale: Southern Illinois University Press, 1989).

29. For example, see the discussion in Bill Crowley, "The Control and Direction of Professional Education," *Journal of the American Society for Information Science* 50 (October 1999): 1134.

30. This definition represents an extension of the definition provided in Loraine Blaxter, Christina Hughes, and Malcolm Tight, *How to Research* (Buckingham, UK: Open University Press, 1996), 185.

31. See the discussion in Sydney J. Pierce, "Dead Germans and the Theory of Librarianship," *American Libraries*, September 1992, 641–43.

32. See John Stuart Mill, "Introduction: An Appraisal of Volume I of *Democracy in America*, Published in the London (and Westminster) Review in 1835 on the Occasion of the First Appearance of the English Translation," in Alexis de Tocqueville, *Democracy in America*, vol. 1 (New York: Schocken Books, 1961) and "Introduction: An Appraisal of Volume II of *Democracy in America*, Published in the Edinburgh Review in 1840 on the Occasion of the First Appearance of the English Translation," in Alexis de Tocqueville, *Democracy in America,* vol. 2 (New York: Schocken Books, 1961).

33. William James, "The Will to Believe," in *The Writings of William James: A Comprehensive Edition*, ed. John J. McDermott (Chicago: University of Chicago Press, 1997), 726.

34. John Herman Randall Jr., "John Dewey, 1859–1952," *Journal of Philosophy* 50, no. 1 (January 1, 1953): 12. Quoted in James Campbell, *Understanding John Dewey: Nature and Cooperative Intelligence* (Chicago: Open Court, 1995), 200.

35. Richard Shusterman, "The Perils of Making Philosophy a Lingua Americana," *Chronicle of Higher Education* 46, no. 49 (August 11, 2000): B4–B5.

36. Williams and May, *Introduction*, passim.

37. Clark Kerr, *The Uses of the University*, 4th ed. (Cambridge, MA: Harvard University Press, 1995), 190.

38. Margaret Stieg, "The Closing of Library Schools: Darwinism at the University," *Library Quarterly* 61, no. 3 (July 1991): 271.

39. Michael E. D. Koenig, "Buttering the Toast Evenly: Library School Closings at Columbia and Chicago Are Tragic, but They Don't Have to Signal a Trend," *American Libraries*, September 1990, 723.

40. Christine Pawley, "Hegemony's Handmaid? The Library and Information Studies Curriculum from a Class Perspective," *Library Quarterly* 68, no. 2 (April 1998): 138.

41. Hope A. Olson, "The Feminist and the Emperor's New Clothes: Feminist Deconstruction as a Critical Methodology for Library and Information Studies," *Library and Information Science Research* 19, no. 2 (1997): 183.

42. Bill Crowley and Deborah Ginsberg, "Intracultural Reciprocity, Information Ethics, and the Survival of Librarianship in the Twenty-First Century," in *Ethics and Electronic Information: A Festschrift for Stephen Almagno*, ed. Barbara Rockenbach and Tom Mendina (Jefferson, NC: McFarland, 2003), 105.

43. Crowley and Ginsberg, "Intracultural Reciprocity."

44. Mary Corcoran, Lynn Dagar, and Anthea Stratigos, "The Changing Roles of Information Professionals: Excerpts from an Outsell, Inc., Study," *Online*, March/April 2000, 29.

Chapter Three

The Revival of Pragmatism

SCENARIO: WHAT GOES AROUND COMES AROUND

Although Dominican University regularly adds degree programs to meet student needs, it is still small enough for cross-disciplinary conversations to be a standard part of faculty life. One popular site for these exchanges is the campus dining hall. Here, almost on a daily basis, professors from the Graduate School of Library and Information Science anchor a table where colleagues from other fields and disciplines — and even a number of university administrators — gather for lunch before and after class. Not long ago I was holding forth at lunch, stressing to all who would listen how the European rediscovery of pragmatism was symptomatic of why this particularly American philosophy was renewing itself after a half-century or more of decline. In retrospect, it is clear that my table companions were feeling a bit trapped by such relentless enthusiasm. When I paused for breath, a faculty member from another department, who had been patiently waiting out this extended monologue, smiled and pointedly asked, "Tell me, Bill, how long do you think it will be before pragmatism goes into decline again?"

My first reaction to this question was a rueful grin. It's a bit embarrassing to be caught in a soapbox oration by your colleagues when everyone else at the lunch table is trying to relax. Thus good-naturedly chided, I limited my answer to two quick points. The first was a prediction that pragmatism, in one form or another, will be around until both humanity and its world become totally predictable. Second, I told

Caroline (not her real name) that I agreed with her position that any research philosophy will only have a limited run at the center of the academic stage. Human nature, particularly as it operates in the higher education environment, will insure that interest in a revived pragmatism will be followed shortly thereafter by equal or greater enthusiasm for another research philosophy that will demand its own time in the intellectual spotlight. At this point other faculty joined the exchange, which then evolved into a tablewide discussion addressing the rich complexity of causes—including the possibility of more productive insights, struggles for dominance among paradigms, faculty ambitions, academic fads, and cultural fashions—that both extend and limit the dominance of even the most productive research philosophies.[1]

PARADIGMS IN COMPETITION

In his *Structure of Scientific Revolutions*, Thomas S. Kuhn discusses the myriad roles played by *paradigms* in advancing human knowledge. Paradigms, which may be envisioned as mental constructs or ways of looking at the world, are supplied to individuals by their culture, profession, or discipline. Such models—in essence, functional philosophies—are affirmed, modified, or replaced over time. Yesterday's widely accepted way of envisioning the world can lose its popularity with relative ease when it fails to provide guidance in solving new problems or is seen as passé by intellectual tastemakers. Kuhn himself made a point of emphasizing that the competition between established and emerging paradigms "is not the sort of battle that can be resolved by proofs," that is, logical analyses, laboratory experiments, or statistical data. This is because paradigms inevitably contain assertions that cannot be substantiated and must be accepted as "given." As Kuhn notes, disputes crossing paradigm lines are seldom settled, since "neither side will grant all the non-empirical assumptions that the other needs in order to make its case."[2] This inability to provide "factual" or "objective" tests to settle intellectual disputes *between* paradigms also applies to struggles *within* paradigms as variant interpretations of what the paradigm actually is vie with one another for influence. The recent history of such contemporary philosophies as critical theory, feminism, classical Marxism, and pragmatism clearly indicate that intraparadigm divergence should be expected as a normal component of intellectual life.[3]

CLASSICAL PRAGMATISM

The concept of competition *among* and *within* paradigms to define acceptable mental models of the world is useful in understanding why
there has always been controversy over what pragmatism, perhaps
North America's most influential "homegrown" philosophy, actually
represents. Dating the birth of a philosophy is often an arbitrary exercise. However, it is commonly accepted in American intellectual history
that William James, even as he acknowledged his theoretical debt to
Charles Sanders Peirce, brought the name and philosophy of pragmatism to wider attention during a famed August 1898 lecture at the University of California at Berkeley.[4] Only ten years later, pragmatism had
attracted so many diverse adherents within American culture that Arthur
O. Lovejoy, a sympathetic opponent, cataloged at least thirteen schools
of thought (subparadigms in contemporary understandings) vying with
each other to define the pragmatic paradigm.[5]

Almost a century after Lovejoy's analysis, there seems to be no real
consensus regarding how classical pragmatism, in its pre-1940 formulations, should be understood. However, a summary provided in the introduction to a special issue on contemporary pragmatism in the *Hedgehog Review* provides a good place to start. According to the *Hedgehog
Review* editors:

> For the most part, pragmatists offer us a simple means of thinking, talk-
> ing, and deliberating about the things that matter most to us. They tell us
> to resist abstraction, stay close to experience, allow for mistakes and un-
> certainty, and look to the consequences of what we propose to believe and
> do. Pragmatism can be seen as a way of approaching life, disagreements,
> hurdles and decisions. "Test one hypothesis, answer, or solution against
> another," the pragmatist suggests. "Rather than strive to attain absolutes
> or certainty, try to come up with something that works and makes sense
> of your experiences."[6]

In the nineteenth-century American context, pragmatism's efforts to
achieve philosophical coherence drew heavily on the example of
Charles Darwin's work in the area of evolution. It has been asserted, for
example, that "Darwin's theory of evolution through spontaneous
variation and natural selection" provided such early pragmatists as James
with a "general model of the means by which knowledge itself is

constructed."[7] Pragmatism allows but does not require a belief in God. To create intellectual breathing space for alternatives to Divine Revelation as a means of legitimating knowledge, the new philosophy engaged in an extended struggle with the Christian worldview that dominated a Protestant America. Abraham Kaplan describes this belief system as "an idealist metaphysics transcending the actualities of human experience."[8] At its most extreme, research and intellectual argument in the early and mid-nineteenth-century American college required faculty to demonstrate an awareness of the truths of mainstream Protestant Holy Scripture in addition to understanding current developments within various fields or disciplines. The inherent contradictions in this uneasy living arrangement intensified as the growth in doctoral degrees and rise of the research university transformed often-doctrinaire college teachers into self-confident academic researchers.[9]

After about 1900, theorists in a secularizing American university entered a period where *even the existence of God, as God,* had to be proven by the methods of science, and worldly learning was less inclined to accommodate itself to faith. Yet the separation was not totally complete. The same William James who stressed, "The truth of 'God' has to run the gauntlet of all our other truths,"[10] could also produce a sympathetic study of the religious impulse in *The Varieties of Religious Experience.*[11]

As might be considered inevitable in a philosophy so varied that it offered more than a dozen identifiable schools, the ranks of classical pragmatism contained elements that were hostile to much of traditional Christian (and other) religious belief. Such opposition is most famously evident in the thinking of John Dewey, who, following the death of James in 1910, assumed the mantle of leading pragmatic thinker. In his 1934 work, "A Common Faith," Dewey expresses views of organized religion that were far less charitable than those of his predecessor. In this short monograph he demands the purging of all supernatural aspects in order to set free what he sees as the "elements and outlooks that may be called religious" from what he terms "a load of current beliefs and of institutional practices that are irrelevant" to what is truly valuable in religion.[12]

Classical pragmatism was in the forefront in conceptualizing the theoretical revolution that freed higher education from dominance by theology and put in place more secular standards for validating knowledge. As such, it participated in an early twentieth-century American intellectual climate that was "shaped by a tolerance for error, by a preference for experiment and a respect for the unknown, by an indifference to tradition and inherited truth, by a need for continuous inquiry and continuous verification."[13]

The world of American higher education has changed greatly in the last hundred years of its history. The nineteenth-century college demanded from its faculty recognition of God's continuing role in the world. In the twenty-first century, a professor who brings a religious perspective to discussions of research and teaching in the secular university runs the risk of being labeled as dangerously dogmatic and intellectually suspect.

CLASSICAL PRAGMATISM'S "CORE" ASSERTIONS

If the inevitable claims and counterclaims of intraparadigm (intramural) disputes are set aside, it is possible to discern a minimum of twelve assertions that a plurality of classical pragmatists—and even more contemporary cultural pragmatists—would not dismiss out of hand:

1. Knowledge and meaning are determined by experience.
2. Research is instigated by a problem.
3. Ideas are instruments for defining and solving problems.
4. Philosophy and theory development are human endeavors, subject to human limitations.
5. Propositions are meaningless unless their being either true or false will make a difference in our lives.
6. Meanings always require human context; there are no eternal essences or ideal objects.
7. Theories are, at best, provisionally true and are always subject to further testing in a variety of contexts.
8. What counts is not where ideas come from but what we can do with them.
9. Facts always involve an element of value, and values cannot be conceived in isolation from the world of concrete events.
10. Any attempt to improve the world must begin by finding out how the world actually works.

11. Humans have the most opportunity to develop their capabilities in a democracy.
12. Scientific and other knowledge progresses best in a democratic context that encourages freedom of inquiry.[14]

Classical Pragmatism in Practice

The ideal "classical" pragmatist did not live apart from the world or try to understand it without a background of experience. Thus defined, the exemplary pragmatist may well have been not James or Dewey but that quintessential Midwesterner, Jane Addams. Illinois born and raised, Addams, founder of Hull House, struggled for long decades on behalf of an immigrant community mired in the day-to-day realities of Chicago poverty. At the same time, she regularly took extended vacations to reflect on her experience in dealing with the wide-ranging demands of a multinational and multilingual clientele. She then applied the fruits of that reflection to help make her city and world a better place.[15] Pragmatism, as represented by Addams, was a philosophy of action for those who wanted to reform their world. This preference for effective action would lead to repeated criticism—from radicals and conservatives alike—that the pragmatic emphasis on *doing something well* ignored the more important discussion regarding whether or not something was actually *well to do* in the first place.

Randolph Bourne, a radical pragmatist who broke with Dewey over the latter's support of American entry into World War I, highlights classical pragmatism's inability to solve the "ends-means" issue in his 1917 essay "Twilight of Idols." This perceptive critique, delivered from the perspective of a former believer, is worth an extended excerpt. According to Bourne, although Dewey himself pressed for a public examination of the goals of America's participation in the war, his calls went unheard. This was because

> his disciples have learned all too literally the instrumental attitude towards life [Dewey termed his version of pragmatism "instrumentalism"], and being immensely intelligent and energetic, they are making themselves efficient instruments of the war-technique, accepting with little question the ends as announced from above. That those ends are largely negative does not concern them, because they have never learned not to subordinate idea to technique. Their education has not given them a co-

herent system of large ideas, or a feeling for democratic goals. They have, in short, no clear philosophy of life except that of intelligent service, the admirable adaptation of means to ends. They are vague as to what kind of a society they want, or what kind of society America needs, but they are equipped with all the administrative attitudes and talents necessary to attain it.[16]

Bourne's 1917 leftist critique is remarkably similar to a more contemporary (and more right-wing) analysis offered by Glenn Tinder, an opponent of pragmatism from a traditional religious perspective. Writing seventy-two years later, in the October 1995 issue of *First Things: A Monthly Journal of Religion and Public Life*, Tinder observed, "The stress on action in pragmatism appears simply because there is no other access to reality. There is no truth of the kind affirmed by Plato and Aristotle, or by Augustine and Aquinas: truth possessing intrinsic beauty and accessible to theoretical reason and to faith. There are no foundations."[17]

Over the years, pragmatists would argue that their philosophy, grounded in analyzed experience, did include profoundly moving concepts of truth and beauty.[18] However, pragmatism was consistently attacked by the Bournes and Tinders of the world, who demanded in their lifetimes a fully developed, "coherent system of large ideas." This was a demand that the philosophy refused to meet. At their best, classical pragmatists were critically aware of the imbalanced results produced by even the most extended efforts of humanity to understand its world. As a result, they tended to assert only "provisional" truths, subject to being overturned by new evidence. This self-imposed limitation was and is frustrating for those who need philosophical certainty and who experience intellectual or other discomfort when dealing with context-dependent and often ambiguous "truths."

As a living force, classical pragmatism survived two world wars and a global depression. Nonetheless, by 1963, Johns Hopkins University Press could reissue Lovejoy's half-century-old attack on pragmatism in the confident expectation that his biting criticisms would not discomfort any active philosopher. By that year pragmatism was deemed to be intellectually inert, and few living theoreticians would identify themselves with the tradition of Peirce, James, and Dewey.[19]

If pragmatism was dead, who or what killed the philosophy? Even more interesting, why didn't the paradigm stay buried?

ENTER LOGICAL EMPIRICISM

Just as classical pragmatism supplanted Protestant metaphysics as the leading American research philosophy, it was replaced during the mid-twentieth century by a European-derived positivism flourishing for decades under a succession of such terms as "positivism," "logical empiricism," and "analytic philosophy" and which will be discussed under the label of "logical empiricism." While the transition from metaphysics to pragmatism might be considered to be a conceptual sea change of fundamental significance, the subsequent dominance of *logical empiricism* might better be considered as a fratricidal succession. As late as 1964, the pragmatic philosopher Abraham Kaplan conceived both pragmatism and logical empiricism to be varieties of *semantic empiricism*, in that each sees knowledge and meaning as dependent on experience and emphasizes that "to be meaningful at all a proposition must be capable of being brought into relation with experience as a test of truth."[20]

It is generally held that logical empiricism originated with the 1922 Vienna Circle, a loose association of philosophers and scientists that met periodically for discussions in that city. It was a research paradigm inspired as much by Einstein's twentieth-century physics as pragmatism had earlier been stimulated by Darwin's nineteenth-century biology. In the beginning, logical empiricism's primary focus was on the "verifiability theory of meaning," which held a statement to be meaningful only if it could be "verified" or proven. As a philosophy, logical empiricism waxed dominant in the United States until the latter part of the twentieth century, when, in yet another example of the limited life of paradigms, it "slowed, stopped, and died out." By the 1980s, logical empiricism was no longer a subject for meaningful discussion on the programs of American philosophy of science conventions but was relegated, instead, to social science textbooks.[21] (For a cogent history of logical empiricism's fall from intellectual supremacy to practical irrelevance, see chapters 1 to 3 of Paul Diesing's *How Does Social Science Work? Reflections on Practice*.)

Over the decades, logical empiricism had drifted away from the strong connection with experience shared with pragmatism to become entangled in unproductive arguments over the meaning of words and sentences. In the process, "a philosophy of science that began with the intention of explicating, clarifying the language of a well-known science [physics] ended by issuing prescriptions to largely unknown sciences."[22] Inevitably, abandoning the focus on experience made logical empiricism largely irrelevant to fields outside of the "hard" sciences, where it yet retains considerable influence.

Given that classical pragmatism and logical empiricism seemingly had so much in common in their early years, it seems reasonable to ask why one would replace the other. At a minimum, pragmatism might have reached the end of its "natural" run as the best-known American philosophy. Nevertheless, such an explanation may not be enough. As its unifying principle, pragmatism had replaced certainty, albeit a theological certainty becoming discredited as a guide to research, with a more modest and contingent knowledge dependent on experience and probability. A philosophy that minimized the likelihood of achieving ultimate truth may not have been the best fit for America's self-confident university system, particularly for faculty theorists of the generation that survived the Great Depression, won World War II, split the atom, and dominated the world economy. Particularly in its early manifestation as a self-confident positivism, the philosophy that evolved into logical empiricism reassured both scientists and philosophers that those with the appropriate education and experience could uncover the world's secrets. It thus represented a powerful validation of human capabilities. Pragmatism's more "subjective" vision of a world where truth is a tentative and changing consensus, grounded in humanity's fallible ability to define and comprehend extraordinarily complex natural and social realities, seemed out of step with the times.

THE SUCCESSORS TO POSITIVISM (AND MODERNISM IN GENERAL)

Three Metaparadigms

For convenience in discussion, it is useful to adopt the arbitrary convention that recorded human history has been dominated to date by three *metaparadigms*. Here, a "metaparadigm" will be defined as a paradigm so large and embracing that it constitutes a broad, fundamental worldview and may even give rise to a number of subordinate paradigms or variations in ways of envisioning "reality." In more or less chronological order of appearance on the Western world's intellectual stage, these metaparadigms or worldviews, variants of which are still influential throughout the world, can be termed the (1) traditional, (2) modern, and (3) postmodern.

The Traditional Metaparadigm

The traditional metaparadigm holds that a culture's customs, specifically including its religious revelations, determine what is or is not "true" knowledge. A culture operating with a dominant traditional metaparadigm tends to emphasize continuity. However, in practice, it usually allows knowledge to evolve over time. If accepted, changes in a traditional metaparadigm's fundamental understandings of the world may be defined as elaborations on long-standing or even eternally valid truths. As discussed above, prior to the twentieth century it was expected that intellectual life, including scientific research, in the American national culture would be aligned with a Protestant version of the traditional Christian metaparadigm.

A Brief Overview of Modernism

When so inclined, theorists can give the metaparadigm of modernism a truly extensive genealogy. Modernism, or modernity, is sometimes defined by its adherents through the ways it differs from the traditional metaparadigm. It has been depicted as a Western European–originated, centuries-long effort (sometimes known as the "Enlightenment Project") dedicated to freeing the human mind from the constraints imposed by traditional society and organized religion. Modernism is often dated to the seventeenth century, when Sir Francis Bacon argued for the superior value of knowledge gained through building *up* from evidence, the "senses and particulars," over knowledge secured by the more traditional approach of taking the most general philosophical axioms developed by human reason—held to be "settled and immovable"—and applying them *down* to explain particulars. It was also in the seventeenth century that René Descartes "laid the ground for a secular science, which would be neutral on questions of meaning and value."[23] As already discussed, the effort in the United States to separate scientific research from theology exemplifies the struggle of modernity for independence.

Writing from the contemporary Roman Catholic paradigm, Timothy G. McCarthy emphasizes that "modernity is not a fully precise term or notion. In each period of history thoughtful persons attempt to be in touch with modernity. For example, the attempt in the thirteenth century of Thomas Aquinas to correlate with the new Aristotelianism was the modernity of that period."[24]

Nonetheless, as McCarthy observes, the now traditional version of modernism's story is that

> modernity denotes the mentality or mindset that developed in the seventeenth century as a result of the scientific revolution. This mindset is associated with the Enlightenment of the eighteenth century and it has continued into the nineteenth and twentieth centuries. Modernity unleashed major critiques of the past understanding of the physical sciences, politics, philosophy, economics, and religion, and was concerned with the progressive enhancement of human life by controlling the natural world; by creating a perfect society; by focusing on human reason, dignity, and autonomy; and by rejecting religion, faith, and revelation.[25]

As noted above, for much of the twentieth century a sequence of paradigms within modernism—first pragmatism, then positivism and its daughter philosophical schools—fought the traditional metaparadigm of "religion, faith, and revelation" for control over mainstream intellectual life within the United States. It took a growing dissatisfaction with the ability of positivism to explain realities outside of the natural and experimental sciences to provide the intellectual space necessary for the emergence of the latest metaparadigm or worldview, generally known as postmodernism.

A Postmodernist Theoretical Abundance

Pauline Marie Rosenau, in *Post-Modernism and the Social Sciences: Insights, Inroads, and Intrusions*, describes attempts to consider postmodernism as "quintessentially 'no win' ventures." In her opinion, theorists who support postmodernism's subjectivity against the presumed objectivity of modernism are likely to feel that any assessments will be "unfair" or "misguided" or will constitute attempts to "represent the unrepresentable." Alternatively, opponents of postmodernism can and often do believe that anything that contributes to providing postmodernism with intellectual respectability is unjustified by the "facts."[26]

Unless authors' loyalties to paradigms are specified in their work, it is possible to mislabel as "postmodernists" those contemporary proponents of critical theory, feminism, or pragmatism who believe that they are functioning quite well within the modernist metaparadigm. Paradigms, however new, rapidly develop intellectual traditions that are useful in understanding later arguments. When authors assert adherence to certain paradigms, they provide readers with a level of theoretical awareness that is helpful in the often-difficult task of understanding their arguments. Contemporary theorists who draw on multiple paradigms may be under an even greater obligation to provide their readers with adequate notice of their affiliations or intellectual influences in order to minimize inevitable misunderstandings.

Unfortunately, there is a tactic for securing publication that involves obscuring an author's intellectual affiliations. Its purpose is to avoid offending those journal reviewers whose dislike of a theoretical school may influence, however inadvertently, their vote for or against publication of a given article or book manuscript. This now-classic tactic may gain publication, but it comes at a price. In the postmodern world of multiple and competing paradigms and metaparadigms, a theorist who refrains from declaring her or his intellectual allegiances provides readers with an unnecessary puzzle, forcing them—often with minimum guidance—to discern the underlying hypotheses, understandings, or findings that are central to the author's arguments. The use of "hegemony" or "class consciousness" represents a contemporary example. Does employing such terms indicate that an author is a classical Marxist, critical theorist, or simply a writer employing currently fashionable terminology in hope of securing publication in the leading journals of her or his field?

The need for theorists to assist readers in understanding their work is present even if the author asserts multiple allegiances. How is one to interpret the work of a researcher who informs readers that he or she has adopted a "sensibility that is critical-feminist-pragmatist-postmodernist with an appreciation of world religions as repositories of human experience"? That such a self-definition has yet to be encountered by the author does not rule out its possibility.

Postmodernism "Explained"

The postmodernist movement is "riddled with ambiguity and controversy" and, given the space limits of this work, impossible to describe in more than a cursory fashion.[27] However, the origin of postmodernism as a self-conscious, if loosely defined, movement is often credited to such European literary and cultural critics as Roland Barthes, Jacques Derrida, Michael Foucault, and Jean-Francois Lyotard. According to Barry Smart, these theorists demonstrate a shared concern with the reality that humans as creatures of language can never be truly certain of what we know.[28]

Rosenau has summarized how scholarly activity operates in the actual work of theorizing for a postmodernist world.

> Post-modernists, defining everything as a text, seek to "locate" meaning rather than to "discover" it. They avoid judgment and the most sophisticated among them never "advocate" or "reject" but speak rather of being "concerned with" a topic or "interested in" something. They offer "readings" not "observations," "interpretations" not "findings; they "muse" about one thing or another. They never test because testing requires "evidence," a meaningless concept within a post-modern frame of reference.[29]

Stanley J. Grenz employs the tactic of defining postmodernism against its modern predecessor, stressing that "modernity is built on the assumption that knowledge is certain, objective and good." In postmodernism, knowledge is uncertain and subjective and can be either good or evil. Nuclear technology, for example, can both light the world and destroy it.[30] Grenz's modernist–postmodernism dichotomy is helpful but a bit oversimplified. Classical pragmatism, for example, was self-confidently "modern," even as it saw the world as contingent, defined by agreements within communities, and as good or evil as the humans who inhabit it.

The primary contribution of postmodernism to theory building may lie in its reminder that a paradigm's universalizing tendencies are always being undermined by the complexities and instabilities of multiple languages and cultures. This assertion is a particularly useful stimulus to theory development. There have been times when modernism, particularly in its mid-twentieth-century flourishing as a highly secular positivism, seemed to have inherited the intellectual arrogance of the nineteenth century's idealistic metaphysics. Both, for example, claimed the right to govern America's intellectual life. To adapt and modify observations that Robert Dubin applied in another context to traditional religious understandings of the world, postmodernism reminds the theorist of the need to give up the "preposterous assumption" of being "in a game of trying to understand the universe from God's [the universe's] standpoint." For unpresumptuous postmodernists of the twenty-first century—as well as their reflective modernist and traditionalist colleagues—effective paradigms and their theories "serve human purposes; their creation is motivated and their logic organized by the skills and limitations of human capabilities."[31]

Before discussing the specific philosophies that moved to center stage as the metaparadigm of postmodernism grabbed the limelight and strong positivism declined into irrelevant analytic philosophy, it is useful to remember that neither the modern nor the traditional metaparadigms have vanished from the world. Modernity, more or less recognizing human limitations, still flourishes in many of the university's natural and experimental sciences. In the humanistic, professional, and social science fields and disciplines, scholars asserting at least a loose affiliation with variants of critical theory, feminism, and pragmatism can also claim some level of allegiance to "modernism."

Within the United States, the nineteenth century's traditional religious metaparadigm, long superseded as a guide for new knowledge in the nation's major universities, has now expanded. Buddhist, Catholic, Islamic, Jewish, Orthodox, and other religious understandings of acceptable knowledge now serve to support or contest the paradigm's historically Protestant core. Thus strengthened, the traditional paradigm retains at least a foothold in the academy while continuing to situate itself in the heart of American culture.[32]

Critical Theory

It is useful to conceptualize *critical theory* as a theoretical approach particularly focused on matters relating to issues of class, power, and human freedom. However, one is likely to encounter scholars utilizing critical theory in combination with, or even in contrast to, a variety of other "postmodern" and even "modern" sources of theory. A small yet illustrative example of just such a mix of paradigms occurred while I was serving as Ohio's deputy state librarian for library services and, concurrently, working on a master's degree in English at Ohio State University.

When this example of "theoretical complication" took place, I was participating in a student group dedicated to investigating feminist theory. Such forums for exploring issues by graduate students are often found in a university community, providing a means to examine in greater depth ideas and philosophies that might have been insufficiently covered in class discussions. If its focus is on a topic that is currently fashionable in the university, a group can bring together students from a number of fields and disciplines. This was the case with the feminist theory group, where most of the members were full-time graduate students teaching undergraduate courses in return for tuition waivers and a minimal stipend for the academic year. To save money, the group's discussions were usually held in student apartments, and the refreshments generally consisted of inexpensive varieties of cheese, crackers, and wine contributed by the attendees.

At one such discussion, a graduate student analyzed the agreed-upon readings through applying theoretical "lenses" (approaches) reflecting her dual realities as a woman and a minority ethnic group member. Toward the end of her remarks, this student stressed that American higher education's lamentable history of sexual and ethnic discrimination would undoubtedly hamper her university career. Following these observations, and before further discussion, the group took a short break for refreshments. As I waited my turn to refill a plastic glass from a wine jug, the student ahead of me, who happened to be an older white female, turned and whispered, "Her theorizing was sound but it really doesn't apply in her case. That student comes from really big money. If anything gets in her way when she leaves OSU, her family could just buy her a university of her own."

This lack of solidarity in theorizing was as intriguing as it was unexpected. However, there were simply too many students in the crowded living room to allow me to discreetly pursue this critique of how ruling classes, even those composed of minority group members, take care of their daughters. On the walk back to our cars after the discussion I was able to press my fellow student on her earlier remarks. After looking around to ensure that we weren't being overheard, she asked a fashion question. Had I noticed that the woman who had talked so long and eloquently about gender and ethnic discrimination was wearing very expensive clothing and jewelry? When I replied that I hadn't noticed, she quipped something about my being a typical male and probably more interested in women with their clothing off. Smiling at my discomfort, she then reminded me that most of the women at that night's discussion wore jeans because that was "all we can afford" on a graduate student's stipend. Like her, most of the other students were piling up debt and stretching already extended budgets to contribute their share of the meeting's refreshments. That definitely was not the case with the night's discussion leader, she asserted. According to the graduate school grapevine, the evening's well-dressed critic of American institutional sexism and ethnic discrimination was residing in an off-campus condominium purchased by her father, who was also providing a generous monthly living allowance. As we reached her car, my companion grew more animated, stressing that even in a society with rampant sexism and ethnic discrimination, the majority and minority ruling classes would always take care of their own. "You need to become more familiar with critical theory," she concluded.

On that evening of wine, cheese, and theory, both the wealthy analyst of gender and ethnic discrimination and her critical theorist evaluator drew on their graduate studies for biting assessments of the national and university cultures of America. In "the States," such evaluations have become the prerogative of yet another defined class, the university-trained (and often university-affiliated) intellectual. According to Murray Hausknecht, "the intellectual" is a contemporary phenomenon, differing from past counterparts in that *the role becomes a self-conscious justification for the intellectual's very existence*. For Hausknecht, the modern intellectual's exploration of society, her or his "critical stance," involves "questioning the fundamental premises underlying beliefs, values and behavior as well as specific ideologies and programs."[33] Such an approach can represent a public commitment to nonmainstream ideas when such allegiance is defined as "deviant" by the ruling elites. Intellectuals who do not support their dominant national culture can and do run the risk of being marginalized as, at best, "malcontents" or, at worst, "enemies." In the United States, for example, opposition to the "institutions of capitalism" could very easily place an intellectual in such suspect categories.

The following quotation, describing the market-friendly approach taken by contemporary heads of British universities, can serve as a litmus test to determine whether one might be the sort of intellectual who views present-day society through the perspective of *critical theory*. By way of background, it should be noted that the position of university chancellor in Great Britain has historically tended to be an honorary post held by prominent individuals who may not otherwise be affiliated with the university. The "working head" of the university usually holds the title of "vice chancellor" or its equivalent. Of late, according to Anthony Smith and Frank Webster,

> the offices of vice-chancellors and managers of [university] corporate communications are clogged with press statements and fliers proclaiming the achievements of their students in obtaining employment, how effective their institutions are in inculcating "enterprise skills" into their graduates, how successful in their co-operation with industry, how energetic in their contribution to the wealth-creating resources of the nation.[34]

In nations where students finance all or part of their university studies, the pro-employment orientation of these British vice chancellors, as well as their commitment to creating jobs through economic development, might be applauded by students (and parents) seeking a financial return for the funds and years devoted to earning degrees. In America, it is customary to view such scenarios as positive depictions of a beneficial alliance of two "goods"—the university itself and the "free enterprise" economy that directly or indirectly makes possible higher education. It must be stressed that envisioning higher education as a worthwhile *investment* for the future is not a particularly modern or American concept. In many ways, it is a notion as old as the university itself. So too is an alternative model, one that values the university as a place of study and often-critical reflection. In the European Middle Ages, when a church position was a path to wealth and worldly power for nobles and commoners alike, university-based theologians could be most strident in their attacks on the field of canon or church law. Such theological critics argued that canon studies were both self-serving and careerist since they drew "students away from pure learning towards the path of ecclesiastical preferment." As one historian of the medieval world stresses, "The church was a vast administrative machine which needed lawyers to run it, and a well-trained canonist had a good chance of rising to the highest dignities."[35]

Critical theorists might argue that the above scenario, indeed any scenario where a university boasts of its connection to the marketplace, masks the negative consequences flowing from a mission buttressing the hegemonic rule of the American, British, or Canadian variations of late capitalism's international governing class. For critical theorists, "hegemony," or often "cultural hegemony," is useful for describing environments where a particular class has power over a society's financial, military, and other resources. More fundamentally, the concept of hegemony spotlights how control of language, religion, education, and other cultural "tools" even allows a dominant class to control the very mental categories that people use to think about the world and their places in it. When analyzing a given culture, critical theorists tend to concentrate on exploring such issues as: the maldistribution of resources within a society; how ruling classes reproduce themselves, in part through privileged access to leading universities; the roles of language in obscuring the realities of class-based gains and losses; and "the historical embeddedness of all theory" in trying to examine how a culture and its university system conduct "business as usual."[36]

It cannot be overemphasized that many critical theorists object to the very idea of a university dedicated to preparing students for a market economy dominated by what they see as self-serving elites. For such theorists, the entrepreneurial university concept embodies the naive or even conspiratorial acceptance and replication of the power of cultural elites and the promotion of their goals by the very institution—the university—where elites and their goals ought to be critically examined. Rather than blindly helping to produce more effective capitalists, critical theorists would argue, American university professors, including those dedicated to the study of information transmission and knowledge generation, should analyze whether or not their institution's support of the dominant culture through close connections with business serves to maximize or limit human potential. Similarly, questioning the standards of society should be stressed in the classrooms so that students might learn effective ways to understand, and perhaps change, local, national, or international variants of the "system."

It might be of interest to American readers to know that critical theory was apparently born in America of European intellectual parentage. The philosophy was "launched" in New York in 1937 by Max Horkheimer and others affiliated with the exiled Frankfurt Institute for Social Research, a group of scholars that had fled to the United States to escape Nazi Germany. The term "critical theory" seems to have been a bit of an intellectual smokescreen, developed by these exiles as a less incendiary alternative to Karl Marx's "dialectical materialism." Apparently, the intent was to play down critical theory's close connection with

Marxism, a philosophy that was never really established in the United States outside of the university environment. From such ironic beginnings in a non-Marxist culture, contemporary critical theory has grown to be a vital component of what has been termed the "European hegemony" in the "world development of social theory."[37]

Within the "library" world, pride of place in the application of critical theory undoubtedly belongs to Michael H. Harris, who openly proclaims his adherence to the philosophy. In a chapter written with Masaru Itoga, for example, Harris cogently summarizes arguments for "critical theories designed to emancipate and enlighten; critical theories that will alert librarians to the ideological frame surrounding library service," even while asserting the need for the "librarian-researcher . . . to undertake emancipatory work that is conscious of the contradictions inherent in the delivery of 'free library service' in a capitalist society." These efforts would be undertaken as part of the effort to study the "production and distribution of cultural capital for ideological purposes."[38]

Harris is part of a minority intellectual component when he proclaims himself a critical theorist within the complex and overlapping worlds of information studies, librarianship, and knowledge management. In "Hegemony's Handmaid? The Library and Information Studies Curriculum from a Class Perspective," Christine Pawley attributes the reluctance of faculty in American Library Association–accredited programs to use a critical theory perspective to causes as diverse as a traditional American avoidance of "class analysis," a reluctance to follow the lead of scholars in other fields who have analyzed subjects through a class-sensitive lens, and a regrettable "willingness to comply with a dominant but unstated value that favors the maintenance of inequality."[39] For Pawley, this alliance of library and information education with American ruling elites leads faculty to adopt research perspectives that forgo class analysis and its revelatory interest in the doings of social groups and, instead, embrace the "individual as [their] unit of analysis" (*pluralism*) and/or concentrate on effectiveness in decision making (*managerialism*). Both perspectives, she notes, encourage a matter-of-fact endorsement of the status quo, including undisputed valuation of the worth of the marketplace, promotion of university–corporate cooperation, concern for the maintenance or achievement of professional status, and what might be termed a near-celebration of the capitalistic ("free enterprise") economy as the basis for organizing society.[40]

From the perspective of American culture, with "culture" being defined as a complex system of symbols and their interpretations that helps members of a society structure their experience and categorize their natural and social worlds, critical theory can have great appeal to academics such as Harris and Pawley while being unattractive to the larger society.[41] Indeed, there is a fundamentally important reason why library, information, and media professionals outside of the university context exhibit what seems to be a natural tendency to ignore findings, however valid, that are produced through the class-based analysis that is at the heart of critical theory. In the words of Pawley, whose own work displays a strong sympathy for the paradigm, "The class perspective is not cheering. Short of revolution, it fails to present solutions to problems of exploitation and inequity."[42]

In the United States, issues of "exploitation and inequity" have usually been addressed not by violent revolution but through campaigns for reform. In such circumstances, theoretical studies grounded in the concept of the library as part of "an ensemble of institutions dedicated to the creation, transmission, and reproduction of the hegemonic ideology"[43] may not have an appreciative audience in the ranks of nonuniversity librarians, media specialists, and information and knowledge managers—practitioners whose paths to more effective library, information, and knowledge services rely more on political persuasion than revolutionary fervor.

However, it may be a mistake to follow Pawley in so tying the impact of critical theory to achieving change on a revolutionary scale. Critical theory findings and formulations have the potential to influence university-based scholarship grounded in a range of other philosophies. The contemporary pragmatist Cornel West, for one, relied on a combination of classical pragmatism, African American Protestant liberation theology, and critical theory to formulate his own *prophetic pragmatism*. According to West, his pragmatic variant "promotes a more direct encounter with the Marxist tradition of social analysis."[44] In the postmodern world that so contextualizes West's formulations, it is thus possible for a theorist to be influenced, at one and the same time, by pragmatic, religious, and critical theory traditions.

Supporters of critical theory clearly have a future in providing analyses directed at academic audiences. However, they also have a number of hurdles to overcome if critical theory is to be the primary resource for the development of theory useful outside of the American university.

These hurdles include:

- the unwillingness of American society to support a Marxist tradition. American academics embrace Marxist-derived insights, but the culture as a whole has little or no use for such formulations. This reality is particularly interesting in light of the fact that a million-plus students earn bachelor's degrees in American institutions in any given year and many of them have undoubtedly taken sociology and other courses where Marxist models are discussed.[45]
- the difficulty of applying critical theory in the development of the interlanguages needed for discussions among academic practitioners and practitioners in off-campus contexts. It may be possible to "facilitate mutual understanding and promote trade [in ideas]" when one's potential partners reject Marxist-derived formulations for describing their realities, but it will take extraordinary levels of sensitivity to do so.[46] Critical theory focuses on class dominance and other negative aspects of a society. American culture, for the most part, has avoided emphasizing class divisions.
- the reality that critical theory seems to concentrate overmuch on *dissensus* (disagreement) and too little on *consensus*. For example, anyone who has ever worked to bring a library or other "public good" into existence knows firsthand that, on occasion, secular idealism or religious conviction can and does compete successfully with both individual and class interest. In part, critical theory shares what Edward Shils saw as an unbalanced sociological vision of American society that asserts, among other aspects, "a self-interested, ruthless pursuit of power for its own sake and for the retention of what they already possess among the powerful."[47]
- the problem of critical theory in meeting the requirements that useful theory in the nonacademic environment ought to (1) predict, (2) be in accord with experience, and (3) solve practical problems more effectively (see above discussion).
- the availability of the alternative of a revived pragmatism, an indigenous, non-Marxist philosophy that enabled John Dewey and others to carry out strong and repeated analyses of American culture. Historically, pragmatism, although subject to attack from the religious paradigm, tends to be more acceptable for critiquing reality in off-campus American environments than Marxism in any of its incarnations.[48]

It is worth stressing again that critical theory, as part of a world discourse among information, knowledge, library, and other academics, has a bright future within the national and global higher education communities both as a source of primary theory and as an aid to theoreticians operating from other perspectives. However, it will require the proverbial sea change—Pawley's revolution or at least the presence of widely acknowledged revolutionary conditions—for the larger American culture to view the findings of critical theory as acceptable for decision making in most off-campus environments. Indeed, it is difficult to envision American academic administrators ever choosing courses of action on the basis of critical theory analyses of higher education environments provided by faculty.

Feminism

In a *Partisan Review* article entitled "The Best Man for the Job May Be a Woman," philosopher Susan Haack—who admits to having "individualistic, old-fashioned-feminist" thoughts—describes how both men and women, particularly women, can fail the "fitting in" test for hiring by a philosophy department. After using such categories as "greed" and "fear" to organize her analysis of the role self-interest plays in faculty votes in hiring decisions, Haack asserts:

> Small wonder, then, that "forced to appoint a woman," sometimes departments hire, not the best woman, but the least threatening: the conventional, the conformist, the student of one's own mentor, or, failing that, the specialist in feminist philosophy, who, though not "one of us," needn't, in private anyway, be taken *quite* seriously—and might earn us points with the Dean.[49]

Haack's article, which discusses feminism amid a jewel of a critique of the academic hiring process, demonstrates both why feminist research is needed and why it may have difficulty in communicating its findings outside the feminist community. The latter difficulty applies, as Haack indicates, because a specialist in feminist philosophy need not "be taken quite seriously" by her male colleagues and, by extension, a male-dominated society that has traditionally undervalued women's perspectives in numerous fields and disciplines.

Terry Lovell, self-identified as a "white, middle-class, 'first-world' feminist," has argued that the object of feminist social theory is the "social construction of gender in its effects in determining the social positions of women." In pursuing this object across national boundaries, the international feminist movement supports a number of schools, such as Marxist, postmodernist, poststructuralist, lesbian, maternal, psychoanalytic, liberal, radical, and so on—all offering differing perspectives and insights on issues affecting women.[50] Such a broad spectrum of alternately converging and diverging standpoints under the feminist mantle clearly makes it impossible, short of a series of monographs, to consider how each might contribute to the development of useful theory, even if such an analysis could be limited solely to the United States.

Alternatively, even allowing for the limitations of context, it might be possible to draw some useful lessons from a partial consideration of feminist influences in one broad context. Somewhere near 80 percent of the five thousand or so professional master's degrees from programs accredited by the American Library Association (ALA) awarded each year—to aspiring librarians, information specialists, knowledge managers, media specialists, and competitive data analysts—are earned by women.[51] As might be expected, as professional gatekeepers educating for professions composed largely of women, ALA-accredited programs have developed a number of feminist research agendas that, in turn, have influenced a growing body of feminist inquiries. Patterns of influence, as opposed to patterns of formal recognition, are notoriously difficult to document. However, Susan E. Searing's "Women's Studies for a 'Women's' Profession: Theory and Practice in Library Science" summarizes a range of significant research efforts and provides a useful template for charting feminist research directions in library and information science (LIS).[52] A small sample of other works of interest, particularly to library, information, knowledge, and media educators, would include Jane Anne Hannigan's "A Feminist Standpoint for Library and Information Science Education," Roma M. Harris's *Librarianship: The Erosion of a Woman's Profession*, Hope A. Olson's "The Feminist and the Emperor's New Clothes: Feminist Deconstruction as a Critical Methodology for Library and Information Studies," and Mark A. Spivey's "Feminist Scholarship: Implications for Information Management and Research."[53]

The works of these authors, collectively, can serve to sensitize readers to a spectrum of concerns regarding the historic undervaluation of women and women's experience within the various library, information, and knowledge environments. Fundamental to such analysis is the understanding that patterns of cultural and institutional discrimination have limited women's career opportunities while ignoring—or underreporting—those successes that were achieved by women under often adverse circumstances. In numerous professional contexts, these and other works in what is clearly a burgeoning area of study may have significant implications for both research and practice. For researchers, this developing tradition can lay the foundation for research questioning whether or not the prevalence of women in the field has inhibited its professionalism and limited its status, analyzing the sorting-out process that historically provided males with administrative positions out of proportion to their numbers, and addressing the validity of such impressions as that both male and female LIS students are "overly feminine."[54] In addition, feminist researchers have raised such critical questions as: "What, for instance, can we learn from observing the practice of female school library media specialists, academic librarians, or corporate librarians?"[55] and "Does the insistence on a masters degree perpetuate a homogenous, middle-class, mostly white labor pool?"[56]

All of the above signify areas for inquiry that may be of fundamental importance for the many worlds of library, information, knowledge, and media practice. When sensitized to the prevalence of cultural and institutional barriers to women's careers, both public and corporate employers (out of sheer self-interest) may find it useful to utilize feminist-derived theory as a touchstone for examining such areas as the recruitment of minority women for professional positions in an increasingly multicultural society, the role of child-care assistance in attracting or retaining staff, and the possible impact on employee morale of responding to public demand to offer evening programs for children. Are there similar morale issues in play, for example, when corporate knowledge management centers adopt twenty-four-hour-a-day staffing in order to provide information service to multinational sites in a global environment? Such questions, some newly emerging but others often ignored or deemed irrelevant in the past, address fundamental concerns for the librarians, information specialists, knowledge managers, and school library media specialists hired to provide service in a wide spectrum of academic and nonacademic contexts. Given such opportunities for building useful theory, the relevant questions now include: *Is feminist research within library, information, knowledge, and media studies making an impact on practice? If so, how? If not, why?*

CULTURAL PRAGMATISM

There are several reasons for concentrating on *cultural pragmatism*, rather than attempting to explore all the schools that currently exist within the broad spectrum of *contemporary pragmatism* or the original *classical pragmatism*.

First, John Dewey emphasized the power of culture in 1951 when he wrote that, if given the opportunity, he would rework his famed *Experience and Nature* into something more appropriately titled *Culture and Nature*. Dewey's reasons for wanting to revise the earlier classic seem to be extremely practical: his vocabulary was out of date, readers were having difficulty understanding what he meant by "experience," and the terminology developed to analyze "culture" had become a more appropriate vehicle for conveying his ideas.[57]

Second, cultural pragmatism takes as a fundamental research objective the development of a solution to a crucially important omission in the pragmatic version of truth offered by Charles Sanders Peirce in his landmark 1878 essay "How to Make Our Ideas Clear." For Peirce and mainstream pragmatists in general, *truth* is "the opinion that is fated to be ultimately agreed to by all who investigate."[58] As suggested by both pragmatic theory and much of postmodern theory, all human knowledge, including that gained through investigation and analyzed experience, is subjectively understood. Truth as agreed-upon opinion, albeit repeatedly tested through experience, requires an ongoing effort to achieve concurrence across a worldwide range of languages and cultures. For cultural pragmatists, the degree to which such transcendence of cultural norms is possible is directly related to the ability of humans to craft appropriate interlanguages as mechanisms for working out the cross-cultural understandings (including on-campus to off-campus understandings) that are necessary to define and share knowledge across context. At a minimum, such interlanguages (1) are essential to the growth of useful theory and (2) can form the basis for what Richard Rorty sees as the "marginal, minor but nevertheless helpful role" of philosophy in assisting humans in overcoming "cultural traditions" that base "political decisions on the difference between people like us, the paradigmatic human beings, and such dubious cases of humanity as foreigners, infidels, untouchables, women, homosexuals, half-breeds, and deformed or crippled people."[59]

Third, the term "cultural pragmatism" reflects the much more complex world faced by all twenty-first-century researchers in light of the wide spectrum of "truth" claims raised by positivism, postmodernism, critical theory, and feminism, as well as such popular European philosophies as existential phenomenology, psychoanalysis, phenomenology, and hermeneutics.[60]

Fourth, as a participant in a paradigm that draws heavily from both modernism and postmodernism, even while being open to insights from the more traditional understandings that permeate American life, I believe that even provisional generalizations grow increasingly difficult to sustain when taken beyond the level of national cultures. There are, of course, recognized exceptions to the caution. For example, in decades of investigation into libraries, information centers, knowledge management operations, and other organizations, American and Canadian scholars and practitioners have long felt comfortable sharing the results of their research and experience across international boundaries with some confidence that their findings would be understood even within different national contexts.[61] In contrast to authors who might claim a universal validity for their findings, I believe that the present work will have value for readers in other nations to the degree that their own cultures resonate with the American variants of the traditional, modern, and postmodern metaparadigms and subparadigms that form the raw material for my theorizing.

Any discussion of cultural pragmatism in the national American context needs to address the assertions accepted or tolerated by many classical pragmatists and discussed earlier in this chapter. While the first ten assertions continue to be more or less supported by analyzed experience in a majority of American contexts, the remaining two—"humans have the most opportunity to develop their capabilities in a democracy" and "scientific and other knowledge progresses best in a democratic context that encourages freedom of inquiry"—may simply *not* be verifiable. Although critical to the formulations offered by cultural pragmatism, they seem to fall into Thomas Kuhn's category of the "non-empirical assumptions" that are central to a philosophy but which cannot be proven to be valid to a (hypothetically) objective judge.[62]

Beyond the necessity to accept certain "non-empirical assumptions" in order to embrace cultural pragmatism, there is the further reality that the pragmatic commitment to democracy occasionally conflicts with the equally important value of freedom in research. For example, democracies usually rely on legislatures or other representative institutions to pass laws for the common good. However, the existence of strong legislation against child pornography at the state and national levels within the United States means that scholars seeking to investigate child pornography on the Internet can be convicted of serious felonies if they bring certain images up on their computer screens.[63]

Previously, it was stressed that people and groups tend to base their actions on operative *"if... then"* rules.[64] Cultural pragmatists are aware that differences in *"if... then"* rules, often caused by variations in life experiences, provide the people of the United States with numerous, often diverging, definitions of their shared national culture. In consequence, it is to be expected that individuals living in other national cultures, or even in the various subcultures that collectively constitute "American," can take very different actions based on variant understandings of the nature of a "problem."

Cultural pragmatism is sensitive to the fact that the very process of defining a problem in collaboration with other "stakeholders" spotlights the natural human inclination, shared by theorists and practitioners alike, to confuse one's view of the world with the world's "objective" reality. This is a problem studied by Richard E. Neustadt and Ernest R. May at the level of American national government, where they found senior policy makers "are prone to project upon relative strangers the meanings of things in their own heads, assuming an undifferentiated rationality."[65] In other words, *even when dealing with critical issues of war and peace, government officials routinely commit the fallacy of believing that (1) they, (2) their likely allies, and (3) their potential opponents are all thinking about problems in the same way.*

For the more radical of postmodern theorists, envisioning "meaning" as having many "meanings" underscores the presence of *incommensurability*, defined as the perceived inability of humans to communicate effectively with one another because of a lack of common standards for meaning and other shared cultural foundations. Pragmatic theorists, particularly those who are cultural pragmatists, usually have a different take on the matter. Whenever theories regarding incommensurability are asserted, pragmatists have the option of walking to the nearest window and observing the world. This simple act can lead to the common-sense but reasonable determination—always subject to revision on the basis of new experience—that much of the world seems to "work," even if the planet supports many cultures and subcultures operating with widely varying rules. For pragmatism, cultural complexity can be an intellectual positive, offering a seemingly endless source of remarkably interesting research questions. Such questions can and do include variations on how it might be possible to facilitate the development of the interlanguages necessary to assist American, British, Canadian, or other cultures in solving a spectrum of library, information, and knowledge "problems."

Pragmatism and Research into Library, Information, Knowledge, and Media Questions

Historically, the relationship between pragmatism and the various professions interested in studying library, information, knowledge, and media issues has mirrored the status of pragmatism within the larger world. In the early years of the twentieth century, when pragmatism was the mainstream professional philosophy, its connection with research in the domain of "library" theorists was evidenced in the pages of the University of Chicago's *Library Quarterly*, a journal launched by its Graduate Library School in 1931 to raise the level of scholarship in the field. The very first issue of this journal contained an article by C. C. Williamson, dean of Columbia University's School of Library Service, that celebrated the value of pragmatism as a philosophy, quoting William James with strong approval and praising John Dewey's writings on research, particularly his work on education, as essential models for "library science."[66]

In the competitive academic world, Williamson's effusive praise of pragmatism as a guide for theory development in "library science" begged for a counterargument. Barely two years later, Pierce Butler's influential *Introduction to Library Science* provided one. On one level, this work can be read as a blistering assault on the practitioner world, labeling the progress made in librarianship as being merely "a pragmatic quest for specific improvement," far below what was needed to achieve status as a "professional science" capable of attracting to its ranks the "really intellectually competent." Butler's assault on practitioner "pragmatism" may also be read, on a deeper level, as an open attack on classical pragmatism, a philosophy that valued the professional life of the practitioner as an essential source of the raw material necessary for theory building.[67]

On the surface, the results of a decades-long retreat by pragmatism under the assault of the positivist paradigm is evident in L. Houser and Alvin M. Schrader's 1978 *Search for a Scientific Profession*. As with Williamson and Butler, the authors of this noteworthy work assert that "library science" would come into existence only when a rigorous adherence to scientific method became characteristic of the field. Although Houser and Schrader cite *The Conduct of Inquiry*, written by the influential (and pragmatic) theorist Abraham Kaplan, their arguments reflect the positivist orientation prevalent in much disciplinary and professional research of the time. In consequence, references to the then-unfashionable Dewey, James, and Charles Sanders Peirce, the trinity of giants who formed the foundation of pragmatism circa 1900, are not to be found.[68]

It would be a mistake to confuse missing citations to pragmatic intellectual giants with a lack of pragmatic influence on library, information, knowledge, and media theorizing toward the end of the twentieth century. The only citation to Dewey, James, or Peirce in the numerous essays contained in 1991's *Library and Information Science Research: Perspectives and Strategies for Improvement* is to James's remarks about the PhD.[69] However, a knowledgeable reader of this work can discern a continuing pragmatic influence through numerous citations to the publications of Barney G. Glaser, Anselm L. Strauss, and Donald A. Schon. Glaser and Strauss's "grounded theory" owes a considerable debt to classical pragmatism; Schon's "Ph.D. thesis [was on] John Dewey's theory of inquiry," and his emphasis on the "reflective practitioner" reflects Dewey's lifelong commitment to enhancing effectiveness in professional work.[70]

As the twentieth century drew to a close, a revived fascination with pragmatism in the larger world made its way into the library, information, and knowledge literatures. For example, explicit and highly complimentary references to the value of pragmatism as a research philosophy can be found in both H. M. Gallagher's 1991 article "Dr. Osborn's 1941 'The Crisis in Cataloging': A Shift in Thought toward American Pragmatism" and Michael Gorman's monograph *Our Enduring Values: Librarianship in the Twenty-First Century*.[71]

The Author and Cultural Pragmatism

My own interest in the value of pragmatism in facilitating useful research began in 1993, when I left the position of deputy state librarian for library services with the State Library of Ohio to study for a doctorate in higher education at Ohio University in Athens, Ohio. There, encouraged by Prof. Robert B. Young, I employed pragmatic analysis and theorizing in the research for my 1995 dissertation and subsequent publications.[72] Several more years of theorizing in a postmodern academic context where (1) faculty research continued to lack utility for many "field" practitioners and (2) no single paradigm or even metaparadigm could any longer claim the right to arbitrate intellectual disputes led me to speculate on whether some form of pragmatism could play a fruitful role as an acceptable "middle ground." Convinced that it could, I began researching how one might update classical pragmatism, in the process developing a subparadigm that I choose to call "cultural pragmatism." These ideas were incorporated in an early draft of this work sent to reviewers. My developing ideas about cultural pragmatism were first made public during a presentation on the future of the academic librarian to a March 15–16, 2001, conference on knowledge management for academic librarians sponsored by Dominican University's Center for Knowledge Management. Subsequently, they appeared in the November 2001 issue of *College and Research Libraries*.[73]

Although several graduate students and I were unable to find prior advocacy of the subparadigm of cultural pragmatism in numerous English language databases and indexes, it remains possible that an earlier theorist, perhaps working in another field or writing in another language, can advance a legitimate claim for coining the phrase. Wherever possible, I have documented my influences. Ideas advanced without such references may be assumed to reflect concepts that were independently developed.

THE SITUATION IN INFORMATION STUDIES AND THE VARIOUS WORLDS OF PRACTICE

Nancy A. Van House has claimed, with justification, that the "positivist method" remains the "most widely accepted" within ALA-accredited programs.[74] *By implication, this means that most scholars in these programs are operating with either an acknowledged or implied allegiance to some version of the modernist metaparadigm or worldview.* In the postmodern world, such allegiance can be seen as the predictable result of graduate school socialization and training, intellectual inertia, or, at worst, a deliberate unwillingness to address the implications of the metaparadigm that provides the intellectual foundation for one's research, whether it is quantitative, qualitative, or a mixture in nature.

It is worth recalling that modernism is based on the fundamental, if often unarticulated, claim that knowledge can be "certain, objective and good."[75] Is there a library, information, knowledge, or media researcher operating today who is willing to advance such claims without immediately qualifying their applicability in differing contexts? Or, as practitioners have informed scholars for decades, is the value and applicability of knowledge determined by the specific context of a given library, community, corporation, or nation?

The usual response of researchers to findings that practitioners do not use their research is to assert that both students and practitioners ought to be better instructed on how to understand and employ such faculty studies. Readers will note, of course, that reprimanding potential users for ignoring a product, even an "intellectual product," reverses the market orientation of American culture as a whole and, for consultants in library, information, knowledge, or media areas, represents an extremely odd approach to operating a business. It is also a self-defeating reaction that obscures the more fundamental issue in advancing useful research, that is, whether or not faculty are actually producing studies that are of interest to practitioners. What Peter Jarvis found for the field of education is also true for library, information, knowledge, and media contexts: "Practitioners seldom read the research literature because it was not written for them—it was written for other researchers."[76]

While instruction in research is of clear value and can equip practitioners to understand faculty studies, there is no guarantee that enhanced comprehension will do anything other than underscore the irrelevance of many academic investigations to the working lives of off-campus practitioners. The "blame-the-customer" mentality present in faculty arguments asserting that practitioners with more training in understanding research would undoubtedly use studies produced in ALA-accredited programs ignores what successful consultants have learned about (1) the necessity of relationship building in constructing successful collaborations and (2) the reality that both consultants and practitioners—unlike faculty—are held accountable for their success or failure in defining and solving "real" problems in "real" time.[77] Shifting the responsibility to the potential consumer for nonuse of faculty research was a "solution" that did not work when it was advanced by C. C. Williamson in 1931; it is unlikely to work when attempted in the twenty-first century.[78]

The fact that a positivist orientation has produced a research literature so irrelevant to practice may be the single strongest argument for asserting that library, information, knowledge, and media faculty ought to join, and proclaim their membership in, research paradigms with a greater awareness of context and human fallibility.

CHAPTER SUMMARY

Chapter 3 addressed how worldviews (metaparadigms) and research philosophies (paradigms) have structured the creation and valuation of knowledge in "Western," particularly "American," history. It began with an exploration of the role of classical pragmatism in the effort to free the American university and its research from theological control in the decades following 1900. In the process, it examined the theoretical contributions of such pragmatic theorists as Charles Sanders Peirce, William James, John Dewey, and Jane Addams. Next, the chapter reviewed the replacement of pragmatism as the leading research philosophy by positivism, later known as logical empiricism. After a consideration of the essential components of the (1) traditional, (2) modern, and (3) postmodern metaparadigms or worldviews, the chapter weighed the intellectual guidance for library, information, knowledge, and media researchers that can be gained from such research paradigms as critical theory, feminism, and the author's own cultural pragmatism.

The chapter included a review of how the universalizing tendencies of the positivist paradigm, deemed to still be the dominant mental model operating in ALA-accredited programs, works to distance faculty-generated scholarship from the context-related needs of practitioner communities. The traditional and often-restated recommendation of faculty researchers for bridging this divide—that students and practitioners should be educated in understanding how to use faculty research—was deemed to be an inadequate solution. Although education on how to use research is valuable in itself, emphasizing such education was seen as a "blame-the-customer" approach that avoids the fundamental issue of research relevance and is out of step with the larger American culture's "customer-centered" orientation.

NOTES

1. Although Thomas S. Kuhn would limit his observations to the natural and experimental sciences, his work on the roles of intellectual or disciplinary "paradigms" has long influenced the social sciences, humanities, and professions. See Kuhn's *The Structure of Scientific Revolutions*, 2d ed., enl. (Chicago: University of Chicago Press, 1970), as well as the considerations of paradigms in such works as Joyce Appleby, Lynn Hunt, and Margaret Jacob, *Telling the Truth about History* (New York: Norton, 1994), and Malcolm Williams and Tim May, *Introduction to the Philosophy of Social Research* (London: University College London Press, 1996).

2. Kuhn, *Structure*.

3. See, for example, the analyses of competition within such paradigms or philosophies described in Bryan S. Turner, ed., *The Blackwell Companion to Social Theory* (Oxford: Blackwell, 1996).

4. Jacques Barzun, *A Stroll with William James* (Chicago: University of Chicago Press, 1983), 83, 85.

5. Arthur O. Lovejoy, "The Thirteen Pragmatisms," in *The Thirteen Pragmatisms and Other Essays* (Baltimore: Johns Hopkins University Press, 1963), 2.

6. "Introduction: Pragmatism—What's the Use?" *Hedgehog Review* 3, no. 3 (Fall 2001): 5.

7. Thomas Carlson, "James and the Kantian Tradition," in *The Cambridge Companion to William James*, ed. Ruth Anna Putnam (Cambridge: Cambridge University Press, 1997), 368.

8. Abraham Kaplan, *The New World of Philosophy* (New York: Random House, 1961), 14.

9. See the discussion of this transformation in Christopher J. Lucas, *American Higher Education: A History* (New York: St. Martin's, 1994).

10. William James, *"Pragmatism" and "The Meaning of Truth"* (1907; reprint, Cambridge, MA: Harvard University Press, 1975), 56.

11. William James, *The Varieties of Religious Experience* (1902; reprint, Middlesex, UK: Penguin, 1982).

12. John Dewey, "A Common Faith," in *John Dewey: The Late Works, 1925–1953, vol. 9, 1933–1934*, ed. Jo Ann Boydston (Carbondale: Southern Illinois University Press, 1989), 8.

13. Frederick Rudolph, *The American College and University: A History* (1962; reprint, Athens: University of Georgia Press, 1990), 412.

14. These definitional elements for classic pragmatism were drawn from a spectrum of the literature, including the work of Charles Sanders Peirce, William James, and John Dewey. In addition, the author owes a particular debt to Abraham Kaplan's lecture/essay "Pragmatism," printed in his *New World of Philosophy*, as well as to his better-known *The Conduct of Inquiry: Methodol-*

ogy for Behavioral Science (San Francisco: Chandler, 1964). Useful samplings of the thoughts of these and other pragmatic theorists are found in Louis Menand's *Pragmatism: A Reader* (New York: Vintage, 1997).

15. See William O. Douglas, introduction to *Jane Addams: A Centennial Reader* (New York: Macmillan, 1960); and Jean Bethke Elshtain, "Jane Addams and the Social Claim," *Public Interest* 145 (Fall 2002): 82–92.

16. Randolph Bourne, "Twilight of Idols," in *The Radical Will: Selected Writings, 1911–1918* (Berkeley: University of California Press, 1992), 343.

17. Glenn Tinder, "Review Essay: At the End of Pragmatism," review of *The Promise of Pragmatism: Modernism and the Crisis of Knowledge*, by John Patrick Diggins, *First Things*, no. 56 (October 1995): 43.

18. See, for instance, John Dewey's *Art as Experience* (1934; reprint, New York: Capricorn Books, 1958).

19. George Boas, preface to Arthur O. Lovejoy, *The Thirteen Pragmatisms and Other Essays* (Baltimore: Johns Hopkins University Press, 1963), vii.

20. Kaplan, *Conduct of Inquiry*, 36.

21. Paul Diesing, *How Does Social Science Work? Reflections on Practice* (Pittsburgh: University of Pittsburgh Press, 1991), 3.

22. Diesing, *How*, 22.

23. Martin Hollis, *The Philosophy of Social Science: An Introduction* (Cambridge: Cambridge University Press, 1994), 24–25.

24. Timothy G. McCarthy, *The Catholic Tradition: Before and After Vatican II, 1878–1993* (Chicago: Loyola University Press, 1994), 25.

25. McCarthy, *Catholic Tradition*.

26. Pauline Marie Rosenau, *Post-Modernism and the Social Sciences: Insights, Inroads, and Intrusions* (Princeton, NJ: Princeton University Press, 1992), ix.

27. Barry Smart, "Postmodern Social Theory," in Turner, *Blackwell Companion*, 397.

28. Smart, "Postmodern Social Theory," 399.

29. Rosenau, *Post-Modernism*, 8.

30. Stanley J. Grenz, *A Primer on Postmodernism* (Grand Rapids, MI: Eerdmans, 1996), 165–66.

31. Robert Dubin, *Theory Building*, rev. ed. (New York: Free Press, 1978), 7.

32. See, for example, the extended discussion in Amanda Porterfield's *The Transformation of American Religion: The Story of a Late Twentieth-Century Awakening* (Oxford: Oxford University Press, 2001).

33. Murray Hausknecht, "At First Glance: The Role of the Intellectual," *Dissent* 44, no. 2 (Spring 1986): 131.

34. Anthony Smith and Frank Webster, "Changing Ideas of the University," in *The Postmodern University? Contested Visions of Higher Education in Society*, ed. Anthony Smith and Frank Webster (Buckingham, UK: Society for Research into Higher Education/Open University Press, 1997), 4.

35. Charles Homer Haskins, *The Rise of the Universities* (New York: Henry Holt, 1923), 50.

36. See, for instance, Craig Calhoun, "Social Theory and the Public Sphere," in Turner, *Blackwell Companion*; and the critical theory approach to educating the "librarian-researcher" advocated in Michael H. Harris and Masaru Itoga's "Becoming Critical: For a Theory of Purpose and Necessity in American Librarianship," in Charles R. McClure and Peter Hernon, eds., *Library and Information Science Research: Perspectives and Strategies for Improvement* (Norwood, NJ: Ablex, 1991). Antonio Gramsci, *Selections from the Prison Notebooks of Antonio Gramsci*, ed. and trans. Quintin Hoare and Geoffrey Nowell Smith (New York: International, 1971), is a fundamentally important resource in attempting to understand much of contemporary critical theory.

37. See the discussions in Olaf Hansen, "Introduction: Affinity and Ambivalence," in *Randolph Bourne: The Radical Will: Selected Writings, 1911–1918*, ed. Olaf Hansen; and Goran Therborn, "Critical Theory and the Legacy of Twentieth-Century Marxism," in Turner, *Blackwell Companion*, 56.

38. Harris and Itoga, "Becoming Critical," 350, 353, 354.

39. Christine Pawley, "Hegemony's Handmaid? The Library and Information Studies Curriculum from a Class Perspective," *Library Quarterly* 68, no. 2 (April 1998): 123–24.

40. Pawley, "Hegemony's Handmaid?" 129–31.

41. See the discussions of culture in David I. Kertzer, *Ritual, Politics, and Power* (New Haven, CT: Yale University Press, 1988), especially 79, 84.

42. Pawley, "Hegemony's Handmaid?" 138.

43. Harris and Itoga, "Becoming Critical," 352.

44. Cornel West, *The American Evasion of Philosophy: A Genealogy of Pragmatism* (Madison: University of Wisconsin Press, 1989), 213–14.

45. Hansen, "Introduction," 17. The figures on "Earned Degrees Conferred" are given in the *Chronicle of Higher Education Almanac Issue*, published every year.

46. Steven Roger Fischer, *A History of Language* (London: Reaktion Books, 1999), 177.

47. Edward Shils, "Social Science as Public Opinion," in *The Calling of Sociology and Other Essays on the Pursuit of Learning* (Chicago: University of Chicago Press, 1980), 456.

48. See both James Campbell, *Understanding John Dewey: Nature and Cooperative Intelligence* (Chicago: Open Court, 1995), and Hansen, "Introduction."

49. Susan Haack, "The Best Man for the Job May be a Woman," *Partisan Review* 65, no. 2 (1998): 218.

50. Terry Lovell, "Feminist Social Theory," in Turner, *Blackwell Companion*, 308, 310, and the chapter as a whole.

51. See the "Earned Degrees Conferred" compilations in the yearly *Almanac Issue* of the *Chronicle of Higher Education*. The gender breakdown has remained relatively consistent over the last decade.

52. Susan E. Searing, "Women's Studies for a 'Women's' Profession: Theory and Practice in Library Science," in *The Knowledge Explosion: Generations of Feminist Scholarship*, ed. Cheris Kramarae and Dale Spender (New York: Teachers College Press, 1992).

53. Jane Anne Hannigan, "A Feminist Standpoint for Library and Information Science Education," *Journal of Education for Library and Information Science* 36, no. 4 (Fall 1994): 297–319; Roma M. Harris, *Librarianship: The Erosion of a Woman's Profession* (Norwood, NJ: Ablex, 1992); Hope A. Olson, "The Feminist and the Emperor's New Clothes: Feminist Deconstruction as a Critical Methodology for Library and Information Studies," *Library and Information Science Research* 19, no. 2 (1997): 181–98; Mark A. Spivey, "Feminist Scholarship: Implications for Information Management and Research," *Journal of Academic Librarianship* 21, no. 3 (May 1995): 159–66.

54. Searing, "Women's Studies," 227–28.

55. Hannigan, "Feminist Standpoint," 300.

56. Searing, "Women's Studies," 231.

57. Quoted in Campbell, *Understanding John Dewey*, 68 n. 3.

58. Charles Sanders Peirce, "How to Make Our Ideas Clear" (1878), in *Pragmatism: A Reader*, ed. Louis Menand (New York: Vintage, 1997), 45.

59. Richard Rorty, "Philosophy and the Future," in *Rorty and Pragmatism: The Philosopher Responds to His Critics*, ed. Herman J. Saatkamp, Jr. (Nashville, TN: Vanderbilt University Press, 1995), 204.

60. Richard Shusterman, "The Perils of Making Philosophy a Lingua Americana," *Chronicle of Higher Education* 46, no. 49 (August 11, 2000): B4–B5. In his article Shusterman provides the following definitions: existential phenomenology "claimed to reveal essences by introspective consciousness," and hermeneutics "saw all reality and experience as interpretation" (B4). Psychoanalysis refers, of course, to the school of psychology founded by Sigmund Freud. A useful definition of phenomenology as "a descriptive, introspective analysis in depth of all forms of consciousness and immediate experience" is found in Peter A. Angeles, *The HarperCollins Dictionary of Philosophy*, 2d ed. (New York: HarperCollins, 1992), 226.

61. See the discussion in Bill Crowley, "The Dilemma of the Librarian in Canadian Higher Education," *Canadian Journal of Information and Library Science* 22, no. 1 (April 1997): 4–5.

62. Kuhn, *Structure*, 148.

63. Philip Jenkins, "Bringing the Loathsome to Light," *Chronicle of Higher Education* 48, no. 25 (March 1, 2002), available at http://chronicle.com/weekly/v48/i25/25b01601.htm (accessed April 4, 2002).

64. See John H. Holland, Keith J. Holyoak, Richard E. Nisbett, and Paul R. Thagard, *Induction: Processes of Inference, Learning, and Discovery* (Cambridge, MA: MIT Press, 1987).

65. Richard E. Neustadt and Ernest R. May, *Thinking in Time: The Uses of History for Decision-Makers* (New York: Free Press, 1986), 159.

66. C. C. Williamson, "The Place of Research in Library Service," *Library Quarterly* 1, no. 1 (January 1931): 1–17.

67. Pierce Butler, *An Introduction to Library Science* (Chicago: University of Chicago Press, 1933), 113–14.

68. L. Houser and Alvin M. Schrader, *The Search for a Scientific Profession: Library Science Education in the U.S. and Canada* (Metuchen, NJ: Scarecrow Press, 1978).

69. McClure and Hernon, *Library and Information Science*.

70. See Crowley, "Dilemma," 2–3; Barney G. Glaser and Anselm L. Strauss, *The Discovery of Grounded Theory: Strategies for Qualitative Research* (New York: Aldine de Gruyter, 1967); Donald A. Schon, *Educating the Reflective Practitioner* (San Francisco: Jossey-Bass, 1987), xi; and Anselm L. Strauss, *Qualitative Analysis for Social Scientists* (Cambridge: Cambridge University Press, 1987).

71. H. M. Gallagher, "Dr. Osborn's 1941 'The Crisis in Cataloging': A Shift in Thought toward American Pragmatism," *Cataloging and Classification Quarterly* 12, nos. 3/ 4 (1991): 3–33; and Michael Gorman, *Our Enduring Values: Librarianship in the Twenty-First Century* (Chicago: American Library Association, 2002).

72. See Crowley, "Dilemma," and Bill Crowley, "A Draft Research Model of the Research University Library: Exploring the Scholar–Librarian Partnership of Jaroslav Pelikan in *The Idea of the University: A Reexamination*" (PhD diss., Ohio University, 1995).

73. Bill Crowley, "Tacit Knowledge, Tacit Ignorance, and the Future of Academic Librarianship," *College and Research Libraries* 62, no. 6 (November 2001): 565–84.

74. Nancy A. Van House, "Assessing the Quality and Impact of LIS Research," in McClure and Hernon, *Library and Information Science*, 87.

75. Grenz, *Primer on Postmodernism*, 165.

76. Peter Jarvis, *The Practitioner-Researcher: Developing Theory from Practice* (San Francisco: Jossey-Bass, 1999), 94.

77. See the discussions on American culture's prioritization of both relationship building and achieving results in Harry Beckwith, *Selling the Invisible: A Field Guide to Modern Marketing* (New York: Warner, 1997), and Paco Underhill, *Why We Buy: The Science of Shopping* (New York: Simon and Schuster, 1999).

78. Williamson, "Place of Research."

Chapter Four

Tacit Knowledge: Bridging the Theory–Practice Divide

SCENARIO: IMPROVING REFERENCE EFFECTIVENESS IN MARYLAND

During the 1980s and 1990s, the Division of Library Development and Services of the Maryland Department of Education conducted statewide reference/information studies in public libraries. Over the years, the objectives of these studies became progressively more ambitious; by 1994, they included:

- determining the degree to which a customer received a complete and correct answer to his or her question
- investigating the environmental and behavioral factors that influenced the performance of reference librarians in delivering service
- exploring which activities supported the continued use of behaviors that contributed to a complete and correct answer
- analyzing how perceptions about the model reference behaviors affected the actual use of the behaviors[1]

Twenty-one Maryland public library systems participated in the mid-1990s version of the survey. Study participants were asked forty questions at each of eighty-three outlets, for a total of 3,320 questions asked statewide. The questions were divided into twenty telephone and twenty walk-in questions.[2] Results revealed that the statewide percentage of correctly answered reference questions rose from 55 percent in 1983 to

75 percent in 1994,[3] even as the "model reference behaviors" exhibited by the librarians (see below) that contributed to correctly answering questions remained the same.

If a patron contacts the library, initially asking for information on "local financial matters," the Maryland experience suggests that a more or less effective reference interview could work along the following lines:

1. First the librarian clarifies or paraphrases the question: "Do I have it right that you would like information on the city's finances?"
2. Then the librarian uses an open probe (question) to initiate: "Is it information on the city budget that you might be looking for? Perhaps the current budget? Or maybe information on property tax rates?"
3. Then she or he uses additional open probes after the initial probe: "OK, tax rates. Are you looking for information on how tax rates are computed? Perhaps your tax rate?"
4. The librarian verifies the specific question: "So you would like information on how the county calculates your tax rate? Including specifics on how the city's part of the tax rate is computed?"
5. Finally, the librarian asks a follow-up question: "Because it's tax reassessment time, the library has linked its web page to a very useful web page called 'Tax FAQs, or Frequently Asked Questions, about Property Tax Reassessment.' It's on the website of the county assessor. I can set you up to look at the site on one of our computers if you would like. Since our printing is free you can print out whatever you need. Are you comfortable using the website or would you like me to work with you on getting the information?"[4]

Since the first efforts, a number of accounts of the sequential strivings of the Maryland Division of Library Development and the state's public libraries to upgrade reference effectiveness have appeared in print.[5] In this researcher's opinion, the key to Maryland's success in raising the statewide average of correctly answered questions in the state's public libraries from 55 percent to 75 percent is directly attributable to a multiyear, multiformat approach *to transform tacit into explicit knowledge*, where the tacit knowledge involved includes that of experienced reference librarians, reference supervisors, and reference effectiveness trainers.

During the summer and fall of 1998, I discussed this hypothesis by telephone with two participants in the effort. The first, who wishes to remain anonymous, was initially doubtful and credited the effort to a version of the scientific method described by Jan C. Robbins; however, this same individual requested and copied down several citations to works dealing with tacit knowledge. The second individual interviewed, Lillie Dyson of the Maryland State Department of Education's Division of Library Development and Services, described her state's process as fully in accord with the tacit knowledge approach.[6]

Arguably, the Maryland effort can be analyzed by academic researchers and used as a possible model for bridging the current theory–practice divide. Given the dissimilar responses of individuals familiar with the Maryland effort to the claim that it involved the capturing and use of tacit knowledge, the effort is also a reminder that bridging an intellectual gap should not be confused with its elimination. There will always be a divide of sorts between theorists and practitioners operating in different contexts. The key to minimizing this disparity lies in the willingness of all involved to create a common basis of understanding.

This shared discernment can be advanced, for example, through interlanguages that facilitate the exchange of experience and the avoidance, where possible, of jargon that diminishes the possibilities of useful exchanges. Analyzing and discussing the results of experience is as relevant in the twenty-first century as it was to Gilbert Ryle, who noted, half a century ago, that both Aristotle and Izaak Walton of *Compleat Angler* fame found inspiration for theory in actual practice. In so doing, they gave "to their pupils the maxims and prescriptions of their arts" and provided a lasting precedent for others to follow with profit both to the development of theory and the enhancement of practice.[7]

THE DEBT OF PRAGMATISM TO POSTMODERNISM

As discussed in chapter 2, much current energy in the area of theory development derives from the challenge offered by postmodernism to the positivist search for "universal" truths that dominated higher education for much of the twentieth century. Members of a largely unstructured movement, postmodernists argue, at a minimum, that we are all creatures of various and conflicting languages, whose unstable and multiple meanings ensure that we can never be certain of what we know or understand. Postmodernism is a movement still in progress, and its long-range effects can only be tentatively rendered. Even so, assessments of the implications of postmodernism for how we view the world regularly appear in print.

For example, Bryan S. Turner stresses postmodernism's work in identifying cultural changes, especially the

- globalization of society
- centrality of modern consumerism
- collapse of traditional hierarchies
- undermining of the conventional role of the intellectual through irony and parody
- fragmentation and diversity of society brought about by social complexity[8]

For her part, Pauline Marie Rosenau, while recognizing that these changes may well have been under way before the advent of postmodernism, suggests that the adoption of postmodern perspectives encourages people to

- be more critical and less naive in the employment of science
- operate with lowered expectations of the results of scientific efforts
- recognize the political, social, and economic context of science
- accept and appreciate the use of qualitative approaches[9]

Turner and Rosenau describe postmodern visions of research and theory building predicated on the absence of certainty. Accordingly, postmodernism is an intellectual environment without agreed-upon rules for settling disputes where more or less subjective understandings rooted in class, gender, cultural, and other viewpoints vie with each other to explain physical, mental, and spiritual worlds. Lacking both umpires and referees, the postmodern world can be characterized as an endless series of "language games" that amuse and entertain the participating university and other theorists, even as they bemuse and bore practitioners who demand more practical results when they invest the scarce time available in their crowded professional lives.

On the level of theory and inquiry, postmodernism's fracturing of the claims of modernism to explain how the world operates had quite a number of interesting if unforeseen consequences. For one, it presented pragmatism with a gift of the first magnitude—it helped to bring this hundred-year-old research philosophy back to life. Pragmatism, a research philosophy that once erupted with such intellectual force that Emile Durkheim feared it as a threat to French national culture, had become "dull and out-of-date" by the mid-twentieth century.[10] Out of intellectual fashion, pragmatism languished in certain American philosophy departments until postmodernism cleared the intellectual space for it again to flourish. Through undermining the claims of positivism and its derivatives to produce certain knowledge, postmodernism provided a larger intellectual stage for all theorists. Here, those contemporary pragmatists who build on the "classic" insights of William James and John Dewey, such as philosophers Richard J. Bernstein and Hilary Putnam, now clash with postmodern pragmatists such as Richard Rorty and Stanley Fish, who "present pragmatism as a postmodernist discourse of critical commentary that denies that we can escape the conventions and contingencies of language in order to connect with a world of experience outside texts."[11]

Beyond its role in the intellectual resurrection of its parent philosophy, the "pragmatism lite," or *postmodern pragmatism*, of Rorty and Fish offers all other branches of the philosophy a potentially rich source of recruits. Postmodernists concerned about the difficulties involved in the communication of ideas can be led by their research questions into considering how the process of communication itself can be improved. This can produce "analyzed experience"—the bread and butter of classical pragmatism and an essential component of my own cultural pragmatism. There really are few alternatives to the ongoing analysis of experience if a theorist has difficulties with absolutes and believes that the complexities of human behavior mean that people can act out of motives that transcend even such strong motivating factors as class loyalty and gender. It is supremely ironic that both those who deny the possibility of "objective" knowledge and those yet hoping to achieve it are likely to find great appeal in one or another variant of pragmatism.

The "truth" that a reformed and more inclusive classical pragmatism can be a productive intellectual home for both positivists who have learned theoretical modesty and postmodernists who understand the value of an appropriate level of research rigor is simply another indicator that pragmatism is an open philosophical system that works, a reality that has drawn worldwide attention. According to the University of East Anglia's Martin Hollis:

> Pragmatism insists that the mind is always active in deciding what counts as knowledge. Yet, although that makes all our concepts and beliefs revisable, revisions are to be made in the light of experience. To put it paradoxically, theory governs experience and experience governs theory. This interplay may cause trouble in the end but is immensely fertile in the meantime.[12]

Whatever its other achievements, postmodernism has opened up a wide spectrum of theoretical discourse where positivism and its descendents can be seen as representing a sort of intellectual "right," a conservative federation that more or less affirms the reality of "objective" rules valid across contexts. Alternatively, postmodernist philosophies themselves can be envisioned as embodying something of an intellectual "left," a radical alliance where understandings of the possibility of achieving objectivity may run the gamut from "impossible" to "incredibly difficult." In this enlarged theoretical arena, pragmatism, particularly when it incorporates the insights of postmodernism, feminism, critical theory, and other contemporary philosophies, offers its reliance on analyzed experience as something of an intellectual middle ground.

The new centrality of neoclassical, cultural pragmatism would have undoubtedly irritated Bertrand Russell, the English intellectual giant whose strong opposition undercut the public appeal of classical pragmatism in Great Britain in the early twentieth century. On the other hand, the latest resort to pragmatism would undoubtedly appeal to Dewey.[13] Pragmatism, the practical approach to knowledge that rebelled against the accepted doctrines of the nineteenth-century American higher education establishment—and for a time became the embodiment of a successor system—now claims a more modest place, where it evidences theoretical appeal to moderate establishmentarians and no-nonsense revolutionaries alike.[14]

Pragmatism, in both its postmodern and its neoclassical variants, is not the only research philosophy bidding to replace positivism and its descendents now that postmodernism has opened up the intellectual competition to explain the world. As discussed in chapter 2, critical theory, feminism, and the various postmodernist schools themselves are also in contention for theoretical leadership. Additionally—and this point needs to be stressed—positivism has not gone away. Within numerous contexts it remains in use in the form of an *everyday positivism*, with people and organizations making decisions on the basis of so-called objective facts.

An everyday positivism, defining things as either true or false, seems to thrive in both our personal and our professional lives, even as positivism as a research philosophy operates in varying degrees throughout the sciences. Nevertheless, the reality that positivism is under theoretical attack in the social sciences and has been all but exiled from the arts and humanities leaves many researchers with an interesting problem. Perhaps we will continue to operate on two levels, with this everyday positivism as the norm in "real life," supplemented by seemingly endless disputes over philosophies that have little or nothing to do with our actions. Alternatively, we can try to match our theories with our experiences.

TACIT KNOWLEDGE

Tacit or "private" knowledge is the often-undocumented wisdom possessed by expert practitioners: attorneys, physicians, social workers, professors, teachers, reference specialists, librarian-politicians, information brokers, or corporate and nonprofit administrators cited by peers as exemplifying the "best," however defined, in an organization or specialty. Conceptually, tacit knowledge is a category usually opposed to *explicit* or "publicly available" knowledge of the type found in printed texts, provided through online sources, and taught in traditional or electronic classrooms. On the whole, tacit knowledge represents an underutilized resource for enhancing effectiveness across a wide spectrum of organizations.

The most famous maxim within the tacit knowledge research enterprise may well be "We can know more than we can tell," offered by Michael Polanyi, scientist, philosopher, and author of the influential *Tacit Dimension.*[15] Recent studies in the business, sociological, psychological, military, and other research literatures have expanded this concise definition to include assertions that tacit knowledge is

- personal in origin
- valuable to the possessor
- job specific
- related to context
- difficult to fully articulate
- both known in part and unknown in part to the possessor
- transmitted, where transmission is possible, through interpersonal contact
- operative on an organizational level
- applied, in part, through "*if-then*" rules ("*if* certain conditions exist, *then* apply the following"; see the discussion in chapter 2)
- capable of becoming explicit knowledge and vice versa
- intertwined with explicit knowledge along unstable knowledge borders
- poorly reflected in contemporary knowledge literature[16]

At a minimum, the cumulative effect of the above assertions suggests that issues involving tacit knowledge may not be readily explored using the traditional scientific approach summarized by Jan C. Robbins in 1973:

> The usual research paper consists of a set of highly standardized parts: (1) a problem statement; (2) a review of the literature of the field related to that problem; (3) a statement of hypotheses deduced from that literature or in answer to questions left unanswered by it; (4) a description of research methods used (the "research design"), an explanation of why they were used, and a description of their execution; (5) a statement of findings produced by the methods in support of the hypotheses; and (6) a set of conclusions or implications to be drawn from hypotheses plus methods plus findings.[17]

Several concerns inherent in the model summarized by Robbins are particularly important and need to be addressed. The first lies in the fact that the "scientific model" does not accurately summarize how much research is actually carried out. Research is often a messy process; the approach outlined by Robbins tends to obscure this reality by requiring that research, no matter how it was really done, be reported in a particular fashion. Through defining effectiveness in terms of a prescribed method, Robbins's outline tends to distort, if not actually conceal, the true process of investigation within a number of disciplines and fields. The outline does more or less describe a completed dissertation in a number of disciplines. Yet, while there are undoubtedly exceptions, the process of dissertation research and writing is usually far messier, contingent, and out of sequence than is evidenced in the final document offered to the dissertation committee and the larger scholarly world.[18] Robbins's model is best understood as an accepted *convention* for reporting on the research process. It functions more as a *wholesome myth* that proclaims an ideal even as it obscures the reality experienced by many, particularly those who have gone through the dissertation research and writing process.

Second, the privileging of Robbins's outline as a template for determining the value of an article or presentation can easily breed scorn for work that does not follow the "script." Potentially valuable accounts of the hard-won tacit knowledge of nonacademic practitioners are discounted or misread because they (1) fail the "Robbins test" or an equivalent template or (2) distort what actually happened in order to match the privileged "scientific" criteria. When viewed in the light of tacit knowledge understandings, such depreciation of the "how I do it good" reports of successes found in much of the practitioner literature may actually indicate a flaw in the analytical process, in effect a privileging of surface appearance over underlying reality.

Two cases of misleading analysis neatly illustrate this point. Both involve the examination of papers delivered at Association of College and Research Libraries (ACRL) national conferences.[19] The first such article finds that only one-third of the papers presented at the first ACRL national conference in 1978 were research based. After censuring the offending practitioners for not following Robbins's outline, the authors argue, "There should be no place either in hard copy or in less expensive fiche for repetitions of the success story. One benefit of having criteria which stress the model of scientific papers is that the 'how I do it good' diatribe is by definition excluded."[20]

Yet, contrary to the implications of this hard-line stance, the "'how I do it good' diatribe" is often precisely the type of report of most value to practitioners. As an act of communication, it signals an attempt to convey a tacit knowledge that is difficult to transmit in print or from a podium even in the best of circumstances. Comprehensiveness is not necessary, since, according to conventions established among practitioner communities, such diatribes carry with them an invitation to further dialogue. Accepting this invitation in turn can lead to information exchanges ranging from a telephone call to lunch at a conference, or, more formally, a paid consultation.

The second article to be touched upon appeared in 1991 and examines "181 papers presented at the second, third, and fourth [ACRL] conferences."[21] Concluding that research was on the decline in ACRL presentations, the authors of this article assert:

> If we consider a positive response to questions about sampling, instrument pretesting, statement of hypothesis, and clearly stated and achieved objectives an indication of a paper's possession of research characteristics, it appears that the research papers presented at the ACRL national conferences do not follow the systematic processes of the scientific method.[22]

More civil than the first in disseminating regret rather than condemnation, this second article correctly concludes that ACRL conference papers were not particularly scientific and appeared to be becoming less so. And why not? At best, tacit knowledge is a worldly wisdom that can be articulated only with difficulty. Unfortunately, a previous dearth of research and published analyses on the value of tacit knowledge may have contributed to a climate of opinion that has consistently privileged even ineffectual "scientific" studies while labeling many attempts to convey valuable tacit knowledge as merely "testimony or glad tidings."[23]

At the same time, it is only appropriate to note that not all is well with the preferred "scientific approach." According to Benjamin D. Singer, the present system of peer-reviewed research and publication is (1) arbitrary; (2) discouraging of creativity; (3) producing the most citations "for routine data, rarely for ideas or original perspectives"; and (4) "so unreliable, such a disaster and the subject of so much disdain."[24] When the research agendas of seasoned faculty researchers remain mired in the inconsequential, matters of true substance are left to off-campus practitioners. In consequence, accusations of faculty navel gazing and questions of cost-benefit "from the field"—although seldom from the academy—may be inevitable.

THE GULF BETWEEN ACADEMIC RESEARCH AND PROFESSIONAL PRACTICE

A remarkable paradox is at the heart of the academic enterprise. American higher education tends to value knowledge that is explicit or published, quantified, and replicable—in short, "scientific."[25] Yet, this same academic culture certifies the worth of its universities and colleges, as well as education programs for individual fields and disciplines, largely based on the reports of accreditation teams applying *expert judgment*.[26] Although it can be supported with quantitative data, expert judgment is a category of knowledge that is notoriously tacit and nonquantifiable in nature.[27]

There may be an intellectual double standard in the reliance of faculty on a variant of "educated common sense" for the crucial purposes of program reaccreditation and continued faculty employment. Our dependence on, indeed demand for, expert judgment to evaluate fundamentally important aspects of academic programs, admittedly garnished with occasional quantitative studies of market demands and customer needs, leaves faculty with little basis for complaint when practitioners ignore the "objective" research emanating from academic programs and apply the same commonsense approach to addressing their own critical issues.

An idea of the gulf existing between faculty concepts of useful research and practitioner views can be gleaned through two observations. Nancy A. Van House summarizes the first, held by many faculty, in a review essay published in 1991.

> Evaluation of the *quality* [of] social science research is based on two sets of criteria. One has to do with the conduct of research: Its underlying logic and methodology, and the validity and robustness of its conclusions. The other has to do with the topic of the research: Does it address questions that are useful, interesting, or important?
>
> Research cannot be of good quality in the second sense and not the first. If the results are not valid, then whether or not the purported findings are interesting is irrelevant. However research can be good in the first sense and not the second. For example, there might be a careful and believable study of uninteresting or trivial phenomena.[28]

In Van House's opinion, research "form" is at least as important as research "substance"; in other words, how research is carried out has a value that stands apart from the merit of what is actually researched. This approach exhibits a number of problems for nonacademic practitioners on both the conceptual and practical levels.

The preceding "academic" version of research can be contrasted to the "practitioner" concept as advanced in 1979 by Kenneth Shearer.

> Practice has little use for brilliant explanations of why libraries fail; its eye is on the main chance and the prospect of how to arrive at better results. When and if anyone sees how to present research findings and understandings in the form of a recipe for success, the interest of the audience swells.[29]

Shearer, it can be argued, may be overstating the interest of practitioners in "how I did it good" stories. He seems to be omitting the value of negative example. A presentation or article on "how I did it bad"—preferably with practical suggestions on how to avoid the mistakes perpetrated by the speaker—may conceivably draw an equally large audience from the practitioner community. If the topic applies to the characteristics that contribute to the success or failure of an academic program, it is likely to have great appeal for the separate but occasionally overlapping *academic practitioner communities*, consisting of (1) deans, associate deans, and assistant deans and (2) faculty.

Inherent in both the Van House and the Shearer assertions is the reality of context, a critically important aspect of tacit knowledge. Briefly
stated, if methodology without useful results is valued in the world of
higher education, it is because methodology in and of itself is effective
in advancing faculty careers. In the circumstances of a major research
university, chemists, physicists, and statisticians serving on university
tenure and promotion committees may know and care little about critically important issues facing teachers, social workers, nurses, attorneys,
librarians, knowledge managers, or similar professionals. Consequently, faculty educating future practitioners for these professions may
"know in their bones," or from the negative examples of former colleagues who failed to earn tenure, that research on public service issues
may prove counterproductive during the all-important, sixth-year tenure
review. They also know that at least some members of this critical audience are more likely to relate to "good quantitative approaches," however inconsequential the subject, when such publications are offered in
support of tenure or promotion.

In any consideration of the rules under which faculty research and
theorizing is judged within the academy, we would do well to keep in
mind the "language games" of Wittgenstein and Lyotard.[30] As noted, all
practitioners, including the academic variety, operate under known rules
(language games) to achieve their objectives. Being a successful academic game player is one thing, but one should not forget that the rules
of the academy might not apply elsewhere—in the so-called real world.

Michael Huberman, an American professor with the University of
Geneva, has provided a useful reminder of the limitations of research
validity and transferability. In an article largely devoted to comparing
the use of American quantitative research and European qualitative research protocols in cross-border European contexts, he differentiates
between "research-in-theory (how we make public what we do)" and
"research-in-use (what we actually do)." In his opinion, the true story of
research is carefully kept out of publication. It is shared, if at all, only
in a "purely oral literature" with a select few "in bars, on airplanes, or
during coffee breaks." This protective and continuing self-censorship
hides the "murky conceptualizations, the uneven measures, or the soar-
ing inferences in our most recent study."[31]

However, Huberman did not exhaust his critique with the preceding.
In a scenario that should resonate with anyone who has ever undertaken
a literature review or wondered at the real applicability of variables, he

provides his readers with possible explanations, suggested by his European colleagues, as to why a research project conducted according to the highest standards of American social science proved inclusive in a European context.

> First, in any study, there are only bits and pieces that can be legitimated on "scientific" grounds. The bulk comes from common sense, from prior experience, from the logic inherent in the problem definition or the problem space. Take the review of literature, the conceptual model, the key variables, the measures, and so forth, and you have perhaps 20% of what is really going into your study—from which you will then make a 100% interpretation. And if you look hard at that 20%, if for example, you go back to the prior studies from which you derived many assumptions and perhaps some measures, you will find they, too, are 20% topsoil and 80% landfill.[32]

Given an extended ratio of 20 percent intellectual topsoil to 80 percent intellectual landfill, it is not surprising that off-campus practitioners see faculty research without demonstrable benefit as a luxury that cannot be justified to voters or guardians of the corporate bottom line. In off-campus settings, multiple demands compete for every dollar of finite resources. Robustness in research technique, unless it contributes to meeting priority needs, is not cost-effective and is therefore little valued.

To paraphrase Huberman, we would do well to generate less landfill and more topsoil in academic research if we care at all whether it is accepted by off-campus practitioners. And productive topsoil is just what the study of tacit knowledge is designed to secure.

WE ARE ALL STRANGERS (IN CERTAIN CONTEXTS)

Multidisciplinary explorations of tacit knowledge are now under way. The initial results of these efforts offer new opportunities to bridge the historical gap between faculty practitioners, whose research often has little influence outside of their research communities, and the off-campus practitioners who repeatedly demonstrate an unwillingness to use the results of academic inquiries in their professional lives.[33]

The primary roadblock to the effective collaboration of faculty, consultants, and practitioners in developing and sharing tacit knowledge results from fundamental differences in contexts. Faculty teach and research in and from programs based in higher education. Practitioners build careers in a wide spectrum of organizations, including academic departments. Although practitioners may teach part-time, it is more difficult for some faculty to "practice" part-time. However, the area of consulting offers considerable promise for common context, since the ranks of consultants include faculty who consult part-time, owners and employees of independent consulting firms, others affiliated with major corporations, and practitioners who consult around full-time jobs.

At the present time, with local exceptions and occasional national anomalies such as the noteworthy involvement of faculty and other researchers in exploring the service roles of public libraries through the Public Library Development Program/Public Library Effectiveness Study, it is not the norm for faculty inquirers and off-campus practitioners to be a significant part of each other's human resource networks.[34] In consequence there are not many off-campus affirmations of the value of researcher–practitioner cooperation across the permeable borders that separate professional education from professional practice.

Worse, there does not seem to be a general movement on the part of off-campus practitioners to change the "we–they" status quo, possibly because faculty have not given them a good enough reason to do so. On the more positive side, there is a possibility, although far from a "quick fix," that reorienting a portion of faculty research toward the discovery and refinement of off-campus practitioner tacit knowledge might help to change the situation. Fundamental to any increased interaction through such research is the need for faculty to foster a number of understandings in practitioner communities, specifically the recognition that (1) formalized approaches to professional tacit knowledge are important and have the potential to improve service; (2) service improvements require greater understanding of the role of professional tacit knowledge within organizations; and (3) faculty represent a source of assistance in gaining such understanding. Unfortunately, creating such perceptions where a basis of cooperation does not already exist requires faculty to overcome decades of mild distrust and/or perceived irrelevance. Only repeated successful performance will demonstrate to off-campus practitioners that Kurt Lewin's reminder "there is nothing so practical as a good theory" ought to specifically include faculty theory generated on the basis of practitioner realities.[35]

Early in the twentieth century Douglas Waples, affiliated with the then-new and now-defunct University of Chicago Graduate Library School, observed, "The function of research is to make common sense still more common."[36] This admirable goal can be achieved only if theory produced by research is actually useful to practitioners—something far from guaranteed. It is an educational truism that most students are more interested in learning how to apply effective rules in their professional lives than in understanding and participating in the deeper intellectual conversation that sustains or challenges such rules. This is true even in the highly structured area of cataloging hard copy or electronic materials. Prof. Shelia S. Intner of Simmons College has confessed in print that the "lack of theoretical knowledge among cataloguers scares me silly," and she further observes that "it can't help but have terrible consequences for libraries and their patrons."[37] As Intner herself notes, failure to think about the larger picture—what professors commonly term the "why behind the how"—is a pervasive failure in many off-campus environments. Practitioners are paid to "do"; they are not rewarded and may even be penalized for neglect of their primary responsibilities if they fail to meet quantitative expectations and address quality issues by devoting time to "talk about theory, principles, and assumptions."[38] If avoidance of theory considerations is so prevalent among working catalogers—professionals accustomed to applying formal rules in their working lives—the unwillingness to embrace theory of their colleagues in library administration, youth services, and knowledge management should not be surprising. At least there are commonly accepted rules for assigning subject headings. Effective understanding of the delicate intangibles involved with influencing city councils, managing hormonally challenged teens in poetry slams, and convincing skeptical department heads that the services of a knowledge management center are still worth paying corporate charge-backs in an Internet-facilitated "information environment" are usually much more difficult to acquire and sustain.

For academic theorists to involve themselves in solving practical problems can be a far trickier process, particularly for those who lack the experience of actually doing what they teach. Practitioners want results. Academics without an ongoing history of success in solving real-world problems, or of effectively advising those who have that responsibility, may have more difficulty in getting a hearing from librarians and information analysts who may be puzzled by seemingly intractable problems. Here, language itself can become an additional difficulty. Researchers without experience as practitioners may be effective in discussing issues in the preferred terminologies or "languages" of higher education decision makers and/or grant makers. Yet, using the same restricted languages to try to communicate with practitioners may result in something close to mutual incomprehension.

On some campuses with programs accredited by the American Library Association, the lack of full-time professors with extensive experience in academic, public, or school libraries, as well as corporate knowledge management centers and competitive data analysis units, can mean that the daily concerns of practitioners receive little respect or attention from a faculty interested in more fundamental information issues.[39] Notwithstanding, if a concern for helping practitioners is seen as the logical outgrowth of commitment to long-accepted theory, it can achieve a level of respectability with colleagues lacking practitioner experience, as well as with university administrators and foundation or government grant providers. One candidate for such intellectual support is an influential theory developed by one of the "dead Germans"[40] that Sydney J. Pierce saw as necessary to make the theoretical base of a discipline or field respectable—Georg Simmel's *stranger* formulation. Simmel, a brilliant theoretician forced to carve out a career on the academic periphery in the anti-Semitic atmosphere of Kaiser Wilhelm's Imperial Germany, analyzed society from his standpoint as an outsider.[41] His theory, clearly containing elements of the autobiographical, holds that those knowledgeable about a given human system but not actually an accepted part of it may be able to see the system's operations in a more objective way than those whose lives have long been regulated by its norms. As recently as 2003, Everett M. Rogers, whose sequential editions of *Diffusion of Innovations* have been "bibles" for those attempting to make sense of innovations and the change process, strongly emphasized the value of Simmel's stranger concept as an analytical tool.[42]

For Simmel, the stranger embodies an "objectivity . . . composed of distance and nearness, indifference and involvement."[43] From the point of view of higher education, this claim for a more objective standpoint, or at least a different stance that might produce valid insights, has the advantage of drawing on well-known arguments advanced by an intellectual giant as a basis for claiming value for the understandings that knowledgeable faculty researchers with life histories spent in different professional and even national contexts may import into a library, information, or knowledge "group" in order to help identify and solve its pressing issues. These understandings, which can alternatively be understood as Alfred Schutz's *recipes* "for interpreting the social world and for handling things and men [and women] in order to obtain the best results in every situation," can and do generate productive questions and useful perspectives precisely because they are not "native" to the courtroom, hospital, classroom, library, information center, or other source of practitioner employment under study.[44]

Where university or grant support for faculty research among practitioner communities is involved, the process may require in-depth citations from the work of Simmel, Schutz, and other theorists regarding the value of the stranger approach. But effective communication with practitioners is likely to require another language—one leavened with commonsense concepts, metaphors, and analogies that are understood by academics and practitioners alike. The occasional need to seek assistance with problem solving from those who are not facing an issue on a daily basis may be seen as the most basic, commonsense justification for the consulting industry. The rationales are pervasive. For example, who in American culture has reached a managerial position in a library, information, or knowledge organization without at some point being advised of the "value of a fresh perspective" for overcoming a seemingly intractable obstacle or being encouraged to "get some more feedback," or "take a step back from the problem," in order to advance its solution?

"Selling" the value of the stranger to the very different audiences of higher education and off-campus practice requires the ability to communicate in at least two separate languages and, at times, find or develop a bridge connecting them. It is indeed a theoretical process where an interlanguage, or a dialect that can be understood by faculty researchers and off-campus practitioners alike, achieves a particular importance. Use of an interlanguage, defined by Steven Roger Fischer as "a simplified dialect with which speakers of two or more quite different dialects communicate with one another," requires that "shared features of their language are retained and non-shared features ignored."[45] Interlanguages come into being when groups, large or small, need to cooperate to achieve ends that cannot otherwise be secured without a great deal more difficulty. When communicating among professional colleagues, a discipline or field's jargon is acceptable as intellectual shorthand. However, such terminology often minimizes the potential for communication with other groups with their own jargons and will almost inevitably foster some level of misunderstanding when employed across contextual boundaries. By establishing what is common, an interlanguage can provide the basis for exploring the uncommon, perhaps the newly disclosed, or anything else that requires communication for shared understanding. The use of interlanguages is particularly effective when sufficient incentives exist to make the exchanges of value to all involved. In the context of research, this means that both faculty and off-campus practitioners must see personal and professional value in any shared effort.

It is important to realize that effectiveness in the role of a stranger is not limited to extraordinary persons with unique talents. A broad spectrum of educators, sensitive to the need for a context-based interlanguage, should to be able to perform the critical role which Simonetta Tabboni emphasizes in Simmel's stranger, the ability to create "bridges which link two or more cultures together."[46] In our case, the cultures involved are the often dissimilar realities of academic research and off-campus practice. Here, the practitioner-generated literature can provide points of entry for developing theory regarding the tacit knowledge of off-campus working professionals. Such efforts should be guided by a superficially simple yet ultimately complex question: *What are the implications for practice?*[47]

Contemporary philosopher Stephen Toulmin phrases these implications quite succinctly: "Theoretical explanations and concepts (*episteme*) will increasingly be exposed to a wider analysis, in terms of their general practical efficacy (*techne*) and the prudence (*phronesis*) of putting them to use in particular real life situations."[48] Put another way, tacit knowledge formulations can be envisioned through three overlapping and nonexclusive approaches, distinguished mainly in terms of how intensely the theorist goes beyond the literature to interact with actual practitioners.

Level 1—Armchair Theorizing

The analysis of written texts has a long tradition in the social sciences and those professions that draw on them for theory. In a number of situations, textual analysis is the preferred theoretical method. As noted by Anselm L. Strauss, "Many sociologists prefer to analyze written texts rather than engage in field research or interviewing."[49] Under such circumstances, the analysis of practitioner accounts in a professional literature is simply the continuation of an old tradition for an emergent purpose.

Level 2—Discussion of Tacit Knowledge Theories with Practitioners

Given the reality that tacit knowledge has gained popularity only in recent years, it is to be expected that the professional literatures display uneven coverage. However, the idea of effectiveness in professionals is nothing new. It is thus possible to reexamine selected publications to determine if researchers were in fact dealing with the *concept* of tacit knowledge without exhibiting knowledge of the *term*. One such publication, used by the author in several reference courses, is Sara Fine's article "Reference and Resources: The Human Side,"[50] where she addresses what she sees as "subtle psychological barriers" affecting librarians, users, and "scholars" during reference transactions. In the process, she describes such dynamics as the "Principle of Least Resistance," "Principle of Information Digestion," and "Principle of Crisis-in-Research" and asserts for them (and similar formulations) a clear impact on reference effectiveness.

Of particular interest from the point of view of tacit knowledge research is Fine's explanation that there are

> a set of principles, observations, and assumptions about behavior in the library, few of which have been empirically tested. All of these assumptions have, however, survived the "flagpole" test; they have been run up the flagpole and saluted. Librarians or users, or both, have said of these principles "Yes, that's how it is."[51]

Interesting though it is, Fine's article is at best an initial theoretical offering from the perspective of tacit knowledge. For example, there is no distinction made between the *explicit knowledge* ("These findings actually prove why this happens") and the *tacit or implicit knowledge* ("I just feel it in my gut, but it always seem to work") of the librarians and users consulted to validate her "principles." However, with appropriate theory and technique, it may be possible to determine whether Fine's principles "work"—and to what degree they do so—in selected contexts.

Level 3—Interviews and Other "Fieldwork"

Space constraints make it impossible to "reconstruct" a number of likely candidates for inclusion on this level.[52] However, the "hidden" (tacit) nature of much professional knowledge makes it unlikely that quantitative surveys and Likert scales will produce more than a "sensitizing" effect, alerting the researcher to something undocumented that may contribute to practitioner effectiveness in a given context. More effective techniques are more likely to be drawn from such fields and disciplines as cultural anthropology, occupational folklore, and sociology.[53] Fortunately, works integrating this approach into mainstream research are now part of the literature.[54]

At its best, exploration of tacit knowledge will include analyses of both the functional expertise developed by off-campus practitioners in various environments and the similar knowledge gained by faculty practitioners during careers spent in higher education programs. With greater understanding of the roles of tacit knowledge in professional contexts, new possibilities should arise for scholars to develop theories and fashion methodologies to identify, capture, refine, and utilize a potentially unlimited knowledge resource.

CHARACTER AND CHARACTERISTICS OF THE EFFECTIVE TACIT KNOWLEDGE RESEARCHER

Professional literatures abound with publications prescribing the training that researchers should receive and the theories that ought to guide their inquiries.[55] However, fields can be less forthcoming regarding the personal characteristics that make an effective inquirer. Warnings to guard against personal bias do exist.[56] Nonetheless, there seems to be an unspoken consensus that selection of a theoretical approach by a researcher is an intellectual choice, existing apart from the spectrum of personal, subjective considerations.

Unfortunately, a "hands-off" approach to the emotional component of life, including the life of a faculty inquirer, is unsustainable in researching tacit knowledge. Briefly stated, an area of research that relies to an extraordinary extent on the willingness of practitioners to share known expertise, and to cooperate in transforming tacit knowledge into its explicit counterpart, requires individuals with distinct human relations skills. It would be possible to draw analogies between the capabilities required to produce an effective tacit knowledge inquirer and, for example, an effective reference librarian.[57] In addition, the literature regarding the stranger in cultural anthropology already provides most useful discussions.

As noted above, the researcher involved is a stranger to the innumerable contexts in which practitioners develop and utilize both explicit and tacit (implicit) knowledge. As such, the researcher faces conditions strikingly similar to those described in Dennison Nash's classic "The Ethnologist as Stranger: An Essay in the Sociology of Knowledge."[58] Drawing on a spectrum of studies and his own fieldwork, Nash describes the "Autonomous Man" (equally applicable to an Autonomous Woman), an individual in the stranger role with the flexibility of personality "to adapt rapidly to host norms or to remain in the limbo of marginality."[59] According to Nash, the Autonomous Man's

> characteristic approach to the world may be described as detached-involvement; his frame of reference is tolerant of ambiguity—he does not resort to "authoritarian" closure. The Autonomous Man is the ideal-typical stranger because he can negotiate short or long-term strangership. . . . It may be such a man as he whom Schuetz [and Simmel] had in mind when they spoke of the stranger's objectivity. The Autonomous Man is subject to very little bias by the conditions of any stranger's role.[60]

Authoritarian individuals then are not good candidates for the role of stranger, a role that requires a negotiation of the conditions for its existence. This lack of fit exists since "authoritarian tendencies are strengthened in the stranger's role, and because these are inimical to the kind of perceptual adaptation which the ethnologist-stranger should achieve."[61] Such qualities, it should be noted, are personal and not ideological in nature. A liberal or conservative political ideology, for example, cannot be used as a shorthand method of determining a researcher's suitability in conducting inquiries into practitioner tacit knowledge.[62]

NOTES

1. Maryland State Department of Education, Division of Library Development and Services, *1994 Maryland Statewide Reference Survey: Statewide Objectives, Facts, and Figures* (leaflet; Baltimore: Division of Library Development and Services, 1995).

2. Maryland State Department of Education, *1994 Maryland Statewide Reference Survey.*

3. Maryland State Department of Education, Division of Library Development and Services, *1994 Statewide Reference Survey: Overall Conclusions* (leaflet; Baltimore: Division of Library Development and Services, n.d.).

4. Maryland State Department of Education, *1994 Statewide Reference Survey.*

5. See Lillie Seward Dyson, "Improving Reference Services: A Maryland Training Program Brings Positive Results," *Public Libraries* 31 (September/October 1992): 284–89; Ralph Gers and Lillie J. Seward, "Improving Reference Performance: Results of a Statewide Study," *Library Journal* 110 (November 1, 1985): 32–35; and Sandy Stephan, Ralph Gers, Lillie Seward, Nancy Bolin, and Jim Partridge, "Reference Breakthrough in Maryland," *Public Libraries* 27 (Winter 1988): 202–3.

6. Telephone interviews, August–September 1998.

7. Gilbert Ryle, *The Concept of Mind* (1949; reprint, London: Hutchinson, 1958), 30.

8. Bryan S. Turner, "The Nature of the Social," in Bryan S. Turner, ed., *The Blackwell Companion to Social Theory* (Oxford: Blackwell, 1996), 305.

9. Pauline Marie Rosenau, *Post-Modernism and the Social Sciences: Insights, Inroads, and Intrusions* (Princeton, NJ: Princeton University Press, 1992), 183.

10. See Emile Durkheim, *Pragmatism and Sociology*, trans. J. C. Whitehouse, ed. John B. Allcock (Cambridge: Cambridge University Press, 1983), 1, 13.

11. James T. Kloppenberg, "Pragmatism: An Old Name for Some New Ways of Thinking?" *Journal of American History* 83, no. 1 (June 1996): 101.

12. Martin Hollis, *The Philosophy of Social Science: An Introduction* (Cambridge: Cambridge University Press, 1994), 77.

13. See the John Dewey–Bertrand Russell arguments collected in Samuel Meyer, ed., *Dewey and Russell: An Exchange* (New York: Philosophical Library, n.d.), and Russell's attacks on pragmatism in his *History of Western Philosophy* (New York: Simon and Schuster, 1945).

14. See, for instance, Dmitri N. Shalin's observation that "postmodernisms tend to overlook movements like pragmatism which eschewed both hyperrationalism and irrationalism and sought to combine the Enlightenment's commitment to rational inquiry with Romanticism's critique of rationalism and capitalist modernity" in "Modernity, Postmodernism, and Pragmatist Inquiry: An Introduction," *Symbolic Interaction* 16, no. 4 (Winter 1993): 325.

15. Michael Polanyi, *The Tacit Dimension* (Garden City, NY: Doubleday Anchor, 1967), 4.

16. See, for example, H. M. Collins, "Tacit Knowledge and Scientific Networks," in *Science in Context: Readings in the Sociology of Science*, ed. Barry

Barnes and David Edge (Cambridge, MA: MIT Press, 1982), 44–64; Joseph A. Horvath, George B. Forsythe, Patrick J. Sweeney, Jeffrey A. McNally, John Wattendorf, Wendy M. Williams, and Robert J. Sternberg, *Tacit Knowledge in Military Leadership: Evidence from Officer Interviews*, Technical Report 1018 (Alexandria, VA: U.S. Army Research Institute for the Behavioral and Social Sciences, 1994); and Louis H. Swartz, "Implicit Knowledge (Tacit Knowing), Connoisseurship, and the Common Law Tradition" (paper presented at the faculty workshop of the University at Buffalo School of Law, Buffalo, NY, April 11, 1997).

17. Jan C. Robbins, "Social Functions of Scientific Communication," *IEEE Transactions on Professional Communication* PC-16 (September 1973), 135. There is certain irony in the fact that Robbins's 1971 influential restatement of the manner in which research should be done, and by implication was carried out (see note 9), was followed by the appearance of a number of accounts which debunked this pristine image of scientific research. Two such classic studies are: Karen D. Knorr, "Producing and Reproducing Knowledge: Descriptive or Constructive? Towards a Model of Research Production" *Social Science Information* 16, no. 6 (1977): 669–96; and Ian I. Mitroff, "The Myth of Objectivity; or, Why Science Needs a New Psychology of Science," *Management Science: Application* 18 (1972): B613–B618.

18. This claim reflects numerous conversations with fellow doctoral students and, later, faculty colleagues in the period 1993–2003.

19. Caroline Coughlin and Pamela Snelson, "Searching for Research in ACRL Papers," *Journal of Academic Librarianship* 9, no. 1 (1983): 21–26; and Pamela Snelson and S. Anita Talar, "Content Analysis of ACRL Conference Papers," *College and Research Libraries* 52 (1991): 466–72.

20. Coughlin and Snelson, "Searching," 24.

21. Snelson and Talar, "Content Analysis," 469.

22. Snelson and Talar, "Content Analysis," 470.

23. Quoted in Coughlin and Snelson, "Searching," 22.

24. Benjamin D. Singer, "The Criterial Crisis of the Academic World," *Sociological Inquiry* 50 (1989): 127–43.

25. See Burton R. Clark, *The Academic Life: Small Worlds, Different Worlds* (Princeton, NJ: Carnegie Foundation for the Advancement of Teaching, 1987), and Robbins, "Social Functions," 131–35, 181.

26. See Robert G. Owens, "Methodological Rigor in Naturalistic Inquiry: Some Issues and Answers," *Educational Administration Quarterly* 18 (Spring 1982): 2, for a reminder of how institution-wide accreditation actually works. Examples of specific program accreditation documents include American Library Association, Committee on Accreditation, *Accreditation under the 1992*

Standards for Accreditation of Master's Programs in Library and Information Studies: An Overview (Chicago: Office for Accreditation, American Library Association, 1994), and American Library Association, Committee on Accreditation, *Standards for Accreditation of Master's Programs in Library and Information Studies* (Chicago: Office for Accreditation, American Library Association, 1992).

27. See E. B. Grant and M. J. Gregory, "Tacit Knowledge, the Life Cycle, and International Manufacturing Transfer," *Technology Analysis and Strategic Management* 9, no. 2 (1997): 149–61; and Robert J. Sternberg, Richard K. Wagner, Wendy M. Williams, and Joseph A. Horvath, "Testing Common Sense," *American Psychologist* 50 (1995): 912–27.

28. Nancy A. Van House, "Assessing the Quality and Impact of LIS Research," in C. R. McClure and P. Hernon, eds., *Library and Information Science Research: Perspectives and Strategies for Improvement* (Norwood, NJ: Ablex, 1991), 90.

29. Kenneth Shearer, "The Impact of Research on Librarianship," *Journal of Education for Librarianship* 20, no. 2 (1979): 121.

30. Jean-Francois Lyotard, *The Postmodern Condition: A Report on Knowledge,* trans. Geoff Bennington and Brian Massumi (1979; reprint, Minneapolis: University of Minnesota Press, 1984), 10.

31. Michael Huberman, "How Well Does Educational Research Really Travel?" *Educational Researcher* 16, no. 1 (January/February 1987): 5.

32. Huberman, "How Well," 12.

33. See, for instance, Joe A. Hewitt, "The Role of the Library Administrator in Improving LIS Research," in McClure and Hernon, *Library and Information Science,* 163–78; Daniel O'Connor and J. Philip Mulvaney, "LIS Faculty Research and Expectations of the Academic Culture versus the Needs of the Practitioner," *Journal of Education for Library and Information Science* 37 (Fall 1996): 306–16; and Pierce Butler's classic *Introduction to Library Science* (Chicago: University of Chicago Press, 1933).

34. Brief accounts of both the distinguished history of the researcher–practitioner cooperation in public library planning and the effective products of this extended effort can be found in Nancy A. Van House and Thomas A. Childers, "The Use of Public Library Roles for Effectiveness Evaluation," *Library and Information Science Research* 16 (1994): 41–58.

35. Quoted in Norman A. Polansky, "There Is Nothing So Practical as a Good Theory," *Child Welfare* 65 (January/February 1986): 3.

36. Douglas Waples, "The Graduate Library School at Chicago," *Library Quarterly* 1 (1931): 32.

37. Shelia S. Intner, "From the Editor's Desk: Ah, Yes, the Old Practice vs. Theory Debate," *Technicalities* 15, no. 10 (October 1995): 3.

38. Intner, "From the Editor's Desk."

39. Herbert A. Simon's classic description of professional schools torn by the animosity between faculty who were former practitioners and those whose loyalty was to an academic discipline is well worth a reading. See his *Administrative Behavior: A Study of Decision-Making Processes in Administrative Organizations*, 4th ed. (New York: Free Press, 1997), 345–55.

40. Sydney J. Pierce, "Dead Germans and the Theory of Librarianship," *American Libraries*, September 1992, 641–43.

41. See Georg Simmel, "The Stranger," in *The Sociology of Georg Simmel*, ed. Kurt H. Wolff (Glencoe, IL: Free Press, 1950), 402–8.

42. Everett M. Rogers, *Diffusion of Innovations*, 5th ed. (New York: Free Press, 2003), 42, 290–91.

43. Simmel, "The Stranger," 404.

44. Alfred Schutz, "The Stranger: An Essay in Social Psychology," in *Collected Papers II: Social Theory*, ed. A. Brodersen (The Hague: Martinus Nijhoff, 1964), 95.

45. Steven Roger Fischer, *A History of Language* (London: Reaktion, 1999), 178.

46. Simonetta Tabboni, "The Stranger and Modernity: From Equality of Rights to Recognition of Difference," *Thesis Eleven* 43 (1995): 25.

47. John W. Ratcliffe, "Notions of Validity in Qualitative Research Methodology," *Knowledge: Creation, Diffusion, Utilization* 5 (1983): 159.

48. Stephen Toulmin, "On from 'The Two Cultures,'" in *Skill and Education: Reflection and Experience*, ed. Bo Goranzon and Magnus Florin (London: Springer-Verlag, 1992), 252.

49. See the discussion on "Materials as Data" in Anselm L. Strauss, *Qualitative Analysis for Social Scientists* (Cambridge: Cambridge University Press, 1987), 3.

50. Sara Fine, "Reference and Resources: The Human Side," *Journal of Academic Librarianship* 21, no. 1 (1995): 17–20.

51. Fine, "Reference and Resources," 17.

52. See, for example, the case studies contained in Jack D. Glazier and Ronald R. Powell, eds., *Qualitative Research in Information Management* (Englewood, CO: Libraries Unlimited, 1992).

53. For an occupational folklore approach, see Bill Crowley, "Deviance, Moral Voices, and Group Boundaries: Labeling Perspective and the Occupational Folklore of Night School Education" (master's thesis, Ohio State University, 1991; EDRS, ED333150, microfiche). Unfortunately, this work was done before advances in tacit knowledge research and theory development were disseminated on a wide basis.

54. See for example, Glazier and Powell, *Qualitative Research*; Constance Ann Mellon, *Naturalist Inquiry for Library Science: Methods and Applications for Research, Evaluation, and Teaching* (New York: Greenwood, 1990); and

Herbert J. Rubin and Irene S. Rubin, *Qualitative Interviewing: The Art of Hearing Data* (Thousand Oaks, CA: Sage, 1995).

55. See the various recommendations contained in McClure and Hernon, *Library and Information Science*.

56. Raya Fidel, "The Case Study Method: A Case Study," in Glazier and Powell, *Qualitative Research*, 48; reprinted from *Library and Information Science Research* 6 (1984): 273–88.

57. See Fine, "Reference and Resources."

58. Dennison Nash, "The Ethnologist as Stranger: An Essay in the Sociology of Knowledge," *Southwestern Journal of Anthropology* 19 (1963): 149–67.

59. Nash, "Ethnologist as Stranger," 156.

60. Nash, "Ethnologist as Stranger."

61. Nash, "Ethnologist as Stranger," 159.

62. Nash, "Ethnologist as Stranger."

Chapter Five

The Academic as Practitioner

In the April 15, 2003, issue of *Library Journal (LJ)*, I published a two-page article that generated a more intense response from practitioners than anything else I had written during thirty-plus years as a librarian, manager, state bureaucrat, and library and information educator.[1] Entitled "The Suicide of the Public Librarian," this essay described how a public library with a national reputation—termed for discussion purposes the "Jonestown Public Library" or JPL—maintained a deliberate policy of "deprofessionalizing" its librarian staff. To save on personnel costs, JPL repeatedly downgraded professional positions to paraprofessional levels and stripped away material selection, storytelling, and other cherished responsibilities from public service librarians, in part to justify paying them less. This systematic undermining of librarian status carried by JPL managers, themselves educated in graduate programs accredited by the American Library Association, held out such negative prospects for professional librarianship that I concluded, "From a managerial/educational vantage point, I am reluctantly coming to believe that the JPL case is a strong basis for librarian unionization. Where senior library managers prosper by discounting the value of their own profession, front-line librarian professionals must organize to determine their own survival and future."[2]

The response to the article was immediate and largely divided between the outrage of library managers whose actions had been called into question and the gratitude of frontline librarians that someone had publicly put a name to their mistreatment. However, several library directors concerned about the long-range implications of librarian deprofessionalization wrote or otherwise communicated their agreement with my analysis.

STIRRING UP A HORNET'S NEST

One library director took the points made in "The Suicide of the Public Librarian" so personally that she wrote several letters to my dean impugning my integrity. These personal attacks contained little if any defense of the "deprofessionalizing" actions disclosed in the article. A student taking a Dominican University weekend course taught by the editor in chief of *Library Journal* e-mailed me to report, "John Berry, my instructor for LIS 808-. . . mentioned that your article seems to be causing something of a furor in the library world."[3] Professionals with connections to nationally acclaimed public libraries located as far apart as California, Georgia, Illinois, and Maryland e-mailed to nominate their present or former employers as the library discussed in the *LJ* article. In an August 2003 conversation I had with *LJ*'s Berry, he noted that the article responses received in his New York office were often protests by library managers.[4] On the level of the state of Illinois, I was informed by several public library administrators that my modest consulting sideline was dead. This was not unexpected; any academic who taught courses in library and information management and publicly argued for unions as a response to management-inflicted deprofessionalization should simply forget about off-campus consulting opportunities.

From its inception, "The Suicide of the Public Librarian" was a deliberate attempt by an academic removed from day-to-day library operations to disseminate useful theory to library and information practitioners. That was the reason the piece was developed for *Library Journal,* a leading professional magazine aimed at an audience of working professionals. The *LJ* article translated fundamental findings from the language of the university to that of off-campus practice. In part, it also popularized points made in an earlier, more theoretical work entitled "Intracultural Reciprocity, Information Ethics, and the Survival of

Librarianship in the Twenty-First Century." The latter was first developed as a shared presentation with Deborah Ginsberg at the "Ethics of Electronic Information in the Twenty-First Century" symposium held at the University of Memphis, October 28–30, 2001; later it became a jointly authored chapter in *Ethics and Electronic Information: A Festschrift for Stephen Almagno*.[5]

In the back of my mind while writing "The Suicide of the Public Librarian" was a growing concern about library managers who rhetorically support the idea of librarian professionalism even as they undermine its reality through downwardly reclassifying librarian positions and stripping away still-relevant librarian duties. It is becoming a mentality that is pervasive, "accepted as given,"[6] and subscribed to without adequate debate over the likely consequences of such actions for the future of the library profession. Thoughtful consideration of the long-range effects of short-term decisions seemed to be giving way to management by unexamined "cultural axioms."[7] Such unanalyzed assumptions are well captured in a short piece by Bill Whitson in the *CARL Newsletter*. Although written by an academic librarian, it applies equally well to public library contexts.

> On every side, we now seem to be confronted with a new ethos, a "commercial" ethos, geared to rapid change and to accountability in terms of short-term, tangible outputs (or in the case of higher education, "outcomes"). Since we work in relatively conservative and non-commercial institutions, many of us have not yet been affected much. But the tide seems inexorable. The new ethos respects only the ability to do the job at hand. The commercial spirit wants to pay people what they are worth, in terms of current output, rather than what they deserve, based on past accomplishment. Credentials and degrees—even employment status or "job classification"—seem less important than what people can do to solve the latest problem in an imaginative way. Flexibility, imagination and the ability to learn quickly become pre-eminent values. Tenure, degrees, credentials and job "classifications" can all seem like archaic impediments to creating adaptive and efficient organizations.[8]

As a popularized work of useful theory, "Suicide of the Public Librarian" seems to have introduced a number of the readers of *Library Journal* to theoretical understandings of managerial decisions negatively affecting their daily working lives. The article's too-short discussion of "process theories of professionalism," for example, appears to have given some readers a greater comprehension of the disingenuousness—whether intentional or unintended—evident when employers strip away still-relevant duties that have long defined professional librarians in order to downgrade their positions.[9] Readers of the *LJ* article took its points and used them to explain their own professional circumstances. Christine Holmes, for example, put in print many of the concerns privately e-mailed to me by line librarians from around the country. Having summarized the contents of the article for the *Alum News* of San Jose State University's CSU School of Library and Information Science, Holmes writes:

> I'll go one step further than Crowley in his assessment of the situation and what the future offers. Despite increased enrollment in library schools and the anticipated graying of the profession, I wonder if we can expect a mass exodus or a critical shortage of librarians fed up with the a system that demoralizes and undervalues them just as we have witnessed in the nursing profession.[10]

When practitioners and practitioners-to-be build on a theorist's writings to reflect their own understandings of issues fundamental to their working lives, the transmission of "useful theory" seems to be demonstrated. Agreement with the points made by the theorist is not necessary for this process. Whenever practitioners find a theorist's formulations worthy of being either embraced or attacked, it is likely that something of substance has been communicated.

COMMUNICATING WITH
OFF-CAMPUS PRACTITIONERS

Unlike publication in refereed journals, where sufficient space is usually provided to place theories in their necessary contexts, writing for practitioner journals and magazines is often an exercise in abbreviation. First, theorists must confront the reality that magazine editors are more likely to publish pieces describing actionable certainty than scholarly nuance. Practitioners believe that theorists who identify problems have an obligation to help solve them. It was this reality, for example, that led to my suggestion for more union activity. Having been both a union member and a manager who worked in a union environment, I know that unions can prevent, or at least delay, deprofessionalization through embedding the librarian's status in contracts, insisting that such contract provisions be upheld, and addressing management overreaching through arbitration or litigation.

Second, in the two-page *LJ* article, I was unable to provide much historical context. Since I had been published in *LJ* before,[11] I realized that there was no way that academic conventions could be imported into its popular magazine context. There is a *Library Journal* approach to publication, a balance between its dual commitments to advancing the profession and making a profit, and I had to abide by its rules if I wanted to reach *LJ*'s loyal practitioner readership. As a result, I did not explore the reality that privileging a "commercial" ethos even in the public and not-for-profit sectors is not really a "new" phenomenon. Rather, it appears to be a more cyclical occurrence; a similar advocacy of running public service institutions as businesses gripped the United States in the early 1900s.[12] It was a misguided idea, but it took the Great Depression of 1929 to drive home the reality that shortsighted business decisions do not necessarily benefit the general public in the long run.

Third, I did not have the column space to address the pressures that might be leading managers to believe that they must reduce costs, including personnel costs, in order to maintain services and, more recently, increase their ratings in Thomas J. Hennen Jr.'s immodestly titled Hennen's American Public Library Ratings (HAPLR).[13] This was particularly frustrating since several managers have informed me that the rise of HAPLR has been leading public library administrators to replace professional librarians with lower-paid library associates on the grounds that reducing personnel costs was likely to help their rankings. Whether this belief is true or not, long-accepted sociological theory dealing with "the critical importance of perceptions in explaining human behavior"[14] suggests that public library managers and boards obsessed with HAPLR standings will do whatever they feel is necessary — including deprofessionalizing their librarian staff — if they believe it will bolster their national reputations.

Although the context lacking in a *Library Journal* article can be supplied in a book, a fuller analysis of the HAPLR rankings in reorienting public library priorities must await another time. This chapter addresses the academic as practitioner; a few words on how and why twenty-first-century academics have inherited a long-established legacy of problems with producing useful theory are now in order.

WHEN THE GODLY PRESIDED
OVER HIGHER EDUCATION

In a real sense, use of the past tense in this chapter section title simplifies matters more than is appropriate. Religious motivations are still significant in American life. However, a by-product of the continued viability of religious paradigms or models outside of the mainstream academic culture may be a lingering unease about academic curricula again being influenced by the doctrines of a faith community—any faith community. This concern seems to be maximized, for example, in the perception of sociologists that a focus on religious issues could even harm their career prospects.[15] To the degree that this perception is true, it complicates the difficulty of preparing students to work in the many American contexts where religious views of all types continue to resonate. The present reality of keeping religion at arm's length represents a 180-degree change from the conditions prevailing about 1850. At that time the "godly," understood as being mainstream Protestants, presided without significant opposition over America's college-based system of higher education.

It is worth recalling that many of the traditions supplying the childhood rules and models competing with faculty-generated theory in the minds of today's American adults are profoundly spiritual. As a result of more varied sources of immigration and greater opportunities for cross-border communication dating from the mid-nineteenth century, such rules have been drawn from a much wider spectrum of religious traditions. A culture where the study of the Protestant Bible was once the rule has been leavened by Roman Catholic and Orthodox interpretations, as well as, for example, the received scriptures and commentaries of Jewish, Islamic, Buddhist, Hindu, and other faith traditions.[16]

Seymour Martin Lipset's 1996 observations about American religiosity parallel to a remarkable degree the explanations of the religious nature of Americans advanced over a century and a half earlier by both Alexis de Tocqueville and John Stuart Mill.[17]

A majority even tells pollsters that God is the moral guiding force of American democracy. They tend to view social and political dramas as morality plays, as battles between God and the Devil, so that compromise is virtually unthinkable. To this day, Americans, in harmony with their sectarian roots, have a stronger sense of moral absolutism than Europeans and even Canadians.[18]

Recently, 81 percent of the American adults surveyed in a *New York Times* poll reported that they believed in some sort of an afterlife; 38 percent of those polled even claimed to know someone likely to end up in hell.[19] Despite its apparent loss of control of American higher education, religion appears to thrive in American culture as a whole. To cite another example, in the election year 2000, a dispute over the selection of the chaplain of the U.S. House of Representatives led to claims of anti-Catholic bias that were "leaving some [House] members politically vulnerable in their home districts."[20] When elected officials see the genuine possibility that their reelection could be endangered by a controversy over filling the position of a legislative chaplain, the religious sway over American culture ought not to be underestimated.

Consequently, "useful" theory produced in higher education—indeed theory of any kind, whether produced in faculty offices, in consulting firms, or at professional workstations—must come to grips with the religious/spiritual nature of Americans and their shared national culture. To modify Robert K. Merton's favorite "theorem" of W. I. Thomas, there should be no doubt that "if people define religious beliefs as real, they are real in their consequences."[21] This reality was a source of considerable frustration for Abraham Kaplan, a leading social science theorist of the mid-twentieth century. In his classic *The Conduct of Inquiry: Methodology for Behavioral Science,* Kaplan complained that "though the physical and biological sciences have largely won their independence, behavioral science in many parts of the world—including our own—is still subject to the influence, if not the authority, of theological doctrine."[22] To restate the obvious, whether or not a researcher believes in any faith tradition, the religious beliefs of others will often impact how her or his findings are received in American culture.

In 1850, religious authority over American higher education was not controversial—it was taken for granted. Frederick Rudolph, in his *Curriculum: A History of the American Undergraduate Course of Study since 1636,* describes the mid-nineteenth-century system of higher education as consisting of four components held in a rough sort of balance. These aspects included the *college chapel,* and the occasions that sent students (mostly male) to it; the "dying but socially respectable and useful *classical course of study*" centered on Greek and Latin, philosophy, and theology; the *extracurriculum,* whose literary societies, debates, and orations helped students make it through the dry formal curriculum; and the senior class in moral philosophy. This *capstone course*, modified from English and Scottish originals and generally taught by the American college president, addressed ethics, politics, economics, sociology, law, history, and numerous other fields to serve "the happy purpose of bringing into harmony reason, intuition, and Christian orthodoxy."[23]

Still, the growth of science in the college curricula during this time demonstrates that it was often not antithetical to Christian belief in academic contexts.[24] However, by its very definition, orthodoxy implies limits beyond which lie the unacceptable—and the orthodoxy of mid-nineteenth-century Protestant beliefs cut a wide swath. It held, as do its Protestant, Roman Catholic, Orthodox, Jewish, and Islamic equivalents of today, that the world is ruled by a God who is "disembodied, free, all-powerful, all-knowing, the creator and sustainer of the universe, and the proper object of human obedience and worship."[25] In such circumstances, college faculty, who were often clergy or had some theological training, were expected to reconcile their investigations and theories with a pervasive public philosophy supporting the reality of Divine Providence as explained in Holy Scripture.[26] Kaplan has rightly termed this philosophy "an idealistic metaphysics transcending the actualities of human experience."[27]

Although written long after this period, Robert Dubin's discussion of "Theory and Theology," contained in the revised edition of his work *Theory Building*, is useful in understanding the climate in which faculty researched and theorized about the year 1850.[28] As Dubin reminds us, a theological model is grounded in conviction. In a God-centered culture such as that of mid-nineteenth-century America, dominated by mainstream Protestantism, such models are not normally subject to testing. Rather, the "certitude of a theological model rests on the consensual faith of those who accept it." In consequence, when a religion-based rule does not seem to be working in a believer's life, the proper reaction is not to question the rule but to ascribe the failure—the sin—either to one's own limitations or to the Devil's presence in the world.[29] This understanding is in direct contrast to the more secular worldview dominant in much of contemporary Western higher education, where it is expected that theories may occasionally prove inadequate and a theory originator is prepared to modify a given concept when necessary so that its "predictions will accord more adequately with experienced reality."[30]

In comparing the rules of theology with those of theory development, Dubin seems to be working with a variant of Max Weber's "ideal types," an abstract category that downgrades context and localized attributes in order to maximize logical precision.[31] However, not all theologies are as rigid as those Dubin describes. As he himself admits, there may be fewer differences in religious and secular philosophies than some would like to admit. Moreover, models used in nonreligious contexts are often the product of a consensus reminiscent of the one Dubin ascribes to pious believers. In the secular world, the "believers" in question may even be faculty researching a particular profession or subject discipline.

At some point a "consensus" theory used by faculty in secular research may fall out of fashion without any proof that the discarded theory has incorrectly "model[ed] the observable world."[32] Indeed, Karl Popper and Thomas Kuhn, two of the twentieth century's theoretical giants, were involved in just such a transition in the 1960s, when Popper and supporters fought an intellectual rearguard action against Kuhn's emerging formulations.[33] Although both Popper and Kuhn might resist the comparison, paradigm changes without an empirical justification seem to breathe a more theological than scientific air when they represent, as was the case with positivism's triumphant over classical pragmatism, a change in intellectual fashion by those apparently bored with approaches inherited from their predecessors.

But it was the dominance of Protestantism, not Popper or Kuhn, that was replaced in the heart of American higher education in the latter half of the nineteenth century. And it was Charles Darwin and his theory of evolution that paved the way for the ejection of religious orthodoxy from the mainstream of American theory development.[34]

THE RISE OF RESEARCH IN THE PHD UNIVERSITY

Until the late nineteenth century, the American college president was a clergyman, often appointed at midlife from the pulpit of a Protestant congregation. His task (the president was inevitably male at this time) was to ensure that all the faculty members taught and their students learned in an atmosphere that reflected America's core values, including its dominant religious beliefs. This undertaking grew progressively more difficult to sustain as the century progressed, the nation industrialized, and it became common for would-be faculty members to earn PhDs at research-minded German universities. In the process, these well-traveled scholars imbibed and spread among their stay-at-home colleagues the German academic tradition of *lehrfreiheit*, or freedom to teach and research. Until the issue was resolved for a time by privileging research in America's leading academic institutions, the tension inherent in the college president's commitment to community aspirations and the faculty's dedication to academic freedom made for increasingly confrontational situations.[35]

In his famed essay "The New Education," written in 1869 on the eve of becoming president of Harvard, Charles W. Eliot argues that the custom of clergy serving as academic presidents had been justifiable only when colleges existed to "breed ministers and laymen of some particular religious communion." Eliot saw that the purposes of higher education had expanded by the later 1800s and the faculty involved in the transformation had become members of the "profession of education." To Eliot, elevating a clergyman without extensive academic experience to the post of college president was an absurdity, equal to appointing the same individual as a sitting judge or placing soldiers under the command of a civilian without military experience.[36]

Despite the danger of oversimplification, it is still possible to provide a more or less accurate explanation of how research and theory, even theory without practical application, captured the university world. Perhaps the most straightforward explanation for this development is contained in the 1994 *Report of the Regents' Advisory Committee on Faculty Workload Standards and Guidelines*, issued by the Ohio Board of Regents. As described in the report:

> In higher education's recent history, both in Ohio and nationally, research and graduate teaching have garnered greater financial support and professional recognition. Federal, state and local governments, as well as private industry, have provided encouragement and financial support for research and graduate education as a means of realizing their own needs and goals. The results of both basic and applied research at our universities have benefited the state and the nation. In response, faculty effort moved away from undergraduate teaching and toward those activities that were more highly valued and rewarded. At the same time, new faculty and graduate students were often socialized in an environment that gave less status and reward to undergraduate teaching, even though universities were facing increasing demands, and concerns, for undergraduate education.[37]

As this report explains, *behavior that is rewarded is behavior that is sustained*. If the Harvards, MITs, and Yales of the world—or the Oxfords, Cambridges, and Torontos—socialize doctoral students into prioritizing research and theory development during the formative years of their doctoral study, they are likely to carry the same preference with them when taking faculty positions at less prestigious institutions. This process is what Burton R. Clark has called "academic drift," or the "unguided imitative convergence of universities and colleges upon the most prestigious forms."[38] Even now, academic drift, in all its permutations, helps set "national" standards for American higher education as a whole.

Space limitations prevent anything resembling a full account of the associated transformation of the American academy from the model of the denominationally affiliated college with its master's degree faculty to the paradigm of Clark Kerr's contemporary, very secular, and PhD-driven "multiversity."[39] But the extent of such change was remarkably far-reaching. In the area of religious belief alone, only a few years after Eliot's 1869 assertions that progress in higher education meant moving beyond the leadership of clergy, larger American universities reached the point where they "produced a casual style of unbelief if they had any influence at all on religious thought."[40]

Just as the PhD experience inspired in America the concept of academic freedom and contributed to undermining denominational control over higher education, it played a leading role in the subordination of teaching within the flagship institutions of American higher education. In professional schools, for example, it has become immensely more difficult for successful practitioners without a doctorate to move, mid-career or upon retirement, into full-time academic positions. The spread of the PhD has produced the now-unchallenged dominance of the *academic practitioner* in professional education. The academic practitioner, defined as a faculty member who has always embraced university norms or who has moved from identifying with professionals "in the field" to embracing university rules for success, is now the standard within the university. And characteristic of the academic practitioner, particularly in the major research institutions, is a necessity to live by rules that privilege research and theory development over any other academic responsibility.

A number of early twentieth-century intellectual leaders saw this change in emphasis from teaching to research as particularly problematic.

William James viewed it as evidence of a "Mandarin disease," asking the question, "Will any one pretend for a moment that the doctor's degree is a guarantee that its possessor will be successful as a teacher?" Still, James, an MD, recognized that a monopoly of PhDs on a faculty ("No instructor who is not a Doctor") was a competitive approach to building institutional credibility, even in 1903.[41]

The observations of the foreign-born and -educated can be of assistance in helping Americans to understand our own culture. For example, the reaction of Max Weber, the famed German sociologist, to the United States has been described as "at once enthusiastic and detached." Weber visited America in 1904 and lectured at the "Congress of Arts and Science," which was affiliated with the Universal Exposition in St. Louis.[42] His experience in America may well have influenced his 1918 presentation "Science as a Vocation," where he compares the average faculty member to a seller of cabbage.

> The American's conception of the teacher who faces him is: he sells me his knowledge and his methods for my father's money, just as the greengrocer sells my mother cabbage. And that is all. To be sure, if the teacher happens to be a football coach, then, in this field, he is a leader. But if he is not this (or something similar in a different field of sports), he is simply a teacher and nothing more. And no young American would think of having the teacher sell him a *Weltanschauung* [worldview or general outlook on life] or a code of conduct.[43]

It is wise to accept Weber's disclaimer that he had exaggerated conditions so as to emphasize his point. Nevertheless, his comments are suggestive of a cultural frame in which academic careerists, even those in the upper levels of the university world where "prestige" is the "principal operative currency," could be seen as the societal equivalent of the shop owner selling produce.[44] A combination of faculty pride and administrative concern for university reputations led, somewhere about 1900, to the wholesale endorsement of the idea by university leaders that research and publication, not teaching, would constitute the "gold standard" for identifying the nation's foremost institutions.

Larry Cuban's *How Scholars Trumped Teachers: Change without Reform in University Curriculum, Teaching, and Research, 1890–1990* parallels the Ohio Board of Regents report discussed above. Cuban found that the adoption of research effectiveness as the principal criterion for promotion and tenure had contributed to a narrowing of the options for academic greatness "into one model of a research-driven university." As a result, innovations such as a "reduced teaching load, sabbaticals, and large graduate schools spread among the less-prestigious and status-seeking institutions to reproduce an academic culture congenial to research-minded faculty."[45] Although essential to research, the time away from the classroom represented by sabbaticals and course reductions, as well as the model's emphasis on work with doctoral students, could not help but have a negative impact on undergraduates, who found themselves unable to enroll in classes with renowned, yet absent, professors.

Hidden in what scholars term a "killer" or "lethal" footnote, Cuban tells the story of a senior faculty member in Stanford University's School of Education who took a new, untenured colleague to view a plaque listing the names "of professors who had been recognized by students as excellent teachers." According to Cuban's informant, the senior faculty member went through the list and indicated which of the professors honored for teaching had been denied tenure. The moral of the story is both blatant and blunt. Teaching was a dead end, and "publications were everything."[46]

As far as members of the general public are concerned, there is something inherently problematic about a situation where senior professors feel obligated to warn new faculty about spending too much time on teaching. Such rules, when they become known outside of the university environment, invariably generate resentment, since "quality instruction at the undergraduate level is viewed by the public as the most important educational service a university provides."[47] Consequently, the world described by Cuban, where professors are "hired to do research and publish findings yet [are] paid to teach courses to undergraduates,"[48] may be facing pressures to embrace teaching effectiveness, particularly in those colleges and universities that are subject to either market pressure or state government influence, while leading private institutions, those universities with recognized brand names, may be exempt.

Similarly, faculty theorists in institutions subject to competition with for-profit providers may find resources for research less available when the price of education would be increased through their receiving sabbaticals or course reductions. Even in the elite public institutions, the public's demand for responsive, cost-effective, and accessible courses is now threatening the structure erected over the decades to support faculty research efforts. The nature of this "threat," powered as it is by a combination of economics and public policy, can be explored through examining the revolutionary rise in the provision of for-profit higher education as exemplified in the University of Phoenix and the dramatic efforts of the Ohio Board of Regents concerning that state's doctoral education system in the 1990s.

THE SPECTER OF PHOENIX

The same academic system whose inability to produce useful theory was so well chastised for its irrelevance to the worlds of practice by Norman A. Polansky is now under converging pressures from the private and public sectors.[49] To the regret of some theorists, the pressure is not for functional theory. Rather, in different ways and for variant reasons, the private sector (profit) and public sector (responsiveness) are now pushing American higher education in the direction of treating students as "customers." As a result of this new orientation, pressure is rising to teach undergraduates through courses and via technologies that are effective, convenient, reasonably priced, and "student-centered instead of 'tenured faculty centered.'"[50]

The competition from the for-profit sector, *indirectly and in the long run*, threatens the university's ability to generate the resources necessary to reduce teaching loads, hire substitute instructors, approve sabbaticals, and fund the stipends necessary for professors to leave the classroom to undertake research.[51] The nature of this competition has been well documented in the *Chronicle of Higher Education*, higher education's "trade" publication. For example, in its December 19, 2003, issue, the *Chronicle* recounted that the University of Phoenix, an institution operated by Apollo Group, Inc., "reported enrollments topping 200,000, an increase of 27 percent over 2002."[52] A preliminary — and very admiring — analysis of the privatizing phenomenon represented by the Apollo Group and related companies was provided in 1999 by Stuart Crainer and Des Dearlove in their book *Gravy Training*. Under the chapter subheading "Welcome to the Future," the authors stress economist Milton Friedman's observation that the present university system is run by the faculty for the faculty's own benefit. According to Friedman, higher education thereby encourages or tolerates "many activities that have very little to do with higher education, namely athletics and research." The cost of these expensive elements is such that their elimination, coupled with the heavy use of part-time faculty, enables the Apollo Group's University of Phoenix to spend only about one-fifth of the money needed by Arizona State University per credit hour of education. For Crainer and Dearlove, "the key to distribution is the new technology. The key to the economics is the area of faculty salaries. Part-time faculty cost less."[53]

In addition to relying on part-time faculty, the University of Phoenix uses a "top-down" approach whereby courses are centrally developed for such instructors as they teach online, in strip malls, or elsewhere around the country. For Phoenix course developers, these largely inexperienced educators are envisioned as a prototypical instructor named "Joe," who lives in small-town Texas and has never before taught a course. To help "Joe," curriculum developers at the University of Phoenix "leave little to chance, guiding Phoenix's instructors in exactly what to teach and how to teach it." Such "Joes," wherever and however they instruct students, "teach from the same detailed syllabuses and faculty notes," may never have to develop a lesson plan, and have to be reminded to actually read the course textbook.[54]

In the November/December 2002 issue of *Across the Board*, business consultant E. J. Heresniak reports on taking part, without pay, in an online training course for would-be instructors in the University of Phoenix Online program. The article describes how the University of Phoenix recruits "facilitators" with such a need to teach that they are willing to conduct an average of six online courses per year while being paid piecework rates of about $950 for an undergraduate course and $1,100 for a graduate offering. Since each online version of a University of Phoenix course typically demands twenty to twenty-five hours of instructor time per week in its four- or five-week duration, despite using prepackaged, standardized curricula, Heresniak estimates that six courses produce earnings of $6,000 for six hundred to eight hundred hours worked. It is a figure that does suggest piecework at somewhat more than the federal minimum wage. Heresniak reports that he was "dropped from the training course after completing 50 hours, apparently for asking too many probing questions about philosophy, fees, ROI [return on investment], the term 'facilitator,' and the wisdom of requiring our group to be online and working over Labor Day weekend."[55]

The July 7, 2000, edition of the *Chronicle of Higher Education* describes the transformations that will become possible as a result of proposed and ongoing changes in the standards for accreditation maintained by America's regional accrediting associations. These regional associations, as well as their discipline-specific equivalents for such fields as business, medicine, law, social work, library and information studies, and so on, provide American students with the certification of quality that, in other nations, is the responsibility of government agencies. Proposed changes in accreditation standards include the elimination of the requirement for on-site libraries, as well as "placing more emphasis on what students learn, and less on how they learn it; accepting the growth of part-time faculty members; developing ways to evaluate the effectiveness of distance learning; [and] letting colleges tailor the accreditation process to their own concerns."[56]

Clearly, money-saving developments such as the use of part-time faculty and the elimination of on-site libraries, with the implied threat to both the jobs of academic librarians and the valuable assistance these librarians provide to researchers, are not likely to encourage a research-friendly climate. The economics work against it. If nothing else, in a climate where students can secure degrees across state and national borders via their home computers, or can earn them from local branches of institutions marketing on the basis of low price and customer convenience, university tuition revenues will become more limited. But the nature of research is also likely to change. Even as they demonstrate greater flexibility with the modes, times, and sites for twenty-first-century teaching, higher education faculty may also need to exhibit in their research what William James, in an unfortunate choice of words, termed "cash-value."[57]

Such research, in a word, may need to become *useful*.

THE GHOST OF OHIO

Academics tend to feel put upon when university administrators, boards of trustees, state legislators, and members of the general public want to make decisions about how they do their work. The traditional argument over the years has been that it takes a PhD, as well as experience in teaching, research, and publication in a discipline, field, or profession, to be a "player" in making important decisions affecting its operations within any university or college setting. There is thus a sense of intrusion, of somebody unfairly changing the rules, when, for example, the Ohio legislature, finding that the time spent by professors in a classroom had *decreased* by 10 percent over a decade, passed a law directing its public-university system to *increase* professors' time in the classroom by the same percentage. To insure that the legislative intent would be carried out, the provisions of the law restoring faculty teaching time even removed the subject from the area of collective bargaining.[58]

This law, and the subsequent court challenges to its constitutionality, took place in an atmosphere where the Ohio legislature and general public had become aware that the public's priority of undergraduate education was seemingly not shared by the state university system. Of particular concern was the revelation by the Ohio Board of Regents that *over half of the "new" money appropriated by the state for higher education instructional subsidies since 1990 had gone to support doctoral education.* In actual dollar terms, the general assembly had voted a total of $92.3 million in "new" money for higher education instructional subsidies in the 1990–1995 period. Of this amount, the universities allocated $53.1 million, or 57.6 percent, to support students in PhD, EdD, and other doctoral programs. Viewed another way, in the 1990–1995 period, enrollment in Ohio's state-assisted doctoral programs increased by *40.4 percent* FTE, or "full-time equivalent"—a common method of providing a total that includes both full-time and part-time students. In the same period, overall student enrollment had increased by just *3 percent* FTE.[59]

As an immediate response to the fiscal imbalance in the direction of doctoral education, the Board of Regents asserted the need for a temporary cap on the number of doctoral students in state universities until it completed its review of all their doctoral programs in nine fields of study—history, psychology, computer science, English, education (leadership), chemistry, biological sciences, physics, and business. This intense review was undertaken at the suggestion of a "blue ribbon panel" appointed by the Board of Regents "at the request" of then-governor George V. Voinovich to respond to the perception, backed by "some evidence," that there was "unnecessary duplication among some doctoral programs in Ohio."[60]

The law increasing teaching time by 10 percent and the statistics on funding provided by the Ohio Board of Regents constitute a rare public revelation of the gulf separating the faculty's vision for a university that privileges research and the public's prioritization of university undergraduate teaching. Such exposures are dangerous for higher education, since they carry with them the risk that the public may see a university or university system as unresponsive to its demands, a perception that rarely has positive implications for funding.

This threat should be kept in mind in considering the first-rate effort at damage control undertaken by the Ohio Board of Regents and the state's university administrators. The process, among other components, stressed that Ohio's state-assisted doctoral programs were instrumental in bringing a half-billion dollars in sponsored research to the state every year.[61] In addition, the regents began a process of paring down the number of doctoral programs, with the stated aims of insuring program quality, insuring relevance to state needs, and minimizing duplication. As one press release noted, "The Regents reviewed more than 100 doctoral programs in 1995–1996. State support was removed from 13 programs. An additional 15 programs will face 'viability reviews' in three years. Twenty-nine programs are required to file 'three-year reviews,' and nine programs were required to restructure as a condition of continued state support."[62]

Removal of the state subsidy is usually a death sentence for a doctoral program at a state university. It means that the program has to be either self-supporting or funded with other university resources. Since full-time doctoral students usually require tuition remission in addition to a stipend, and part-time students may well balk at increased fees, maintaining the program with locally controlled resources would require a substantial, and ongoing, drain on the university budget.

Whatever else might be said about the Ohio law, it is clear that these actions were spurred by a negative public judgment on the faculty's successful efforts to prioritize research and theory development—represented by high enrollment in doctoral programs—over undergraduate teaching. In this context, it is interesting to note that the Board of Regents provided a wealth of advice to state universities on how the law's requirements could be met while protecting the more productive researchers through, for example, authorizing uneven teaching loads.[63]

The elimination of subsidies for a doctoral program, whatever the perceived quality, has negative implications for both the lost students and the affiliated faculty. Obviously, students cannot attend a PhD program that no longer exists, and the elimination of that program may work to the detriment of their potential careers. Closing a doctoral program could also have severe implications for the research agendas of an entire department. In the sciences and professions, doctoral students often form a vital component of the teams necessary to conduct research funded by government or industry. Further, students in science, social science, humanities, and professional programs frequently teach introductory courses, enabling professors to concentrate on research and/or to teach upper-division undergraduate or graduate students. Finally, and most problematically, not all tenured professors are effective teachers of undergraduate students. Conducting seminars for PhD students—in effect, exploring subjects of mutual interest with near-colleagues—may well fit the talents of such faculty more than standing at a podium, or in front of a camera or computer screen, attempting to convey basic concepts to new undergraduates. In short, when a PhD program dies, the loss has more than monetary implications. In the absence of doctoral students, the hopes of faculty to secure the time and resources necessary to achieve research recognition may be similarly affected.

Playing the "What if?" game is always problematic. However, there are lessons to be learned from Ohio's actions to reduce faculty research commitments and the support of doctoral students while redirecting resources and attention to undergraduate teaching. Undergraduate instruction offers a payback to the general public that is delivered on a very personal basis. Taxpayers experience benefits on the "checkbook level" when their daughters and sons receive state-subsidized educations. Supporting faculty research agendas and the education of doctoral students does not provide such immediate benefit. Few members of the public may even know the faculty or the students involved even in large doctoral programs or in multimillion-dollar research efforts.

Still, there are exceptions to the lack of popularity of faculty research. For example, the perception of the benefits delivered to the farming community by results-oriented university professors affiliated with state agricultural extension networks is near legendary. The research of such faculty regularly changes to meet the perceived needs of its public. As such, it is both appreciated and supported. I find it significant that those who have studied American agricultural research assert that the key to its gaining and sustaining public support over the decades lies in the fact that "all participants in the research/transfer process pull together to produce utilizable knowledge, and to get it diffused and adopted."[64]

It is not my suggestion that all faculty researchers should orient their research toward the agricultural sector. But here too, as in the proceeding section, faculty research must appear to be "useful."

NOTES

1. Bill Crowley, "The Suicide of the Public Librarian," *Library Journal*, April 15, 2003, 48–49.

2. Crowley, "Suicide," 49.

3. E-mail message to author, June 8, 2003.

4. John N. Berry III, editor in chief, *Library Journal*, personal communication, August 23, 2003.

5. Bill Crowley and Deborah Ginsberg, "Intracultural Reciprocity, Information Ethics, and the Survival of Librarianship in the Twenty-First Century," in *Ethics and Electronic Information: A Festschrift for Stephen Almagno*, ed. Barbara Rockenbach and Tom Mendina (Jefferson, NC: McFarland, 2003), 94–107.

6. Robert K. Merton, *Social Theory and Social Structure*, enl. ed. (New York: Free Press, 1968), 524.

7. Merton, *Social Theory*.

8. Bill Whitson, "From the President: Do We Have a Future?" *CARL Newsletter*, September 1995, 1–2, available at http://www.carl.acrl.org/Archives/NewsletterArchive/1995/news95-9pres.html.

9. Crowley, "Suicide," 48.

10. Christine Holmes, "The Dirty Little Secret," *Alum News* (CSU School of Library and Information Science, San Jose State University), Fall 2003, 7.

11. Bill Crowley, "Dumping the 'Library,'" *Library Journal*, July 1998, 48–49.

12. See the section entitled "Business Models for Educational Enterprise" in Laurence R. Veysey, *The Emergence of the American University* (Chicago: University of Chicago Press, 1965), 346–56.

13. See Thomas J. Hennen, "Great American Public Libraries: The 2003 HAPLR Rankings," *American Libraries*, October 2003, 44–48.

14. Everett M. Rogers, *Diffusion of Innovations*, 5th ed. (New York: Free Press, 2003), 219, 223.

15. See the discussion in D. W. Miller, "Measuring the Role of 'the Faith Factor' in Social Change," *Chronicle of Higher Education* 46, no. 14 (November 26, 1999): A21–A22.

16. For one example of the dialogue resulting from this multiplicity of religious views, the reader is referred to F. E. Peters, *Judaism, Christianity, and Islam: The Classical Texts and Their Interpretation* (Princeton, NJ: Princeton University Press, 1990).

17. See John Stuart Mill, "Introduction: An Appraisal of Volume I of *Democracy in America*, Published in the London (and Westminster) Review in 1835 on the Occasion of the First Appearance of the English Translation," in Alexis de Tocqueville, *Democracy in America*, vol. 1 (New York: Schocken Books, 1961), and "Introduction: An Appraisal of Volume II of *Democracy in America*, Published in the *Edinburgh Review* in 1840 on the Occasion of the

First Appearance of the English Translation," in Alexis de Tocqueville, *Democracy in America*, vol. 2 (New York: Schocken Books, 1961).

18. Seymour Martin Lipset, *American Exceptionalism: A Double-Edged Sword* (New York: Norton, 1996), 63.

19. "The Way We Live Now Poll: Spirituality," *New York Times Magazine*, May 7, 2000, 84.

20. Lizette Alvarez, "After Months of Rancor, Speaker Names a Catholic Priest as House Chaplain," *New York Times*, March 24, 2000.

21. W. I. Thomas's original theorem, "If men define situations as real, they are real in their consequences," was cited in Robert K. Merton, "The Self-Fulfilling Prophecy," in Robert K. Merton, *Social Research and the Practicing Professions*, ed. Aaron Rosenblatt and Thomas F. Gieryn (Cambridge, MA: ABT Books, 1982), 248.

22. Abraham Kaplan, *The Conduct of Inquiry: Methodology for Behavioral Science* (San Francisco: Chandler, 1964), 5.

23. Frederick Rudolph, *Curriculum: A History of the American Undergraduate Course of Study since 1636* (San Francisco: Jossey-Bass, 1977), 90, 98.

24. See the relevant pages in Frederick Rudolph, *The American College and University: A History* (1962; reprint, Athens: University of Georgia Press, 1990).

25. Philip L. Quinn, "Philosophy of Religion," in *The Cambridge Dictionary of Philosophy*, ed. Robert Audi (Cambridge: Cambridge University Press, 1995), 607.

26. In 1868, seven of the ten members of the Princeton faculty were Presbyterian ministers. See Rudolph, *American College*, 160.

27. Abraham Kaplan, *The New World of Philosophy* (New York: Random House, 1961), 14.

28. Robert Dubin, *Theory Building*, rev. ed. (New York: Free Press, 1978), 222–24.

29. Dubin, *Theory Building*, 223.

30. Dubin, *Theory Building*.

31. H. H. Gerth and C. Wright Mills, "Introduction: The Man and His Work," in *From Max Weber: Essays in Sociology*, trans. and ed. H. H. Gerth and C. Wright Mills (New York: Oxford University Press, 1946), 59.

32. Dubin, *Theory Building*, 223–24.

33. Thomas S. Kuhn's famous questions regarding the disagreements between himself and Sir Karl Popper are relevant in this context. "How am I to persuade Sir Karl, who knows everything I know about scientific development and who has somewhere or another said it, that what he calls a duck can be seen as a rabbit? How am I to show him what it would be like to wear my spectacles when he has already learned to look at everything I can point to through his own?" The remarks can be found in Thomas S. Kuhn, "Logic of Discovery or Psychology of Research?" in *Criticism and the Growth of Knowledge*, ed. Imre Lakatos and Alan Musgrave (Cambridge: Cambridge University Press, 1970), 3.

34. Rudolph, *American College*, 346–47.

35. Christopher J. Lucas, *American Higher Education: A History* (New York: St. Martin's, 1994), 194–95.

36. Charles W. Eliot, "The New Education," *Atlantic Monthly* 23 (1869): 366.

37. Ohio Board of Regents, *Report of the Regents' Advisory Committee on Faculty Workload Standards and Guidelines: February 18, 1994*, available at http://summit.bor.ohio.gov.plandocs.workload.html (accessed March 24, 1999).

38. Burton R. Clark, *The Academic Life: Small Worlds, Different Worlds* (Princeton, NJ: Carnegie Foundation for the Advancement of Teaching, 1987), 143.

39. Clark Kerr, *The Uses of the University*, 4th ed. (Cambridge, MA: Harvard University Press, 1995), 102.

40. Veysey, *Emergence*, 281. See also the account of the transformation contained in Rudolph's classic *Curriculum*.

41. William James, "The Ph.D. Octopus," in *Memories and Studies* (1911; reprint, New York: Greenwood, 1968), 333, 334, 337.

42. Gerth and Mills, "Introduction," 14–15.

43. Max Weber, "Science as a Vocation," in *From Max Weber: Essays in Sociology*, trans. and ed. H. H. Gerth and C. Wright Mills (New York: Oxford University Press, 1946), 149–50.

44. The role of prestige in contemporary faculty careers is reviewed in Clark, *Academic Life*, especially 187–89. For a historical perspective, see Veysey, *Emergence*, and Rudolph, *Curriculum*.

45. Larry Cuban, *How Scholars Trumped Teachers: Change without Reform in University Curriculum, Teaching, and Research, 1890–1990* (New York: Teachers College Press, 1999), 2–3.

46. Cuban, *How Scholars Trumped Teachers*, 246 n. 32.

47. Ohio Board of Regents, *Report of the Regents' Advisory Committee*.

48. Cuban, *How Scholars Trumped Teachers*, 14.

49. See Norman A. Polansky, "There Is Nothing So Practical as a Good Theory," *Child Welfare* 65 (January/February 1986): 14.

50. Florence Olsen, "Phoenix Rises: The University's Online Program Attracts Students, Profits, and Praise," *Chronicle of Higher Education*, 49, no. 10 (November 1, 2002), available at http://chronicle.com/weekly/v49/i10/10a02901.htm (accessed December 30, 2003).

51. Goldie Blumenstyk, "Companies' Graduate Programs Challenge Colleges of Education: For-Profit Institutions Find a New Market—Schoolteachers," *Chronicle of Higher Education* 50, no. 2 (September 5, 2003), available at http://chronicle.com/weekly/v50/i02/02a03001/htm (accessed December 30, 2003).

52. Goldie Blumenstyk, "Financial Outlook 2004: For-Profit Colleges: Growth at Home and Abroad," *Chronicle of Higher Education* 50, no. 17 (December 19, 2003), available at http://chronicle.com/weekly/v50/i17/17a01201.htm (accessed December 30, 2003).

53. Stuart Crainer and Des Dearlove, *Gravy Training: Inside the Business of Business Schools* (San Francisco: Jossey-Bass, 1999), 215–17.

54. Elizabeth R. Farrell, "Phoenix's Unusual Way of Crafting Courses: The For-Profit Giant Uses a Systematic Grid and a Guy Named 'Joe' to Set Curriculum," *Chronicle of Higher Education* 49, no. 23 (February 14, 2003), available at http://chronicle.com/weekly/v49/i23/23a01001.htm (accessed December 30, 2003).

55. E. J. Heresniak, "Adventures in Cyberspace: The Business of Education—A Higher Calling? For Higher Profits, Maybe," *Across the Board*, November/December 2002, 61–62.

56. Beth McMurtrie, "Accreditors Revamp Policies to Stress Student Learning: Agencies Say They Are Responding to Years of Complaints about Regulations and Paperwork," *Chronicle of Higher Education* 46, no. 44 (July 7, 2000), A29–A31.

57. William James, *"Pragmatism" and "The Meaning of Truth"* (1907; reprint, Cambridge, MA: Harvard University Press, 1975), 31.

58. Robin Wilson, "Supreme Court Says Ohio Can Bypass Collective Bargaining in Push to Raise Faculty Workloads," *Chronicle of Higher Education*, "Today's News," March 23, 1999, http://chronicle.com/daily/99/03/9903230 1n.htm (accessed March 24, 1999).

59. These figures are contained in Ohio Board of Regents, "Board Resolution 1/13/95—Ohio Board of Regents—Agenda Item 8," http://www.regents.state .oh.us/newsitems/news4.html; and Ohio Board of Regents, "Board of Regents Recommends Temporary Limits on Doctoral Program Enrollments" (press release, January 13, 1995), http://www.regents.state.oh.us/nessitems/news5.html (both accessed January 11, 2000).

60. Ohio Board of Regents, "Board of Regents Recommends."

61. See, for example, the emphasis on the half-billion dollars in sponsored research in such documents as Ohio Board of Regents, *Report of the Commission on Graduate Education: July 17, 1998*; and Ohio Board of Regents, "Regents Actions" (press release, July 17, 1998), http://www.regents.state .oh.us/bdmeet/jul98/nr071798.html (accessed January 11, 2000).

62. Ohio Board of Regents, "Regents Approve Restructured Doctoral Programs in Educational Administration and English" (press release, April 11, 1997), http://www.regents.state.oh.us/newsitems.news153html (accessed January 11, 2000).

63. See the discussions on setting university, college, and departmental "workload policy" in Ohio Board of Regents, *Report of the Regents' Advisory Committee*.

64. Everett M. Rogers, *Diffusion of Innovations*, 4th ed. (New York: Free Press, 1995), 361.

Chapter Six

The Practitioner as Academic: Adjunct Faculty/Lecturers

SCENARIO: TRICKS OF THE TEACHING TRADE

Many ALA-accredited programs have been enrolling record numbers of students. The reasons for this influx include the realization on the part of business executives that program graduates are valuable guides to information-rich environments and a paradoxical increase in the number of corporate refugees looking for greater personal satisfaction in public-service jobs. Traditional sources of recruitment, ranging from the early influence of public and school librarians on youth, an individual's love of reading, and a fascination with information and its uses are also in play. Strangely enough, this surge in student enrollments occurs at a time of significant faculty shortages, with multiple positions open for every qualified applicant.[1] The combination of rising student counts with faculty scarcity has led some ALA-accredited programs to rely more than ever before on recruiting public library managers, reference librarians, school library media specialists, or corporate knowledge managers to teach evening classes in addition to their "day jobs."

Programs such as Dominican University's Graduate School of Library and Information Science have long benefited from their locations in major metropolitan areas. Being within driving distance of many successful practitioners with an interest in teaching enables them to provide students with often-unique educational experiences; they are frequently taught by highly paid professionals whose classes can resonate more with job-hungry students than courses taught by full-time faculty whose own "real world" experience is nonexistent or receding into the past. But teaching, particularly when it involves the mature students who dominate enrollment in many ALA-accredited programs, can be harder than it looks from off campus. Prudent practitioners agreeing to become part-time instructors have learned to ask full-time professors—or experienced adjunct faculty—for assistance on how to fill forty-two or more semester hours with effective student learning. Those who have failed to seek such help have sometimes learned the painful truth of an old joke long told in professional schools:

Professor: So, how are you going to teach your course?

Practitioner: I'm going to tell the students everything I know.

Professor: And what will you do for the second class?

As a member of Dominican University's Institutional Review Board, I was asked recently to speak with a number of adjunct instructors teaching for the Graduate School of Library and Information Science about how class assignments involving student interviews with "human subjects" might be carried out within university guidelines. As I was preparing my remarks, I learned that several of the new instructors had never taught a class—anywhere. On an impulse, I decided to add to my dry remarks on the "tricks of the teaching trade" that I had learned since coming to Dominican University in 1996 to teach my own first-ever classes. The following observations were among the many offhand comments I made that evening.

- Teaching is performance, and students expect to be entertained as well as to learn. Bore them at your peril.
- In a teaching university like Dominican University, full-time professors without tenure can feel that they live or die on the basis of their student evaluations. It's not quite as bad for adjuncts, but if your scores on the end-of-semester forms filled in by students are too low, or you have too many negative comments on the qualitative evaluation sheets, you may not be invited back.
- At the first class, hand out questionnaire cards asking students for their education to date and work history, as well as their aims for the class and for their own careers. Then ask the students to introduce themselves and share their answers with the rest of the class before

taking them though the course syllabus. Go over the cards after class to determine if student expectations are in line with your own plans for teaching. Make adjustments where appropriate and possible. If students do not get a hard copy of the syllabus but are expected to print it out and take it to class, bring a few hard copies of the syllabus to the first session for those who forget to make copies.

- Students regard the syllabus as their contract with the instructor, so take them through the course requirements at the first class. Feel free to make changes in the syllabus during the first session in response to new information volunteered by the students. Afterward, once it is "adopted," do not add new written or oral assignments to those already in the syllabus without subtracting something from the workload.

- Use well-selected scenarios that can raise a number of issues for discussion, and require students to write a one-page reaction paper to the scenario assigned for a particular class. At the start of each session have the students discuss the scenario in small groups and then bring the full class back together for a further exchange of ideas. More than a few students may actively participate. At a minimum, you can be fairly sure that scenarios will be read if there is a short paper attached to them, even if students don't read any of the other assignments.

- Allow a variety of subjects for class papers. Students will spend more time working on a project that interests them than on an assignment that seems to appeal only to the instructor. Since you don't know where they are going to work, it's better to make sure that they learn a research process that can be useful in a number of contexts.

- Instructors usually don't get the class and syllabus "right" until they have taught a class at least three times. It seems to be pretty much a tacit knowledge "given."

- Even the best instructor will occasionally have a course that struggles through an entire semester or will experience a session of a "great" class that bombs for seemingly inexplicable reasons. Sometimes you can never figure out why. So set up an occasional campus lunch or dinner meeting with another instructor, make sure that passing students can't overhear, and swap horror stories. We all accumulate them.

To my surprise, these tricks of the teaching trade, written out as a last-minute addition to a talk on research using human subjects, produced much positive feedback at the session and resulted in e-mail contacts from new adjunct instructors for several weeks thereafter. In retrospect, I shouldn't have wondered why such offhand comments were so appreciated. Although far from the best instructor in Dominican University's Graduate School of Library and Information Science, I am experienced at the "trade." Even better, I was the only full-time professor in the room when new part-time instructors first realized the magnitude of what they were facing and suddenly needed to ask questions. Sharing my tacit knowledge about what seems to work for me with practitioners-turned-instructors met an unarticulated but very intense need for reassurance. In addition to providing some tips that might actually help, I admitted to a number of my own classroom failures, stressing that they were going to happen even to the best full-time and part-time instructors.

"THEORY VERSUS REALITY"

In *Rules for Radicals: A Practical Primer for Realistic Radicals*, Saul D. Alinsky, the famed mid-twentieth-century community organizer, relates an incident in the higher education context that may tell us more than the author intended. It happened while Alinsky was a visiting professor at "a certain Eastern university."

> Two candidates there were taking their written examinations for the doctorate in community organization and criminology. I persuaded the president of this college to get me a copy of this examination and when I answered the questions the departmental head graded my paper, knowing only that I was an anonymous friend of the president. *Three of the questions were on the philosophy and motivations of Saul Alinsky. I answered two of them incorrectly. I did not know what my philosophy or motivations were, but they did!* [2]

This story of the obliging department head—one willing to grade exams on demand!—was not meant as a general attack by Alinsky on higher education. Rather, Alinsky placed the head's perceived failure to understand him within the larger problem of distinguishing "between fact [what really happened] and history [what the record says happened]." To this end, he relates another story where a Chicago reporter asked him whether holding a massive community-organizing meeting on July 14—France's Bastille Day—might be "too revolutionary" a choice. Alinsky himself had overlooked the meaning of the date as symbolic of the radical spirit and had selected July 14 only because it fit the schedules of participating labor unions, a local bishop, and a Chicago park department field house. But he seized on this information and immediately briefed all the speakers to emphasize the Bastille Day connection in their remarks, turning a lucky coincidence into the revolutionary call to action recorded in the published history of Chicago's *Back of the Yards Council*.

As Alinsky saw it, both the Chicago reporter and the "Eastern university" department head were making the same mistake. They injected "reason, purpose and order" into situations where his actions were "part accident, part necessity, part response to reaction, and part imagination" or "tactical sensitivity." More often than not, contingency and luck overtake planning; and "when the 'accident' happens, the imaginative organizer recognizes it and grabs it before it slips by."[3]

WHAT ALINSKY DIDN'T WRITE

Saul Alinsky's explanation of the complexities impacting community organizing is a fine example of the difficulty of capturing *tacit knowledge* and turning it into the *explicit knowledge* that is so often what is conveyed to students in academic environments. Worse, the apparent one-upmanship game played by the department head and Alinsky over the test questions on the latter's "philosophy or motivations" may have diminished any real possibility of a successful knowledge transfer.

THE ACADEMIC AS PRACTITIONER

Throughout this book, we have assumed that all who work in higher education, including faculty theorists, are properly described as *academic practitioners*. Our individual responsibilities may differ, but we perform in our colleges and universities in the same sense as do physicians in hospitals, attorneys in courthouses, teachers in elementary schools, social workers in local government departments, children's librarians in branch libraries, or knowledge managers in corporate offices. As with any practitioners, we grow and flourish, or decline and wither, according to whichever rules govern our individual working contexts or organizational cultures. These cultures can be extremely influential in encouraging or discouraging the building of useful theory. This last point is worth stressing. In organizational cultures where research is not normally rewarded, as in those American community college environments where teaching five classes a semester is the norm, a commitment to the development of theory demonstrates an extraordinary level of dedication.[4]

As discussed in chapters 1 and 2, even in environments where research and theory development are encouraged, at least two models of "useful" theory are potentially in play. Instead of attempting to uphold unproductive distinctions between the faculty "basic theory" that prizes understanding over usefulness and the practitioner "action theory" that privileges solving problems, this work has argued that theory development is nearly always pragmatic. It would not be attempted at all unless it benefited the developer in some context. This work has further stressed that the relationship between the faculty-centered *internal effectiveness model of useful theory* and the practitioner-inclusive *external effectiveness model of useful theory* has been stretched to the point of breaking by the application of different rewards systems. The internal effectiveness model values theory on the basis of how well it assists a faculty member in achieving the goals of tenure, promotion, and continuing influence on the direction taken by a profession or discipline. The second model, the external effectiveness model builds on the success of the internal model. Even though it is outwardly directed and aims to solve off-campus problems, it cannot be pursued unless a researcher makes her or his peace with the rules of the campus culture. As previously observed, professors who do not meet campus expectations for research can lose their faculty appointments. Unless they join the world of corporate research, it is likely that they will either give up theory development or become "independent scholars" lacking a continuing connection with higher education and its support system. To remain on campus, theorists have become quite realistic about taking care of themselves first, even if they subscribe to John Levett's dictum that the "primary task—and, indeed, the only justification—for research is the amelioration of the human condition."[5]

On the other hand, too much adherence to academic mores will virtually guarantee the *inapplicability* of academic research and theory to off-campus environments. It is a natural result of the power of the inwardly looking internal effectiveness model to shape the interests and standards of those who employ it. It is understandable that academics want to be retained by their employers and equally comprehensible that they produce just the sort of research and theory needed for tenure, promotion, and continuing influence.

Although appreciating the campus criteria of elegance and novelty in theory development, the alternative external effectiveness model of useful theory would accept less of both qualities if the result were theory more relevant to the messy, complicated worlds of off-campus concerns. The second model also recognizes the negative roles that certain academic criteria, in effect the "rules" of the faculty "language games," play in reducing theory's off-campus usefulness. When faculty theorists "speak" in the languages of higher education, they tend to be heard more by other academics than by practitioners.

Let us return to Alinsky. Undoubtedly, he knew best what his motivations were at the time he was a visiting professor. But, is it not possible, indeed likely, that the department head had intensely studied Alinsky's writings and had taken his statements, including his imaginative reconstructions regarding the Bastille Day mass meeting, at more or less face value? In truth, if one studies an individual whom one admires, it is a bit disconcerting to constantly view her or his written communications as the elaborate fabrications that Alinsky admitted to in his book. Such lies aside, the department head might have visited communities where Alinsky had organized, or even interviewed his past or current associates, in the process learning that Alinsky had once espoused quite different beliefs. It is even possible that the department head might have had greater knowledge about what the larger world—including higher education—perceived Alinsky's "philosophy or motivations" to be.

As interpretations vary, so do models of useful theory. Thus, it would be highly inappropriate, even arrogant, to suggest one research philosophy or one theory-development method would suit faculty, consultants, and practitioners alike. Many roads lead to "there" from "here." It is worth keeping in mind the already discussed injunctions for humility, tolerance, and respect advanced by William James and Abraham Kaplan (see chapter 3). At the same time, it is equally relevant to adapt more contemporary insights, such as Zygmunt Bauman's observation that in a world where the certainties of modernism are increasingly under criticism, effective "intellectual work" needs a change of metaphors. No longer is it realistic to conceptualize the theorist as *legislator*, someone who proclaims a universal validity for her or his "rules." Rather, a faculty-theorist should be viewed as an *interpreter*, building knowledge through facilitating communication among systems that operate on the basis of often-diverging knowledge traditions.[6]

Although the philosophy of positivism seems to have been discredited to a greater or lesser degree, its practical operation can still be discerned throughout higher education. It exists, for example, in often-tenuous claims made about the applicability of data gathered through the quantitative surveys that support so many PhD dissertations and faculty studies. Even though many of us share in a long-standing and "rather widespread skepticism surrounding the ability of conventional data collection techniques to produce data that do not distort, do violence to, or otherwise falsely portray the phenomena such methods seek to reveal," we continue to sample, randomize, and control our variables as ever before.[7] Whether or not we formally claim to believe that the world can be known "objectively," our actions often proclaim that we indeed believe it to be the case.

In the basic and applied sciences, a reliance on data collection techniques is not seen as much of a problem. Instruments either measure or they do not. Water boils or it doesn't. Nuclear reactions in stars take place, and their temperatures, within limits, can be ascertained. Outcomes can be expected and the methods for their achievement can be standardized. Granted, there are concerns regarding the social contexts of science and who controls its purposes, but the day-to-day operation of science continues.[8] However, it is not wise to portray the domains of science too mechanistically or as too isolated from other knowledge contexts. Analogies and metaphors useful in scientific theorizing—such as Sir Isaac Newton's famed apple or Charles Darwin's "living tree" metaphor—are regularly drawn from other fields or everyday life and can be immensely productive.[9] Philosophy and research theory can be fruitful, even in physics. As observed by physicist Lee Smolin, "Philosophy cannot settle scientific questions, but it has a role to play. A bit of philosophical thought may prevent us from getting hung up on a bad idea."[10]

This is a work about the development of useful theory written by a former *off-campus practitioner* turned *academic practitioner*. In the continuing transition from one status to another, I often find "real-world" tacit knowledge, learned in many contexts over several decades, being displaced by the understandings necessary to exist in a small university environment. Where I was once involved with decisions affecting dozens of full-time staff, divisional budgets in the millions of dollars, or the complexities of chairing statewide legislative efforts, I now teach, advise, revise syllabi, explore curriculum relevance, consult with or without charge, serve on numerous committees, debate more effective ways to recruit a diverse student body and faculty, evaluate potential courses, research, write the occasional article, deliver presentations to on- or off-campus audiences, and worry about both student assignments and evaluations. Despite long hours spent reading the practitioner-generated literature and the occasional consultation, there are times when I feel I am losing "field" credibility. This makes it increasingly necessary to invite guest speakers to my classes, who often tell students the same things I would say but with greater authority. They are, after all, describing their current working environments. Still, I do look forward to hearing off-campus practitioners recount their use of emerging technologies, employment of more-effective approaches to motivating staff, or delivery of programs that may not even have existed when I worked with the mass media as a public relations representative, staffed a reference desk, administered a division of state government, or negotiated legislation with state or federal lawmakers.

ACADEMIC LIBRARIANS

Part of the Problem? Or Part of the Solution?

For the very practical reason that a publication record is usually necessary for achieving tenure in colleges and universities, academic librarians and library and information educators tend to be "the two major contributors to LIS literature."[11] However, analyses of the value of such contributions, as research exemplars or as practical aids to practice, have generally been negative, even to the point of degenerating into efforts "more to assign blame than to present solutions."[12] On the faculty side, a frustration with the disregard of librarians for theory deemed irrelevant to their working lives has fueled complaints about practitioner resistance to theory since Pierce Butler's 1933 remarks about the librarian being "strangely uninterested in the theoretical aspects of his profession" and standing alone "in the simplicity of his pragmatism."[13]

Sixty-two years later, this same exasperation was evident in Blaise Cronin's assertion that the ideological demands of librarians were causing sympathetic "library science" faculty—but not their "information science" equivalents—to embrace "professional values and fuzzy philosophical ideals rather than theory building and rigorous research."[14] For Cronin, the connection with librarianship is a negative; it does not provide information science researchers with fruitful areas of potential study but actually hampers the development of their theories. Setting aside the tuition and state assistance flowing to those programs that teach librarians-to-be, Cronin asserts that there has developed "a pretty solid academic justification for eliminating librarianship programs from major research universities and locating them in vocational education institutions."[15]

Where Cronin claims that information science has adhered to the "value neutrality" asserted to be a scholarly norm,[16] academic librarian Joe A. Hewitt takes a markedly different approach, seeing values as being omnipresent in a librarian's working life: "Research may never become the controlling factor in the majority of important, value-laden politically conscious decisions which must be made in libraries."[17] For Hewitt, LIS scholarship has an "almost nonexistent" impact on practice.[18] Disillusionment with faculty researchers is evident in his assertion:

> An effective bridging mechanism [between the world of research and the arenas of practice] must rest heavily on a committed group of professionals who are conversant in both worlds and positioned as decision makers in the arenas in which new knowledge is to be applied. Most importantly, they must be prepared to deal sensitively with the conditions, limitations, values and complexities of the world of practice. Such requirements disqualify most academic researchers for a direct role in assimilation and point emphatically to the library administrator/manager as the key agent.[19]

Restricting the evaluation of the worth of research to practitioner-administrators is likely to bring with it another set of problems. Thereby disqualified from filling a "direct role," faculty theorists would also be prevented from playing the function of Georg Simmel's "stranger" and raising the critical, even fundamental, questions that are so often glossed over by the conventional wisdom of practice. As "strangers" to a given practitioner context, faculty researchers are less likely to have their mental horizons controlled by the same "habit, piety, and precedent"[20] that holds the questioning of certain assumptions to be unacceptable in a given practitioner context. Managers are members of administrative systems, and their socialization into an organization's culture—no matter what their intellectual capabilities—may prevent them from "introducing alternative possibilities," let alone taking necessary actions that "violate the values of the bureaucracy."[21]

For example, refocusing the library profession to again embrace the educational role of the library and librarian[22] is likely to be problematical in an academic environment unless such efforts find ways to deal with the unwillingness of students to read. As reported in *The Teaching Professor*:

> Students discuss with each other what it takes to succeed in a given class. And they listen intently to advice that *conforms to what they'd like to believe. Many college students today are not strong readers; they regularly report that they don't like to read.* So if it turns out that peers report reading in a given course isn't all that essential, students are only too ready to kick back and do the reading half-heartedly just before the exam.[23]

A focused effort to redefine the academic library as an educational resource with value beyond the basic provision of information would benefit from the application of such student learning studies,[24] as well as the cooperation and advice of campus teachers and learning researchers. For library, information, and knowledge issues, this would be particularly the case where an ALA-accredited program was present on campus. Hewitt to the contrary, without providing for friendly experts able to raise the questions that subordinates may not be likely to bring to the attention of the managers who write their evaluations, transformation efforts can be doomed from the start. Someone has to be in a position, if necessary, to inform library managers that their cherished projects are simply not doing the job.

Academic Librarian Research Inapplicability?

If practitioners see research by theorists in library, information, and knowledge as problematic, there are equally strong assertions that research conducted by practitioners rivals that of university scholars in its lack of usefulness. First, for Peter Hernon, this lack of usefulness results from the reality that "librarians conducting research may not have an adequate foundation in reflective inquiry, research design, the use of quantitative and qualitative methods of data collection, and report writing as a form of communication. Providing that foundation sufficiently is beyond the scope of any library and information science program at the master's level."[25]

For his part, Donald E. Riggs, who identifies academic librarians as major contributors to the disciplinary literature, also stresses that their research often lacks merit in an environment where "best practices articles and books are displacing publication based on research and intellectual inquiry."[26] He also regrets that research is marred by a too-intensive concentration on statistical approaches, because "we tend to be mesmerized by measuring everything with numbers, and place too little emphasis on the meanings of words and feelings provided via qualitative research."[27] Riggs's identification of an emphasis on the statistically measurable in library, information, and knowledge research is understandable in a "field hankering for academic respect," where the "pressure to be conventional, quasi-scientific, and carefully piecemeal is powerful."[28]

Contrary to the assertions of Riggs, the rise in the number of "best practices articles" is likely to be a positive influence for the development of useful theory. First, such publications perform the valuable function of filling the off-campus "usefulness gap" that seems to arise so often when faculty scholars produce works meant primarily for other scholars and secondarily, at best, for practitioners. All too frequently, information, knowledge, and library researchers ignore the fundamental contradiction inherent in expecting practitioners to prefer faculty intellectual products, often shorn of vital context, over the published experience of other practitioners, many times in similar situations, reporting how they identified, analyzed, and solved real problems.

Second, an abundance of the "how we did it good" articles provides theorists with a wealth of raw material for analysis. If a number of practitioners are reporting positive results for similar actions in comparable contexts, there may be a pattern, a potential model in play. If properly explained in their contexts, such models could become an important part of the intellectual tool kits of theorists, consultants, and practitioners alike.

AN IMPORTANT CAVEAT

It will take a transformation in academic values to allow campus-generated theory to become more relevant to practitioner realities. Whether managing systems of hiring and promotion, or the interweaved process of making decisions on what is acceptable for publication in leading journals, campus and disciplinary leaders will need to sanction the development and testing of theory that is derived, not from original faculty research, but from a researcher's analysis of practitioner "how I did it good" or "best practices" stories. Promotion and tenure bodies operating within departments, schools, colleges, and universities will need to adjust academic research priorities in order to facilitate the active engagement with the real world that Gerald Graff saw, with pardonable exaggeration, as offering the "long-awaited salvation of higher education from ivory tower marginality and irrelevance."[29]

NOTES

1. Remarks of Ann L. O'Neill, director of the ALA Office of Accreditation, to the Colorado Association of Libraries annual conference in October 2002. Published as "Library Education in the West," *Colorado Libraries*, Summer 2003; available at http://vnweb.hwwilsonweb.com/hww/results/results_single.jhtml?nn=9 (accessed November 11, 2003).

2. Saul D. Alinsky, *Rules for Radicals: A Pragmatic Primer for Realistic Radicals* (New York: Vintage, 1971), 169; emphasis mine.

3. Alinsky, *Rules for Radicals*, 168.

4. See the discussions of the lives of community college faculty in Burton R. Clark, *The Academic Life: Small Worlds, Different Worlds* (Princeton, NJ: Carnegie Foundation for the Advancement of Teaching, 1987), and Arthur M. Cohen and Florence B. Brawer, *The American Community College*, 3d ed. (San Francisco: Jossey-Bass, 1996).

5. John Levett, "A Critical Nexus: The Link between Research and Practice," in *Public Librarianship: A Critical Nexus: Proceedings of the Public Library Research Forum, Monash University, 8 April 1994*, ed. B. J. McMullin and Radha Rasmussen (Melbourne, Australia: Ancora Press, 1995), 4.

6. Zygmunt Bauman, *Legislators and Interpreters: On Modernity, Post-Modernity, and Intellectuals* (Ithaca, NY: Cornell University Press, 1987), 4–5.

7. John Van Maanen, "Reclaiming Qualitative Methods for Organizational Research: A Preface," *Administrative Science Quarterly* 24, no. 4 (December 1979): 522.

8. C. G. Prado's exploration of the role of tools and scientific explanations in *The Limits of Pragmatism* (Atlantic Highlands, NJ: Humanities Press International, 1987) is well worth reading.

9. Roy Dreistadt, "An Analysis of the Use of Analogies and Metaphors in Science," *Journal of Psychology* 68, first half (January 1968): 97–116.

10. Lee Smolin, *The Life of the Cosmos* (New York: Oxford University Press, 1997), 12.

11. Donald E. Riggs, "Writing for the LIS Profession: Introductory Comments and Questions," in *How to Get Published in LIS Journals: A Practical Guide*, ed. Lisa Janicke Hinchliffe and Jennifer Dorner (San Diego, CA: Elsevier Library Connect, 2003), 2.

12. Charles R. McClure and Ann Bishop, "The Status of Research in Library/Information Science: Guarded Optimism," *College and Research Libraries* 50, no. 2 (March 1989): 133.

13. Pierce Butler, *An Introduction to Library Science* (Chicago: University of Chicago Press, 1933), xi–xii.

14. Blaise Cronin, "Cutting the Gordian Knot," *Information Processing and Management* 31, no. 6 (1995): 897.

15. Cronin, "Cutting the Gordian Knot," 899.

16. Cronin, "Cutting the Gordian Knot," 897.

17. Joe A. Hewitt, "The Role of the Library Administrator in Improving LIS Research," in Charles R. McClure and Peter Hernon, eds., *Library and Information Science Research: Perspectives and Strategies for Improvement* (Norwood, NJ: Ablex, 1991), 177.

18. Hewitt, "Role," 165.

19. Hewitt, "Role," 166.

20. Georg Simmel, "The Stranger," in *The Sociology of Georg Simmel*, ed. Kurt H. Wolff (Glencoe, IL: Free Press, 1950), 405.

21. Robert K. Merton, *Social Theory and Social Structure*, enl. ed. (New York: Free Press, 1968), 273.

22. As described in Gretchen V. Douglas, "Professor Librarian: A Model of the Teaching Librarian of the Future," *Computers in Libraries* 19, no. 10 (November/December 1999); and Robert S. Martin, "Returning to the Center: Libraries, Knowledge, and Education," address to the annual meeting of the Colorado Library Association, October 29, 2001, available at http://www.imls.gov/scripts/text.cgi?/whatsnew/current/sp102901.htm (accessed April 24, 2003).

23. "Reading Assignments: Can We Persuade Students They Matter?" *Teaching Professor*, February 2003, 3; emphasis mine.

24. Dominican University's subscription to *The Teaching Professor* allows this valuable resource for practical teaching theory to be accessed from faculty offices.

25. Peter Hernon, "Research in Library and Information Science: Reflections on the Journal Literature," *Journal of Academic Librarianship* 35, no. 4 (July 1999).

26. Riggs, "Writing," 2.

27. Riggs, "Writing."

28. George Keller, "Academic Duty: The Role of the Intellectual," *ASHE Newsletter* 16, no. 2 (Winter 2002): 3. Although applied to scholarship in the field of higher education, Keller's remarks are regrettably appropriate to many library, information, and knowledge management "scholarly" endeavors.

29. Gerald Graff, "Introduction: Public Intellectual and the Future of Graduate Education," *Minnesota Review*, nos. 50–51 (Spring and Fall 1998), 163.

Chapter Seven

Other Worlds of Practice: The Field Practitioner

SCENARIO: "PILED HIGHER AND DEEPER"

A number of winters ago, I was seated in the baggage area in the Columbus, Ohio, airport, avoiding the frigid outside air while waiting for the small van that provided what passed for deregulated "bus" service to Athens and Ohio University. I had just returned from the annual meeting of the Association for Library and Information Science Education (ALISE), where I had tried without success to convince several search committees that I could complete a PhD with just two years of work. Frankly, I needed a job, since my decision to study full-time had meant giving up the more than adequate salary of an Ohio deputy state librarian. In return, I received a graduate assistant stipend (about 10 percent of my old income), tuition remission (a significant savings), and the opportunity to discuss important ideas with some first-rate minds, including the university president (incalculable value). A year and a half into the process, my savings account was a small fraction of its former self. Where once I had had enough money for a down payment on a modest house, I was now approaching the poverty level of the average doctoral student. Even my meager income as a graduate assistant was scheduled to end with the award of a PhD. It was only to be expected that I would be concerned about how to pay my bills while waiting for the next academic hiring season to begin in the fall.

Several recent conversations had made me feel even less positive about my future. The ALISE conference coincided with preconference workshops and other activities preceding the midwinter meeting of the much larger American Library Association. That overlap was how I had run into a library recruiter who, in the past, had regularly contacted me regarding vacant positions heading public or state libraries. After learning that I was studying for a PhD, this headhunter first frowned, and then informed me that I would be deleted from his contact list.

"I can't help it," he apologized. "Board members have it in their heads that PhDs are so filled with theory that they have no room for common sense. I could never get you interviewed."

The second conversation occurred just minutes after my plane landed. A man and a woman, apparently coworkers at a Columbus company, had also traveled on my plane. While waiting for their luggage they discussed the new department head joining their firm. The male had a bitter edge to his voice. "That job should have been mine," he declared. "I have twice as much experience as he does."

"But he has a PhD," she pointed out. "And you don't."

"And you know what PhD means, don't you?" he countered. "It stands for 'piled higher and deeper.' It's a b—s— degree for people who can talk lots about the job but who can never really do it." That conversation ended abruptly when the horn sounded and the conveyor belt bringing in our luggage started to move. But it had lasted just long enough to remind me of my second reason for worrying. I could rationalize why I wasn't receiving offers of faculty positions—I was still working on the PhD and happened to be a "mature" student with decades of experience and the habit of questioning absurd statements, even those voiced by members of search committees. I realized that I might not be the best fit for academic cultures that prized youth and malleability. Yet, I had always assumed that I could return to library management if a faculty position didn't work out. Now I was facing the unanticipated possibility that studying for a PhD had eliminated my backup job option. After the van for Athens finally arrived, the seventy-five-mile drive through scenic central Ohio and the historic Hocking Hills was unusually depressing.

USEFUL THEORY IN SEARCH OF A NAME

Years before these conversations, I was assigned by the Alabama Public Library Service to attend a meeting called by residents of a small Alabama town to discuss forming their own public library. The session took place in a room at the local hospital, and those present included doctors, lawyers, and other community leaders. I had spent quite a few hours preparing to lead the evening's discussion on both the value of a public library and how it could be brought into existence. However, I soon discovered that my duties would be far less significant. The other people around the table, most locally born and raised but experienced with libraries from being educated elsewhere in the state or country, already had their own ideas of what a public library could provide. It was a personal knowledge that they freely shared with one another as the discussion developed. There really was little for me to do. After being thanked for making the long drive from Montgomery, I saw my role during the meeting quickly becoming that of the professional librarian and state bureaucrat who could answer the occasional technical questions and provide information on state support for new libraries.

Ever so politely pushed to the edge of the library planning conversation, I was free to consider what was happening in the room. Neighbors were coming together to communicate their library experiences, explore differences and similarities, and arrive at common conclusions concerning the services they would like their proposed library to provide. After an ideal model was finally agreed upon, they applied the lessons learned from other political battles in a poor county in a low-tax state with lots of pride but few public dollars. In this second part of their planning session, the participants boiled their ideal library model down into an achievable reality, in the process producing a plan with time lines, contacts, and reporting structures. In short, they had crafted a viable strategy for bringing a local public library into existence.

At the time I didn't have a name for what these local residents were doing. Now, I know they were engaging in a process involving the (1) establishment of a common language and framework for discussing a shared concern, (2) surfacing of a spectrum of individual tacit and explicit knowledge about libraries for collective analysis, and (3) addition to these hitherto uncompiled and unanalyzed private understandings of a more public and shared knowledge of their local environment, all for the purpose of defining and achieving the shared aim of a public library. Theoretically speaking, it was a textbook illustration of the powerful role of tacit knowledge in defining and solving problems.

THE ISSUE OF RELEVANCE

During a subsequent conversation, one of the participants at that Alabama library-planning meeting apologized for the fact that I had been "deprived of [my] soapbox," explaining that the schedules of the busy professionals involved in the planning left them no time to "hear from you what they already knew." As the discussion had revealed, collectively the local planners had a pretty good idea of what a library could do, and the local attorney was clearly conversant with Alabama's relatively simple library laws. These local leaders knew what they wanted and what was involved in achieving it. They wanted a public library. To get it, they needed to develop a reasonably specific and affordable plan that could be achieved within local political realities. As a state consultant in their town for the first time, I was an outsider who lacked their knowledge of local conditions. They hadn't the time to bring me up to speed—not if they wanted to outline their strategy in a single planning session.[1]

Although this emphasis on understanding local circumstances is an undoubted strength in practitioners' carrying out of their daily operations in the library, information, and knowledge professions, it may also be a fundamental weakness. As with faculty and consultant environments, practitioner cultures seem to be almost hardwired to look internally for solutions to problems. This can be taken to self-defeating extremes. For example, there is a body of research on personnel recruitment demonstrating that, even in times of personnel shortage, potential employers will not readily hire professionals—at least not for senior positions—seeking to transfer in from a different type of library, information, or knowledge organization.[2] Rather than concentrating on skills that may be transferable across occupational boundaries, many employers, perhaps overly influenced by their organizational or professional cultures, want to hire only candidates who already share their values and who require little or no additional training in order to do the job on "day 1" of their employment.

More on the Nonuse of Theory

The resistance of practitioners to faculty-generated theory, so striking and so long-standing, has been addressed throughout this work. It is a resistance arising from the reality that approaches taken by practitioners to solving problems, such as (1) working from analogies to relevant issues in their past, (2) using interpersonal communications networks for advice, and, when such options fail, (3) turning to the professional literature as a "pointer" to other individuals or institutions that might be able to help, seem to do the job most of the time.[3] Many students enter ALA-accredited programs having already worked in library, information, and knowledge environments. In the process, they have likely experienced contexts where the formal theory developed and publicized by library, information, and knowledge educators through the refereed literature was simply not a factor in solving organizational problems. Too often, when reviewed, that literature has been judged by practitioners to be lacking in relevance. On the whole, our students have learned to trust the "personal lessons of experience derived from the school of hard knocks"[4] over the recommendations generated through academic studies. This mindset may help explain John M. Budd's observation that "it is not uncommon for those who teach in LIS programs to hear students say that they only want the practical in their course work, not theory, as there is some chasm between the two that stands in the way (necessarily) of their intermingling."[5]

This resistance by practitioners to one variety of abstract thought—*theories*—is in distinct contrast with their frequent embrace of another equally abstract concept—*values*. This prioritization has been seen as a source of intellectual weakness, with the values of librarianship, such as "service, intellectual freedom, stewardship, literacy, etc.,"[6] being attacked for their dependence on "fuzzy rhetoric and feel-good value statements."[7] Ironically, those calling for reorienting professional education toward the "theoretical foundations and analytic rigor"[8] ideal cherished by many twentieth-century library, information, and knowledge researchers may be playing their own value games. Much of what passed for "truth" in the past is no longer considered to be objective and universally applicable. At present, the "problem of truth" has even been defined as "finding any, getting agreement that you have it, and then someday having to revise it."[9] Knowledge is now understood to be socially constructed, with values playing a significant part in its production. Rather than dismissing values, the truly observant faculty theorist is likely to be more inclined to study their effects, both positive and negative, in setting the conditions for delivering library, information, and knowledge service.

It is a research problem in itself to determine how the issue of values has been embraced by those who would use librarianship to change the world.[10] Drawing for inspiration on the fundamentally important work of Richard Hofstadter, Michael Winter describes an American professional context where intellectuals come in two types—the ideologue and the expert. He continues:

> Librarians have much less trouble with the first kind, and even show a kind of constant affection for the moralist (witness our embrace of various forms of identity politics and our love of intellectual freedom), but have a suspicion of expertise which shows up most dramatically in our [negative] attitudes towards professional education and in our readiness to embrace general management as a kind of value system.[11]

Within a national culture where ideologues will readily find library, information, and knowledge audiences willing to embrace their value assertions and where less doctrinaire "experts" may encounter greater suspicion about their work, faculty researchers can easily blame practitioners for their choices. A more effective response would be for theorists to embrace another cherished American value—a "tough-minded pragmatism"[12]—when disseminating their theories. If effectiveness is a widely accepted criterion for judging whether or not a theory has truly captured aspects of the world, a "useful theory" is likely to be embraced, used, and modified to practitioner benefit. The pendulum of practitioner support can be moved in the direction of theory at any time. All that is required is for theorists to produce theories that can actually be used.

SOLVING THE "PROBLEM" OF PRACTITIONERS AND THEORY

If the results of a recent, "unscientific survey" by *Library Journal* are any guide, it is highly unlikely that students will graduate from ALA-accredited programs with an interest in developing theory. As reported by John N. Berry III in *LJ*'s May 1, 2003, issue: "Students long for more practice in the curriculum, yet the programs veer into more theory. The students ask for teachers from the practice, yet the programs increasingly hire faculty with no ties to practice and often little practical experience."[13]

AND FINALLY

It is fairly safe to assert that library, information, and knowledge practitioners with an interest in conducting research and developing theory will always emerge from ALA-accredited programs. However, even with required research classes embedded in their courses of study, the majority of graduates will learn to be effective practitioners largely on the basis of professional tacit knowledge and the reading and writing of "'how we did it good in our library' pieces" or "best practices articles and books."[14] Articles by people like themselves about issues similar to those they are facing, written in a reader-friendly style, will continue to be a preferred guidance for practitioners. From the point of view of practitioner influence, the last thing the library, information, and knowledge literatures need is an increase in the number of articles written in the formal academic fashion that faculty members adopt in order to influence promotion and tenure committees.

However, practitioners can join with faculty and consultants to reorient the library, information, and knowledge literatures in ways that are likely to facilitate the development of theory that is more useful to the "real world." In addition to conducting original research, practitioners could join with faculty and consultants to ponder the larger implications of those practitioner and faculty writings offering solutions to professional problems, including the notorious (from a faculty perspective) "how we did it good"/"best practices" articles and books. In the process, they might ask such questions as: Are there patterns to be discerned? Are practitioners able to report success in applying similar solutions to problems encountered in divergent contexts? If so, what are the human and technological forces at work that may account for such successes—or failures? In essence, this approach represents an opportunity to draw on practitioner tacit knowledge in order to help determine if common theories, models, or paradigms can explain success and failure in a multiplicity of contexts. By definition, this represents second-level analysis and is writing at the theory level.

In his *Idea of the University: A Reexamination*, Jaroslav Pelikan identifies as a continuing problem "the temptation of the university faculty . . . to present the results of their own research as the latest revelation, or even the final revelation."[15] Arguably, this applies as much to the library, information, and knowledge literatures as it does to the record of any other field or discipline.[16] For Pelikan, one solution would be for research librarians to prepare bibliographical essays that summarize the state of knowledge in a given field or subfield. Who better to prepare such an analysis of literatures reporting on successes and failures of prior attempts to bring teenage males into a public library or serve the information needs of employees of a multinational corporation than staff who must routinely address the same issues during their working days?

It is to be acknowledged that practitioners trying to capture the results of prior attempts to solve issues in their professional subfield will face the same problem identified by John Henry Newman as facing the teaching faculty in the middle of the nineteenth century: "To discover and to teach are distinct functions; they are also distinct gifts, and are not commonly found united in the same person. He, too, who spends his day in dispensing his existing knowledge to all comers is unlikely to have either leisure or energy to acquire new."[17] Regardless of their gender, not all librarians, information specialists, and knowledge managers are both able and willing to examine the relevant literature, analyze its implications, and report on their findings as a contribution to the store of their profession's useful theory. Additionally, if they are both willing and able, their contributions will not be universally appreciated or acknowledged. The latter, however, is a reality that faculty theorists have been living with since they first started to offer their own answers to important professional questions.

NOTES

1. Rachel Riedner and Noreen O'Connor, eds., "Activism and the Academy," *Minnesota Review*, nos. 50–51 (Spring and Fall 1998).

2. See the cross-national discussion in Peter Dalton, Glen Mynott, and Michael Shoolbred, "Barriers to Career Development within the LIS Profession," *Library Review* 49, no. 6 (2000): 271–76.

3. See the relevant summary in Bill Crowley, "Building Useful Theory: Tacit Knowledge, Practitioner Reports, and the Culture of LIS Inquiry," *Journal of Education for Library and Information Science* 40, no. 4 (Fall 1999): 285–86.

4. Joseph A. Horvath et al., "Experience, Knowledge, and Military Leadership," in *Tacit Knowledge in Professional Practice: Researcher and Practitioner Perspectives*, ed. Robert J. Sternberg and Joseph A. Horvath (Mahwah, NJ: Lawrence Erlbaum Associates, 1999), 41.

5. John M. Budd, "The Library, Praxis, and Symbolic Power," *Library Quarterly* 73, no. 1 (2003): 20.

6. Michael Gorman, "A Profession That Looks Like America," *SRRT Newsletter*, December 2003, 2.

7. Blaise Cronin, "The Dean's List: The Dreaded 'L' Word," *Library Journal*, March 15, 2001, 58.

8. Cronin, "Dean's List."

9. Joyce Appleby, Lynn Hunt, and Margaret Jacob, *Telling the Truth about History* (New York: Norton, 1994), 280.

10. Ann Sparanese, "Activist Librarianship," *Progressive Librarian* 22 (Summer 2003), available at http://www.libr.org/PL/22_Sparanese.html (accessed January 15, 2004).

11. Michael Winter, "Garlic, Vodka, and the Politics of Gender: Anti-Intellectualism in American Librarianship," *Progressive Librarian* 14 (Spring 1998): 2, available at http://www.libr.org/PL/14_Winter.html (accessed January 15, 2004).

12. Winter, "Garlic," 1.

13. John N. Berry III, "LIS Recruiting: Does It Make the Grade?" *Library Journal*, May 1, 2003, 5, available at http://libraryjournal.reviewsnews.com/index.asp?layout=artiiclePrint&articleID=CA292594 (accessed June 2, 2003).

14. Donald E. Riggs, "Writing for the LIS Profession: Introductory Comments and Questions," in *How to Get Published in LIS Journals: A Practical Guide,* ed. Lisa Janicke Hinchliffe and Jennifer Dorner (San Diego, CA: Elsevier Library Connect, 2003), 2.

15. Jaroslav Pelikan, *The Idea of the University: A Reexamination* (New Haven, CT: Yale University Press, 1992), 115.

16. See Riggs, "Writing," 2, where he observes, "Research in library and information science (LIS) appears to be uneven, fragmentary, and non-cumulative." As a former editor of *College and Research Libraries*, *Library Administration and Management*, and *Library Hi Tech*, Riggs can be acknowledged as someone with a unique tacit knowledge of the characteristics of such professional literature, even if one occasionally differs with him on the nature of its larger meanings.

17. John Henry Newman, *The Idea of a University* (1873; reprint, Notre Dame, IN: University of Notre Dame Press, 1982), xl.

Chapter Eight

Other Worlds of Practice: The Consultant

SCENARIO: BIAS IN THE LIBRARY BOARD ROOM

Some time ago I was consulting with a public library board in the aftermath of a dispute that sent its director to another state, one step ahead of being sacked. The cause of the departure is all but irrelevant. Most public library boards have the legal authority to hire and fire head librarians, and a departure is inevitably the case when the board–director divide becomes unbridgeable. It was late in the evening and I was tired, primarily because I had been up long before dawn to attend another meeting the length of the state away. Nonetheless, my incipient attention problem ended quickly when the board reached the agenda item calling for discussion of the search for a new director. Almost immediately one trustee, a businessman retired to the area from another state, insisted that the board must avoid its previous mistake of "hiring a Catholic director for a Protestant community."

There were audible gasps in the room at these words. Several of the other board members appeared as stunned as I felt at this open display of bigotry. Legalities of hiring aside, religious discrimination violates some fundamental understanding in American culture. It's not that it doesn't occur; it just isn't acceptable as an option for discussion by public bodies at open meetings. As several of the other board members began voicing their objections to this comment, I looked around the room for a reporter. There were none at the start of the meeting. Fortunately, none had shown up since.

Before I took up consulting work, my resume included years of employment in public relations. From experience, I knew the negative possibilities when a publicly supported institution is perceived as being infected with bias of any type. That trustee's remarks had the possibility of garnering a lot of attention. If they became public—and a murder or a worldwide disaster didn't grab column space or airtime—local news editors would find it hard to resist running headlines or televising stories asking the question, "Are bigots running your public library?" If it was a really light news day, the story could "go national" through an Associated Press feed. With wire-service editors baptizing the story as respectable, media in other cities and states would look for local angles and press their own public libraries for comment. Someone would probably contact the American Library Association in Chicago, and ALA would trot out the appropriate staff, who would point out that, if the story were true, a biased public library was an unfortunate anomaly. Libraries, ALA would insist, are bastions of freedom, disowning all prejudice, not merely the religious variety.

In short, this trustee posed the potential to be a real disaster. He had to be stopped—soon—and his words had to be buried quickly, before they festered and drew the wrong kind of attention.

Even as I assured myself that the media wasn't present and that no one in the room would be dumb enough to turn whistle-blower after the meeting, I realized that several board members were staring at me. A stranger until only a few weeks before, I was still something of an unknown quality. How was I taking that remark? Wondering what my expression had already signaled, even if inadvertently, I concentrated on appearing to be calm yet appropriately concerned.

While busy trying to hide my strong irritation with the offending board member, I thought about whether it would be better to inject myself into the meeting or sit back and watch the chair handle the airing of his colleague's prejudices. There was a particular fascination in imagining what the chair's response might be since he was still wearing the "dog collar" of his day job as a minister in a mainstream Protestant denomination. Would the chair ignore the comment and continue the meeting? Alternatively, would he condemn such views as unacceptable bias in a trustee of the public's library? Or would he ask the offending member to submit his resignation and leave the board? How would the chair react to the fact that there was an outsider—me—present and witnessing his board's embarrassment?

Finally, the chair began to speak, in a calm, measured voice. Looking particularly thoughtful, he offered his view that the former director's relative youth and inexperience, not her religion, generated the problems that caused her departure. "She was clearly over her head," he stressed. "And it really was the board's own fault. We should have never appointed her director in the first place."

Keeping his tone of voice matter-of-fact, the chair mused aloud about local Catholics who had earned local praise for their extensive community work. "I've served with many Roman Catholics on boards, committees, and task forces devoted to making our community better," he reflected. "What they seem to take from their religion, in my view, is almost inevitably positive."

His own position thus asserted, the chair then turned to the offending board member and offered him an out. "Do you really believe what you said or were you just overly tired and venting a bit?"

Grasping the verbal lifeline, the board member with the prejudicial views mumbled something that sounded like "just venting." The chair smiled and suggested, "Unless anyone objects, I will ask our board secretary to leave this part of our discussion out of the minutes." With this unanticipated crisis thus defused, the board members spent another hour productively deciding what they needed in a new library director.

A CONSULTANT'S RUMINATIONS

In curiously reinforcing ways, both the unexpected eruption of bias from the one board member born and raised in another community's local culture and the tactful manner in which the chair papered over a public rift reflect the ongoing tension between an organization's established values and beliefs and the private views of the sometimes notoriously independent trustees who donate their time to public service. While never a truly easy task, maintaining organizational norms is a bit simpler when library directors or knowledge management heads socialize new employees into how their employing organization "thinks" in its interactions with the world.[1] For better or worse, people with jobs to lose have a stronger incentive to conform to organizational norms than trustees who could volunteer their time elsewhere.

In reflecting on the board meeting during the long drive home, I marveled at just how smoothly the chair had used local traditions of civility and graciousness to defuse such a divisive issue. Whatever their private views, the colleagues of the offending board member were clearly embarrassed by the public demonstration of bigotry they'd witnessed. Yet, given the heated debated over the forced departure of the previous library head, the chair's options for a response had been unusually limited. Passing over the remark without comment would have allowed such bias to fester, perhaps poisoning future working relationships. A public condemnation of the offending board member might have been justified by the facts, but that option also risked negative repercussions. It had the potential to further tear apart a board whose members had only recently reestablished effective working relations after the emotionally debilitating episode over the fate of the former library head.

Since this incident was not included in the adopted minutes of the board meeting, it officially never happened. Unofficially, the chair's response could be characterized as subtle, pragmatic, and, above all, effective. Morally and ethically opposed to religious bias, this minister, in his volunteer capacity as an appointed public official, later elected as board chair by his colleagues, advanced an inclusive vision about tolerance in the community. At the same time, he demonstrated his understanding of the ebb and flow of emotions in the operations of a library by providing a wayward board member with the opportunity to retract his comments and thereby maintain a fragile board collegiality.

The restraints of confidentiality inherent in a consulting relationship prevent me from writing more about this board meeting, although it is an incident potentially rich in contributing to useful theory. I believe that my extended work with the board enhanced its effectiveness and thereby benefited the community it was appointed to serve. However, the difficulties that I have in discussing the specifics of this incident make it a "textbook" illustration of the problem that consultants have in contributing to the "knowledge base" of a given discipline, field, or profession.

THE THEORETICAL SILENCE OF CONSULTANTS?

In his review of the impediments preventing consultants from regularly contributing to public knowledge and potentially advancing theory, Douglas L. Zweizig focuses on the field as a "secret science."[2] His primary contention is that the confidentiality inherent in the process so minimizes its value for the larger world that consulting projects should not be permitted to compete for the relatively few dollars available to advance research. Consulting, he observes, is the "research equivalent of releasing sterile Mediterranean fruit flies."[3] Its effect on the growth of knowledge is actually negative, since it diverts dollars that could be used to support more public research efforts.

In *Why We Buy: The Science of Shopping*, Paco Underhill, an academic turned full-time consultant, stresses what he sees as a fundamental difference between his world and that of higher education, emphasizing that consultants "actually stick our necks out and are held accountable for the success or failure of our suggestions."[4] A variant of the historic "town–gown" divide is also present in the ways that part-time consultants operating out of the university and full-time consultants making their living in the "real world" identify and solve the problems of their clients. Professors as part-time consultants inevitably bring some consciousness of higher education's standards to their work. They are thus likely to see it as a positive when praised by others for demonstrating that "consulting does not exist in a vacuum—as a bag of tricks totally unrelated to theoretical underpinnings."[5] Conversely, full-time consultants turned authors have been known to advise their readers to avoid the pitfalls of too much intelligence and "think dumb."[6] They have also gloried in their status as refugees from higher education, even complaining about an academic world that indoctrinates their potential employees with "unproductive" higher education values, including an interest in proving or disproving a particular theory.[7]

ON THE OTHER HAND . . .

From personal experience and years of discussions with others who have consulting backgrounds, I have become convinced that theory, theory of virtually any type, can and does play a particularly useful role in sensitizing consultants to the possibility of alternatives. In the process, it widens the options for action they present to their clients. In their fundamentally important *Thinking in Time: The Uses of History for Decision-Makers*, a work that summarizes the lessons of years of work with government and military leaders, Richard E. Neustadt and Ernest R. May describe an everyday, decision-making reality where overreliance on "common sense" and *unanalyzed* experience regularly contributes to multiplying problems instead of solving them.

Whatever the locus of action, from national government down to precinct, whether in an executive body or a legislative committee, some participants are almost sure to start with favorite, long-developed schemes. Their inclination will be to ignore whatever seems not to fit and to define the problem as one calling for solutions they have handy. Their arguments will be supported, more than likely, by analogies.[8]

Neustadt and May propose a number of methods for minimizing the possibility of basing present actions on inappropriate past experience. As will be seen, these approaches are actually variations on techniques long used within consulting communities.[9] Such approaches include the simple expedient of separating "elements of the immediate situation" into columns labeled "Known," "Unclear," and "Presumed" and listing "Likenesses" and "Differences"[10] in order to determine the real significance of past incidents for current decisions. The examples provided by Neustadt and May involve national policy. From a more local library, information, or knowledge management perspective, their relatively simple process of analysis might prevent such foreseeable actions as

- billing a corporate knowledge management center's internal clients at last year's rates without determining if new factors have negatively or positively changed this year's information- and knowledge-provision environment ("We've got a rush analysis job for the CEO on that proposed merger. There isn't time to do a reliable SWOT [Strengths, Weaknesses, Opportunities, and Threats] analysis. Just tell the financial people to use last year's numbers and adjust for inflation.")
- attempting to work out software upgrade problems solely on the basis of previous experience without determining if new factors are in play ("It's just like that circulation module problem that we solved last year. Get the same committee together again.")
- planning strategies for defending library ownership of controversial materials on the basis of an unexamined assumption that opponents of the public library's possessing certain books operate out of the same mindset as those who support Internet filtering ("Those people on the city council supporting the Supreme Court's filtering decision on library user access to the Internet are every bit as bad as the religious fanatics who protested Judy Blume before the board last summer.")

Basing present actions on past experience may indeed be appropriate in these examples. However, such action ought not to be taken without an adequate assessment to determine the true relevance of past models to current problems.

As is evident, Neustadt and May advance the theory that humans frequently use analogies from the past, even inappropriate analogies, to solve contemporary problems. Their formulation is useful precisely because it surfaces for review a decision-making process that is often accepted as a matter of course. Applying their thinking to a given situation may actually lead to better problem definitions and more useful solutions. Still, while employing a theory that supports the analysis of experience in relevant contexts, Neustadt and May hesitate to embrace grand theories of how the world works, since

> underneath each [grand theory] is a model, bolstered by pieces of history, controlled by presumptions about future trends, and reflecting the theorist's values. A few years hence prevalent presumptions may be different, along with predicted trends and implicit values. From that future vantage point what now seems "right" may well look "wrong." Or vice versa.[11]

The progressive unfolding of a "contingent truth" through the ongoing analysis of experience advocated by Neustadt and May is, of course, a vital component of virtually all schools of pragmatism, specifically including cultural pragmatism.

IF THEORY CAN BE USEFUL, HOW SHOULD CONSULTANTS DEVELOP AND EMPLOY IT?

Deirdre Moore has defined "consultant" as "someone who is hired to provide expert advice to the person or organization requesting this service."[12] This is a short, useful definition that does not address whether or not such advice includes an acknowledged theoretical standpoint. This may be a self-protective approach, since "generalist" consultants and their theories have been summarized as "MBAs and lots of business jargon." People who have never actually worked in the field they claim the ability to consult with represent to many practitioners a source of "expertise" that is best avoided.[13] However, "specialist" consultants, those who "have actually toiled in the vineyard" of a particular profession, can be seen as genuine sources of assistance for the very practical reason that the specialist consultant is likely to have seen a wide range of flaws and problems in his or her own experience (and has personally made many mistakes in the process of becoming a seasoned veteran). Consultants have also observed many similar organizations, large and small, that are flawed in countless ways. And of course, they know that an invitation to visit is often triggered by internal difficulties.[14]

From the perspective of most practitioners, the true value of consultants seems to lie in their ability to provide practical results. As Kathryn Sullivan, CEO of Blue Cross Blue Shield of Louisiana, asserted: "At the end of the day, a successful [consulting] engagement can be characterized as one where you can see the recommendations incorporated into daily operations of the business. I don't want a report with academic recommendations that I'm just doing to put into a drawer."[15]

From the perspective of higher education, consulting by faculty members, particularly in their early years of struggle to secure promotion and earn tenure, is best undertaken if it furthers academic, not practitioner, objectives. For example, the experience of consulting offers the credibility of actually having "seen the workings of government and industry" and "can also provide a faculty member with research support, additional income, and help with the placement of students."[16]

A review of the reports on consulting and theory development in the library, information, and knowledge literatures reveals some level of practitioner support for consultant use of theory. However, this support is lukewarm at best. As stressed by Vera Fessler, "consultants can be theorists, purists—and properly they should be—while library managers must be pragmatists; library managers must deal with a complex of responsibilities and personalities, capabilities, funding levels, and political realities."[17] For the most part, practitioners leave theory to those academics who are rewarded for such work by their higher education environments and demand from their paid consultants practical results that can be implemented in very short order.

REDEFINING THEORY—AGAIN

In the previous chapter dealing with practitioners, it was stressed that consultants can join with faculty and practitioners to reorient the library, information, and knowledge literatures in ways that are likely to facilitate the development of theory that is more useful to the "real world." As was noted above, "specialist consultants" with practical experience, here emphasizing experience in library, information, knowledge, and related environments, may have "been there and done that" in a sufficient number of contexts to discern the critical patterns that often form the basis of useful theory. Even without revealing the identity of clients, it can and should be possible for consultants to contribute to the relevant literature a number of insights that may serve as valuable signposts for organizations seeking to enhance service. At a minimum, experienced consultants may be superbly equipped to examine practitioner "how we did it good" accounts to discern larger patterns or to determine when accounts of success may have occurred in contexts so specific that they have little to offer other communities of practice. The questions asked in the previous chapter are relevant when posed by experienced consultants: Are there patterns to be discerned? Are practitioners or consultants able to report success in applying similar solutions to problems encountered in divergent contexts? If so, what are the human and technological forces at work that may account for such successes—or failures? To again make a critical point, such considerations are, by definition, second-level analyses and writing at the theory level.

NOTES

1. See the discussion of organizational culture and the challenges posed to its suasion ability by increasing diversity in William Sannwald, "Understanding Organizational Culture," *Library Administration and Management* 14, no. 1 (Winter 2002): 8–14, available at http://vnweb.hwwilsonweb.com/hww/results/results_single.jhtml?nn=17 (accessed January 7, 2002).

2. Douglas L. Zweizig, "The Secret Science: The Role of Consulting and LIS Research," in Charles R. McClure and Peter Hernon, eds., *Library and Information Science Research: Perspectives and Strategies for Improvement* (Norwood, NJ: Ablex, 1991), 212.

3. Zweizig, "Secret Science."

4. Paco Underhill, *Why We Buy: The Science of Shopping* (New York: Simon and Schuster, 1999), 21.

5. W. Charles Redding, foreword to Sue DeWine, *The Consultant's Craft: Improving Organizational Communication* (New York: St. Martin's, 1994), xxv.

6. Harry Beckwith, *Selling the Invisible: A Field Guide to Modern Marketing* (New York: Warner, 1997), 67.

7. Underhill, *Why We Buy*, 14, 247.

8. Richard E. Neustadt and Ernest R. May, *Thinking in Time: The Uses of History for Decision-Makers* (New York: Free Press, 1986), 235.

9. Personal communications, Fall 2003.

10. Neustadt and May, *Thinking in Time*, 235.

11. Neustadt and May, *Thinking in Time*, 208.

12. Deirdre Moore, "Consultancy: A Career Option for Professional Librarans," *Argus* 34, no. 3 (September/December 1995): 1.

13. Mark Sexton, "Why a Consultant?" *Scholarly Publishing* 20, no. 2 (January 1989): 90.

14. Sexton, "Why a Consultant?"

15. Quoted in [Melissa Master,] "A Sharper Look," *Across the Board* 40, no. 6 (November/December 2003): 2, available at http://newfirstsearch.oclc.org /images/WSPL/wsppdfl/HTML/04816/QRGWD/TF6.HTM (accessed January 12, 2004).

16. Richard M. Reis, "When Faculty Consulting Helps—and When It Hurts—Your Career," *Chronicle of Higher Education,* "Career Network Catalyst," October 22, 1999, at http://chronicle.com.jobs/99/10/99102202c.htm (accessed June 22, 2000).

17. Vera Fessler, "Consulting Products and Library Processes," *Library Hi Tech* 8, no. 2 (1991): 108.

Chapter Nine

Theory and Revelation

SCENARIO: GOD AND RESEARCH
IN A CATHOLIC UNIVERSITY

Not that long ago, I took part in an informal discussion with a number
of other Dominican University professors on the impact of Catholic religious dogma on teaching and research. As is almost inevitably the case
with such exchanges, it occurred over a weekday lunch in the dining
hall shared by faculty with staff, students, and the regular (and often
noisy) celebrations and commemorations that mark important milestones in a vigorous academic community. Behind the conversation was
a common awareness that the nation's Roman Catholic bishops, following years of dispute with officials in the Vatican over American national realities regarding intellectual freedom, had reluctantly issued
regulations attempting to define what it means to be a "Catholic" college or university in the context of the contemporary world. As might
be expected, several involved in the discussion were Catholics. However, people from other faith traditions were present and felt comfortable sharing their views. There were even significant contributions from
a professor whose religious affiliation, if any, was unknown to others at
the table.

As the exchange progressed, it became clear that a strong consensus
existed on certain fundamentals. First, we all had a great deal of sympathy for Dominican University's theologians. Alone on the campus,
these professors had to reconcile the American tradition of academic

freedom with the Vatican's insistence that they seek a *mandatum*—formal authentication that they taught "authentic Catholic doctrine"—from Chicago's Roman Catholic cardinal.[1] But the theologians were elsewhere that day; nobody at our lunch table expected any pressure at all from the university administration to follow Catholic dogma in our teaching and research. All at the table, undergraduate and graduate professors, arts and science faculty, social scientists, and educators for the professions alike, fully intended to exercise our usual right to critique the actions of all individuals and organizations as they impacted our own corners of the intellectual world. As might be expected, the strength and believability of such assertions tended to resonate with a faculty member's tenured or nontenured status.

This adherence to the norms of academic freedom by Dominican University faculty was far from a rejection of the mission of the institution. As a group, we had found a congenial home. Regardless of our spiritual and/or secular affiliations, we enjoyed the university's intellectual climate and supported its declared mission of educating students for lives of achievement and service, grounded in strong ethical, intellectual, and moral understandings. Backing this purpose was seen as fully in accord with faculty freedom. Each of us made this point in her or his own fashion. My remarks, in retrospect more than a little defensive, went something along the lines of:

> Our graduate students tend to be mature individuals with their own belief systems. They enroll at Dominican because our reputation is good, we have the only American Library Association–accredited program in the Chicago metropolitan area, and many don't want to do their degree online. The Graduate School of Library and Information Science faculty make a point of addressing relevant ethical and moral issues. But, even if we wanted to proselytize some sort of Catholic view it would be a little difficult to do so. Unlike the rest of the university, most faculty members in our program aren't even Catholic.

Time can pass quickly in faculty discussions, particularly when the participants get carried away with their own eloquence. Shortly before 1:00 PM, we began leaving to teach our afternoon classes. At this point, another faculty member, a devout Protestant who also possesses a PhD from one of America's leading universities, calmly observed that he saw no problem in combining a belief in the literal truth of the Bible with the skeptical attitude, the willingness to doubt anything and everything, that he saw as essential to advancing knowledge.

That comment grabbed my attention. Putting my tray back down on the table, I challenged, "That's impossible, and you know it. You can either believe in the literal truth of the Bible or you can be open to new evidence. The approaches are mutually exclusive."

My lunch companion smiled.

> Bill, you weren't really listening to me. I said that I believe that the Holy Scriptures, *as given to us by God*, were error-free in their original forms. But we don't possess the original works. All we have now are copies, more precisely, copies of copies as far back the historical eye can see. And every one of those copies was written down, compiled, or edited by fallible human beings. Since we don't have the inerrant original works, the only way we can confirm or disprove what we think we know from the Bible—or from anywhere else—is through research.

The faculty member concerned with aligning the Bible with his scholarly inclinations had been hired on the basis of an ability to teach and research. He was certainly not employed for the primary purpose of reconciling his Protestant faith with his commitment to the scientific method. But it is important to stress that this professor felt free to articulate his views in an open discussion at a Catholic university. There is a certain amount of irony in the reality that Catholic institutions such as Dominican University can, at times, appear to support a wider range of views than either sectarian colleges with a strict test of orthodoxy for employment or those public universities where "God talk" generates a strong level of unease and spirituality is tolerated only if private or exotic in nature.

WHY THIS CHAPTER?

In the course of the twentieth century, much of the Western world stopped envisioning libraries—particularly public and school libraries—as arbiters of "good" reading for the elevation of the masses. Instead, the staff of many libraries became vocal proponents of the public's right to read, view, hear, or otherwise access information and ideas regardless of age or condition. In the process they openly contested in favor of strong

positions in support of intellectual freedom, often against people motivated by received, including religious, beliefs that might privilege a certain way of thinking about the world. Consequently, the literatures of
the library, information, and knowledge professions have reflected this
struggle, often producing works that saw interactions with people of
faith as involving

1. resistance to censorship[2]
2. avoidance of giving offense[3]
3. ensuring certain levels of fairness by requiring that religious perspectives are appropriately represented in library collections[4]

In a distinctly minority approach within the professional education
sanctioned by the American Library Association, Richard J. Cox of the
School of Information Sciences at the University of Pittsburgh has recently drawn on his religious faith to analyze or "approach the promises
of the Information Age,"[5] even as reference librarian and Christian pas-
tor Mike Wessells has strongly advocated closer connections by libraries with local religious traditions, as well as writing of "balancing a
spirituality that mandates 'witnessing' with the neutrality ethics of librarianship."[6] Although intriguing contributions to the minor component of the mainstream library, information, and knowledge literature
that can be termed "proreligion," the Cox and Wessells articles are not
likely to resonate with information, library, and knowledge faculty
members educated in the scholarly tradition of doubt who, nevertheless,
seek an intellectual bridge across the secular–religious divide in education and practice.

   As will be discussed, there is a certain irony in the fact that construction of that intellectual bridge is going to require creative theorizing. It
is also likely to require reliance on pragmatism, a philosophy fundamentally opposed to absolutes that nevertheless holds the undoubtedly
optimistic view that "no disagreements among human beings are absolutely irreconcilable, for we share a common humanity; and equally,
no agreements are entire, for we are distinct individuals occupying different contexts, viewing the world in different perspectives, and so pursuing different values."[7]

   The author is a cultural pragmatist and has regularly proclaimed this
affiliation at Dominican University. This connection has not negatively

impacted a career where the university recently promoted me to full professor. In a context where I have rightfully been challenged to justify particular positions taken at faculty seminars, there have never been questions raised regarding my right to adhere to a century-old pragmatic tradition holding that the "meaning of life . . . must be answered by each of us, not in terms of meanings already provided, but only in terms of the meanings, which, with the deepest sensibilities and fullest exercise of intelligence, we ourselves can provide."[8]

In common with their brethren in other pragmatic traditions, cultural pragmatists believe in an evolving truth, always contingent and perennially being subjected to the test of analyzed experience by those most knowledgeable in a given field. Even this test has its limits, since pragmatists are very much aware that our oldest resource, human reason, "is never 'mere' or wholly 'pure'; it is always related to interest, passion, and desire."[9] However fallible it may be, reason is probably the best analytical tool humans can employ. And that same reason has convinced me that library, information, and knowledge theorists can no longer ignore a significant aspect of their worlds—religious belief. To be more precise, they will be increasingly required to understand, and at times finds ways to cooperate with, a multilayered, complex, growing, and progressively more disconcerting religious dynamic that is impacting practitioner environments and, to a lesser extent, higher education contexts.

THE REVIVAL OF RELIGIOUS UNDERSTANDINGS OF THE WORLD

In the preface to the 1980 collection of revised essays entitled *Philosophy and Public Policy*, the pragmatic and very secular philosopher Sidney Hook asks, "Who would have thought a generation or two ago that there would be something of a revival of a religious interpretation of culture or that we would be hearing again that without commitment to some transcendent religious principle there would be neither a just social order nor genuine social peace and progresses?"[10] Although written a quarter-century ago, that question has proven to be an understatement. From the standpoint of cultural pragmatism, contemporary religion has exploded in its influence, in the process becoming both a critical problem for study and an unavoidable factor in a broad range of cultural and societal interactions. Whether one supports or fears the development, since the 1980s, "religious traditions throughout the world—Protestantism, Catholicism, Judaism, Islam, Hinduism, and Buddhism"—have been on the rise, abandoning acceptance of a secondary status and refusing "to accept the marginal and privatized roles that theories of modernity, liberal political theories, and secularist ideologies had reserved and prescribed for them."[11]

As stressed by José Casanova, the rejuvenated efforts of faith traditions to expand their roles mean that

> religions throughout the world are entering the public sphere and the arena of political contestation not only to defend their traditional turf, as they have done in the past, but also to participate in the very struggles to define and set the modern boundaries between the private and public spheres; between legality and morality; between family, civil society, economy, and state; between nations, states, and civilizations in the emerging global system. Insofar as this politicization of religion has assumed a global character, one can understand it as a religious response to the challenges and opportunities that processes of globalization present to all religious traditions.[12]

In practical terms, the revival—or, more realistically, the enhanced public presence—of religious doctrines and their exponents in national and international contexts means that the compromise under which research and theory development has taken place in American and other contexts has broken down. Prior to the twenty-first century there were a number of very practical reasons explaining why openly religious perspectives were usually absent from the process of developing theory for library, information, and knowledge studies; other professional fields; and the social and experimental sciences. The first reason was the need to avoid the "Which religion is right on this issue?" question. This query reflects the existence of a large number of faiths with sometimes-conflicting truth claims.[13] In much of the twentieth century, potential conflict arising from the question of which believer's religious dogma would take precedence in a research project was avoided through the seldom articulated but widely understood agreement among faculty to set aside diverging denominational teachings and rely on "scientific evidence and empirical data." Such an approach proved to be enormously attractive as the world of university researchers and theorists expanded from its liberal Protestant base to include Catholics, Jews, and Muslims, as well as a spectrum of other believers and nonbelievers. The reliance on what is conventionally termed the *scientific method*, with an emphasis on the seemingly objective process of experiment and replication, advanced human knowledge through supplying "standards for truth on which people of many persuasions could agree." In so doing, it allowed scholars from a spectrum of faith traditions to "suspend or subordinate their sectarian religious beliefs . . . [to] work together and treat reality as the product of natural forces susceptible to empirical investigation."[14]

Within mainstream higher education as a whole, there seemed to exist a fundamental consensus that applying religious approaches to research questions was intellectually irresponsible. Living in what was perceived to be an increasingly secular world, a number of researchers and theorists even defined religion as a category that was becoming merely of historical interest—at least in a university environment. Science, in short, was deemed to provide more respectable answers to all truly worthwhile questions.

In the academic world, the perspective that religion is in a permanent state of decline is usually termed "secularization theory." Originally developed to explain the process through which Western Christianity lost its cultural dominance in much of Europe, secularization theory stresses, "As a society becomes modern, it becomes more secular."[15] Prior to the twenty-first century, secularization theory did seem to explain much of what had occurred in the states of Western Europe and in various other nations with a significant European influence. However, prosecularization analyses proved far less successful in explaining religious developments in the United States, where local public libraries and librarians have observed some denominations in their communities decline in numbers while others, in multiple domestic and imported religious variations, evolved, mutated, and expanded.[16] The ramifications of the American example of combining progress with religiosity are well captured by Peter Berger, who observes: "If modernity and secularization go hand in hand, how does one explain the United States? It is a vibrantly religious society, yet it is difficult to maintain that it is less modern than, say, the Netherlands."[17]

Of late, rather than being a formulation useful for understanding multiple environments, secularization theory seems to be geographically applicable primarily to parts of Europe and intellectually appealing elsewhere to cultural elites with a "Western-style" higher education. Otherwise, secularization theory has difficulty addressing an international reality where "most of the world is as religious as it ever was, and in some places is more religious than ever."[18]

In a world where the multiplying streams of world religiosity interact with the expanding processes of globalization, it is now becoming imperative within the library, information, and knowledge fields to address the question, *"How can theorists provide constructive guidance to practitioners who must interact in the religiously influenced environments supported by the various information, library, and knowledge professions?"*

AN AUTHOR'S LAMENT

It must be stressed that it is only with considerable reluctance that I am theorizing about how secular and religiously influenced scholars may collaborate in environments where the underlying components of both science and revelation may be in play. This work on useful theory already questions current academic standards for valuing research and is hardly likely to benefit by giving critics ammunition for attacking the author for either a perceived lack of faith or creeping denominationalism. However, I was unable to find a secular source to which I could refer current or would-be theorists for guidance in cooperating in theory development with adherents from the twenty-first century's increasingly influential religious traditions. Arguments for such collaboration from a religious perspective abound. Indeed, the theoretical physicist-turned-theologian John Polkinghorne has developed a virtual cottage industry devoted to seeking a religious–secular research accommodation.[19] In truth, sales of this present work might be larger without this chapter. However, for me, failing to address the reality of the proverbial eight-hundred-pound gorilla sitting at the theory table would have been a severe ethical lapse. Someone has to bite the bullet and attempt to use secular intellectual tools to build a tentative structure for collaborating with religiously influenced colleagues to address issues in a world where issues of faith are clearly in play.

PRAGMATIC JUSTIFICATIONS FOR TESTING FAITH ASSERTIONS IN LIS THEORY DEVELOPMENT

The research philosophy of cultural pragmatism offers a number of justifications for opening up the theory development process within the library, information, and knowledge fields, as well as within other fields and disciplines, to collaboration with researchers with faith-based connections. First and foremost, religious traditions have not gone away. They still impact matters ranging from international war and peace to decisions to protest books in local school library media centers. Such powerful traditions cannot be ignored—and they refuse to be subsumed. In consequence, they must be engaged with, preferably in a mutually rewarding manner.

Second, the fundamental tenets of cultural pragmatism include the extension to religious traditions of William James's assertion that "all philosophies are hypotheses."[20] For a cultural pragmatist, all religions, indeed all of humanity's traditions, may have the potential—*the word "potential" is here emphasized*—for providing testable assertions about the world. At a minimum, faiths and their stories may offer a fruitful source of the analogies and metaphors (Garden of Eden, widow's mite, Armageddon, and so forth), that capture the experience of daily life, contribute to the advancement of science, and draw attention to desirable or even threatening states of being.[21] In this context, a third fundamental tenet of cultural pragmatism—shared at many levels with classical pragmatism—asserting that *consequences or results determine if an idea is true* now comes into play. Under this criterion, the "origin, logic, and elegance of an idea are secondary to its practical outcomes."[22] Here, cultural pragmatism seems to be more inclusive than its intellectual parent. A contemporary cultural pragmatist can see the early twentieth-century assault on religious belief and practices by the otherwise genial John Dewey—particularly in his 1934 publication of *A Common Faith*—as reflecting less of Dewey's pragmatic reliance on analyzed experience and more of what can only be termed "dated cultural baggage" and lack of understanding of religions and the purposes they serve.[23] Unfortunately, the work seems to be the product of a time when both pragmatists and religious believers were focused so much on their surface differences that they failed to understand the deeper, more unifying aspects of their shared national culture. In the twenty-first century, cultural pragmatists understand that all dogmas of religious traditions, at a minimum, have the potential to contain insights reflecting centuries or millennia of accumulated, and more or less adequately analyzed, experience. In consequence, it makes little sense for cultural pragmatists to ignore the possibility, however remote, that even dogmatic assertions advanced by a given religion can suggest useful explanations of the physical and social universes for testing in a given context.

A fourth culturally pragmatic reason for not ruling out the possibility of theory collaboration with religious believers involves the reality that the shared culture of the United States supports religious adherence, with the notable exception of significant aspects of the secular university environment. Here, for much of the twentieth century, what Martin Marty has termed a "secular only" attitude left religious issues underexplored and religious studies departments "underfunded and underappreciated."[24] With the necessary assurances of confidentiality, it might be a productive study in itself to investigate whether or not scholars with both strong faith affiliations and appointments in "inhospitable" university environments draw on their religious traditions to generate questions for research but report the results of such research in what might be seen as the more acceptable intellectual languages of critical theory, feminism, or classical pragmatism. If religious faith is suspect on a given campus, using secular language to describe the research process may be required in order to attract favorable attention from promotion and tenure committees, as well as academic administrators. For their part, contemporary cultural pragmatists prefer to avoid any pressures for "theory source concealment" by according religious traditions a more open respect as possible—again the key word is "possible"—generators of testable hypotheses.

A fifth reason for potentially collaborating with the religiously influenced flows from the reality that pragmatism recognizes that all truths, including its own, are "fallible, situated in history, and open to revision."[25] This intellectual self-restraint allows pragmatists to be periodically disquieted when the alternative theoretical lens of critical theory, feminism, or religious dogma reminds them that accepted definitions of analyzed experience may have become outdated. For pragmatism, at least in its cultural variety, this awareness of limitations means that it would be intellectual hubris of the worst sort to rule out religious or other traditions as potential sources of useful explanations for understanding the world and how it works. Without religiously inclined associates able to serve as "translators," for example, a pragmatist may have difficulty in theorizing for the contemporary United States, where "a growing body of literature documents how religious beliefs and commitments inform political values and behaviors."[26]

As William James noted nearly a century ago, "We are all biased by our personal feelings."[27] A cultural pragmatist, whether atheist or believer, is likely to need intellectual balance from critical theorists, feminists, and even scholars with faith connections to compensate for her or his own prejudices, in order to theorize with greater chances of success for environments where faith traditions are in play. The same need for balance, it must be stressed, applies to scholars from faith communities who, for example, seek to develop hypotheses describing the library, information, or knowledge experiences and perceptions of believers from other traditions or nonbelievers with secular orientations.

A sixth culturally pragmatic rationale for being open to the possibility of collaboration with scholars and others who are also faith adherents results from the understanding that members of such traditions can exhibit a high degree of flexibility, possibly in response to an American national culture that "encourages a mixing of religious themes."[28] In this context, it is worth noting the everyday pragmatism in religious affairs of American adults, who agree at a 42 percent approval level with the statement "The best religion would be one that borrowed from all religions."[29] Even in the hierarchically inclined Roman Catholic Church, numerous American Catholics apparently embrace "autonomy of conscience" as the "ultimate judge in decision making"[30] in their religious and secular lives. Orthodox Catholic theologians assert that this exercise of freedom in belief ought to take place in the "context of faith and the faith community."[31] However, the question of whether or not a scholar from the Catholic tradition has dutifully followed internal religious prescriptions in developing possible hypotheses will be of far less interest to cultural pragmatists than that same scholar's suitability for participating in the intellectual give and take necessary for success in a collaborative theory development environment.

COLLABORATING IN THEORY DEVELOPMENT WITH FAITH ADHERENTS

The processes through which LIS cultural pragmatists and scholars from other research philosophies may cooperate with scholars from faith traditions in theory development for library, information, and knowledge issues are precisely the same methods through which scholars adhering to different research philosophies may collaborate over any intellectual boundaries. One such approach, far from exhaustive of the possibilities, involves focusing on the first factor in a model that the author has entitled "A Nine-Step Model for Pragmatic Research." The components of this model are:

1. Confirm, or establish and maintain, a common language for identifying and solving the problem.
2. Identify the problematic situation.
3. Frame (define) the research "problem" from elements of the larger problematic situation.
4. Identify how analogous problems may have been resolved in other contexts.
5. Devise one or more provisional solutions to the "framed" problem through a "useful theory" construction process.
6. Field-test, fine-tune, or reject the provisional solution(s).
7. Implement the successfully field-tested solution(s) on a broader basis.
8. Monitor the continued effectiveness of the solution(s).
9. Decide when changes in contexts may require a revised identification of the problematic situation, another effort at problem definition, or new or different solution(s).

The first step in this collaborative theory development process directs the collaborating partners to "confirm, or establish and maintain, a common language for identifying and solving the problem." Potential partners in theory development, be they critical theorists, feminists, or faith adherents, need to demonstrate flexibility in the preliminary and subsequent discussions called to determine the feasibility of collaboration in the usually ego-driven, frequently intense, and always demanding theory development process. If such discussions make it clear that a common language for discussion does not exist and is impossible to negotiate, or that potential associates for a project believe that their research philosophies or religious traditions already provide all the necessary answers, then alternative partners should be sought or the collaborative project should be abandoned in favor of individual efforts.

NOTES

1. See the discussion in Beth McMurtrie's "Silence, Not Confrontation, over the 'Mandatum,'" *Chronicle of Higher Education* 48, no. 40 (June 14, 2002): A10–A11.

2. See Kenneth Jost, "Libraries and the Internet," *CQ Researcher* 11, no. 21 (June 1, 2001): 465–68; Joe Landrum and Dorothy White, "Intellectual Freedom in Public Libraries," *Louisiana Libraries* 62 no. 2 (Fall 2001): 15–16; Richard E. Rubin, *Foundations of Library and Information Science*, updated version (New York: Neal-Schuman, 2000); and Nicolle O. Steffen, "Challenging Times: Challenges to Materials in Colorado Public Libraries," *Colorado Libraries* 28, no. 3 (Fall 2002): 9–12.

3. See Barbara Schleihagen, "Intellectual Freedom and Libraries: German Perspectives," *IFLA Journal* 28, no. 4 (2002): 185–89.

4. See Robert P. Doyle, "Islamic Resources for Libraries," *ILA Reporter* 20, no. 6 (December 2002): 4–6; and Linda R. Silver, "Up for Discussion: Judging Judaica," *School Library Journal*, January 1, 2002, available at http://slj .reviewsnews.com/index.asp?layout=articlePrint&articleID=CA188165 (accessed July 5, 2003).

5. Richard J. Cox, "Testing the Spirit of the Information Age," *Journal of Information Ethics* 10, no. 2 (Fall 2001): 62.

6. Mike Wessells, "Faith at the Front Desk: Spirituality and Patron Service," *American Libraries*, May 2003, 43.

7. Abraham Kaplan, *The New World of Philosophy* (New York: Random House, 1961), 49.

8. Kaplan, *New World*, 45.

9. Sidney Hook, *Philosophy and Public Policy* (Carbondale: Southern Illinois University Press, 1980), 268.

10. Hook, *Philosophy and Public Policy*, ix.

11. José Casanova, "An Interview with José Casanova," by Krishan Kumar and Ekaterina Makarova, *Hedgehog Review* 4, no. 2 (Summer 2002): 95.

12. Casanova, "Interview."

13. R. Stephen Warner, "Approaching Religious Diversity: Barriers, Byways, and Beginnings," *Sociology of Religion* 59, no. 3 (Fall 1998): 193–215.

14. George M. Marsden, "Theology and the University: Newman's Idea and Current Realities," in John Henry Newman, *The Idea of a University*, ed. Frank M. Turner (New Haven, CT: Yale University Press, 1996), 311.

15. Robert D. Putnam, *Bowling Alone: The Collapse and Revival of American Community* (New York: Simon and Schuster/Touchstone, 2000), 69.

16. Warner, "Approaching Religious Diversity."

17. Peter L. Berger, "Globalization and Religion," *Hedgehog Review* 4, no. 2 (Summer 2002): 10–11.

18. Berger, "Globalization and Religion," 10. See also the discussion in Abdulaziz Sachedina, "Political Islam and the Hegemony of Globalization: A Response to Peter Berger," *Hedgehog Review* 4, no. 2 (Summer 2002): 21–29.

19. See, for example, John Polkinghorne's works *Belief in God in an Age of Science* (New Haven, CT: Yale University Press, 1998); *Quarks, Chaos, and Christianity: Questions to Science and Religion* (New York: Crossroad, 1994); and *Science and Theology: An Introduction* (Minneapolis: Fortress Press, 1998).

20. William James, "Absolutism and Empiricism," in *Essays in Radical Empiricism* (1912; reprint, Lincoln: University of Nebraska Press, 1996), 279.

21. For a now-classic discussion of the employment of secular analogies and metaphors in the development of theory, see Roy Dreistadt's "An Analysis of the Use of Analogies and Metaphors in Science," *Journal of Psychology* 68, first half (January 1968): 97–116.

22. Robert B. Young, *No Neutral Ground: Standing By the Values We Prize in Higher Education* (San Francisco: Jossey-Bass, 1997), 35.

23. Milton R. Konvitz, introduction to *John Dewey: The Later Works, 1925–1953, vol. 9, 1933–1934*, ed. Jo Ann Boydston (Carbondale: Southern Illinois University Press, 1989), xxxi.

24. Martin E. Marty with Jonathan Moore, *Education, Religion, and the Common Good: Advancing a Distinctly American Conversation about Religion's Role in Our Shared Life* (San Francisco: Jossey-Bass, 2000), 111.

25. Danny Postel, "Sidney Hook, an Intellectual Street Fighter, Reconsidered," *Chronicle of Higher Education* 49, no. 11 (November 8, 2001): A19.

26. Darren E. Sherkat and Christopher G. Ellison, "Recent Developments and Current Controversies in the Sociology of Religion," *Annual Review of Sociology* 25 (1999): 4.

27. William James, "A World of Pure Experience," in *Essays in Radical Empiricism* (1912; reprint, Lincoln: University of Nebraska Press, 1996), 40.

28. Wade Clark Roof, *Spiritual Marketplace: Baby Boomers and the Remaking of American Religion* (Princeton, NJ: Princeton University Press, 1999), 41.

29. "The Way We Live Now Poll: Spirituality," *New York Times Magazine*, May 7, 2000, 84.

30. Timothy G. McCarthy, *The Catholic Tradition: Before and after Vatican II, 1878–1993* (Chicago: Loyola University Press, 1994), 141.

31. McCarthy, *Catholic Tradition*, 142.

Chapter Ten

The Foundations for Building Bridges

SCENARIO: WHEN IN ROME . . .

As a foundation for its deserved reputation as a quality university with a growing number of respected graduate programs, Dominican University maintains a process of faculty evaluation that may be more intensive than those operated by other institutions with ALA-accredited programs. There are no promotion and tenure committees at the school or college level. Instead, as a legacy from the university's earlier decades as the much smaller Rosary College, this faculty appraisal system rests on a process of considering untenured faculty members for retention at the university level based on intensive reviews during their first, second, fourth, and sixth years. These evaluations are carried out by the Committee on Faculty Appointments. Promotions, which involve separate applications, require yet more rounds of paperwork and committee judgment.

Committee on Faculty Appointments assessments of faculty begin with a notice from the university president inviting a formal application for reappointment from untenured faculty members on tenure lines; their paperwork is expected to address certain stipulated criteria. At the same time, the university community as a whole is invited to comment on the faculty member's contributions to the university. This process inevitably results in crammed binders full of supporting documentation created or assembled to demonstrate a faculty member's effectiveness in teaching, research, and service. Particularly valued in this process are student evaluations, publications, successful grant applications, and supportive letters from one's dean and colleagues. The amount of work involved in each application for retention is comparable to that required for tenure at other institutions and, admittedly, is a continuing source of stress for untenured professors. All the same, this system is based on faculty examinations of other faculty and thus incorporates important components of faculty governance. It is primarily for that reason that many senior professors support it. In its review process the Committee on Faculty Appointments looks for and analyzes the quality and quantity of faculty scholarship. Nevertheless, Dominican is a teaching university, and even an outstanding record of research and publication will not insure reappointment if indicators of student learning are less than acceptable.

In 1996, after decades as a librarian, consultant, manager, and state bureaucrat, followed by an educational detour to earn a PhD, I was hired by Dominican University (then Rosary College) through a faculty search overseen by then-dean Peggy Sullivan. When I applied for reappointment for a second year, Peggy's letter of support was strong, even if it stressed my need to stop thinking like a practitioner and start reasoning more as a member of an academic community. Years later, Peggy was kind enough to write another letter, this time supporting my application for tenure. In contrast to her earlier note, this equally positive communication suggested that it was time for me to spend less time at the university and become more involved with off-campus practitioners.

The next time that Peggy and I met was after I had been awarded tenure. She was serving as a search consultant for the Suburban Library System, and I was a new member of the system board who had been elected to represent academic libraries. In a conversation just prior to the start of our Monday night board meeting, I reminded Peggy of the conflicting advice she had given me in her two letters. She laughed and claimed, "I was right both times." And she was. Had I not learned to think as a faculty member in my early years with Dominican, I would not have met the university's expectations for reappointment, tenure, and promotion, most recently for promotion to full professor. Yet the process of being socialized into the university's academic culture had inevitably distanced me from the worlds of library, information, and knowledge practice.

AND OF WHAT REAL USE IS THEORY?

In *How Institutions Think*, a work containing her Abrams Lectures delivered at Syracuse University,[1] anthropologist Mary Douglas advances a number of observations about institutions that may help explain why Peggy Sullivan felt it necessary to advise me first to embed myself in Dominican University's academic culture and later to reconnect with the worlds of practice. According to Douglas, institutions provide their members with "a set of analogies with which to explore the world and with which to justify the naturalness and reasonableness of the instituted rules"[2] as part of the very process of maintaining their continued existence. In addition:

> Any institution [university, public library, corporate knowledge management center, etc.] then starts to control the memory of its members: it causes them to forget experiences incompatible with its righteous image, and it brings to their minds events which sustain the view of nature that is complementary to itself. It provides the categories of their thought, sets the terms for self-knowledge, and fixes identities.[3]

For Americans steeped in a tradition of free will, free choice, and intellectual freedom, the reality that institutions of all kinds, large and small, secular and religious, function through socializing their members to categories of acceptable thought can be disconcerting. Memory, identity, and everything else that defines us as human seem to be affected. Douglas even asserts that humans simply cannot cooperate without devising such controlling entities and ends her book with the observation, "For better or worse, individuals really do share their thoughts and they do to some extent harmonize their preferences and they have no other way to make the big decisions except within the scope of institutions they build."[4]

This reminder of the power of institutions, including colleges, universities, and practitioner work sites, to control the thought processes of people in their organizational cultures also provides an explanation of why faculty research that is irrelevant to practitioner contexts continues to be produced and why it remains so hard to change the academic research and publication process. Academics will persist in researching, writing, and publishing exactly the sorts of publications that they have been socialized into believing will help them achieve the campus aims of tenure and promotion. For their part, practitioners will answer their daily questions and address long-term issues, in part, through utilizing the "how we did it good" literature whenever their own experiences or interpersonal networks lack ready answers.

Ironically, this portrait of a status quo of mutual researcher–practitioner frustration also provides a bottom-line explanation of why theory is helpful. At a minimum, *theory is useful because it can provide methods for addressing issues that may differ from the ways of categorizing and solving problems supported by the institutions in which we work.* Theory can help faculty think like practitioners and assist practitioners and consultants in thinking like faculty. Theory is valuable because it gives us options for achieving "truth," no matter how provisional and limited such truth may actually be.

WHAT KIND OF THEORY IS BEST FOR BUILDING BRIDGES BETWEEN RESEARCH AND PRACTICE?

This volume has spent a considerable amount of time addressing the need to bridge the gaps separating the theoretical perspectives of faculty, consultants, and practitioners. One way to do so, though most certainly not the only approach, is to apply what I term the "Peggy Sullivan Test." This test is defined as a concentrated effort to determine how best to answer two questions: "Which perspective (faculty theorist, consultant, practitioner, or some combination thereof) and what research philosophy (critical theory, feminism, pragmatism, combination, etc.) are likely to contribute most to identifying and solving priority problems at this time?" and "What are the likely short-term and long-term pluses and minuses of the solutions developed through adopting what seem to be relevant perspectives and utilizing what may be appropriate philosophies?"

In contexts where faculty theorists are convinced that practitioners ignore valuable research and practitioners respond with the view that theorists pay no attention to existing realities, the most effective perspective to take may not be one that claims to have all the answers. Rather, it is more likely to be a philosophy grounded in humility and open to other viewpoints, a research perspective that "stipulates that reality does not always lend itself squarely to yes/no judgments and allows practical knowers to say 'perhaps,' 'it depends,' 'who knows,' and to use indeterminate truth values that help us handle situational indeterminacy."[5] Progress in theory effectiveness, particularly in cooperative theory development involving faculty researchers, consultants, and practitioners whose mental models are often sustained by very different organizational patterns of thinking, is likely to require an approach that understands that "inarticulate sentiments, private interests, logical inconsistencies," and other factors frequently distort human communication. No approach to research can be anywhere near as effective as it claims to be if it so prizes its own definition of "pure reason" that it proves to be "intolerant of ambiguity, contemptuous of common sense, disdainful of compromise, proud of its intellectual machismo in dealing with particulars, and arrogantly dismissive of its own blunderings in the practical domain."[6]

In other words, progress in theory development across faculty–consultant–practitioner divides is probably best facilitated by some form of twenty-first-century pragmatism that is open to input from virtually every conceivable source, including critical theory, feminism, and (most controversially) appropriately analyzed religious tradition that is treated as a source—and not a limiter—of potentially useful ideas. I like to think that an effective approach to developing the necessary theory may even lie in the components of the inclusive cultural pragmatism discussed throughout this work.

NOTES

1. Mary Douglas, *How Institutions Think* (Syracuse, NY: Syracuse University Press, 1986).

2. Douglas, *How Institutions Think*, 112.

3. Douglas, *How Institutions Think*.

4. Douglas, *How Institutions Think*, 128.

5. Dmitri N. Shalin, "Critical Theory and the Pragmatist Challenge," *American Journal of Sociology* 98, no. 2 (September 1992): 260.

6. Shalin, "Critical Theory," 270.

Postscript

Throughout this work there has been a deliberate effort not to underestimate the difficulties that will be encountered by faculty, consultants, and practitioners embarking on the road to developing useful theory. As might be expected, the rules defining how promotion and tenure can be achieved on a given academic campus are generally well known, even if their interpretation can evidence a remarkable level of subjectivity. However, the guidelines for comprehending and describing the library, information, and knowledge realities of off-campus environments in ways that are useful to various practitioner communities are inevitably less spelled out and more open to differences in interpretation. Indeed, the possibilities for misunderstanding and frustration are such that one might wonder, "Is it really worth the effort?"

Unfortunately for potential and existing theorists who would prefer to concentrate on a campus-centered life, the answers to that question are in the process of being provided by others. The world outside the college or university gates has changed from the more civilized ideal that can linger in the collective memory of the academic world. Higher education has become a competitive business, and faculty members are being asked to be "more productive." Whether it is the state of Ohio emphasizing teaching and wiping out support for doctoral programs that are deemed not to be relevant to the interests of taxpayers, or the University of Phoenix opening up branches in strip malls and purveying lower-prized educational credentials to community residents via the web, the dollars necessary to support an academic life divorced from the off-campus worlds of practice are increasingly scarce.

We are well into a time when demonstrations of relevance, specifically including the production of theory that is actually useful for identifying and solving the critical problems facing practitioners in their varying environments, may be a particularly viable argument for

- faculty wanting to justify not increasing their teaching loads
- consultants seeking to obtain new contracts
- practitioners wanting to create a vision of future success that is attractive to potential and existing employers

To take a less defensive, more positive view of the matter, wouldn't it be a welcome change to be a theorist whose theories are actually used?

Glossary

Note: The definitions in this glossary are offered from the author's philosophical perspective of cultural pragmatism. Theorists, consultants, and practitioners from other research traditions may have alternative definitions for any or all of the topics defined below.

Americanization The process through which the shared culture of the United States socializes individuals and groups into supporting such national values as democracy and individualism.

context For the purposes of theory development, "context" is the total of cultural, emotional, intellectual, linguistic, physical, and other circumstances within which thoughts are formulated and actions are taken. In the words of John Dewey, "We are not explicitly aware of the role of context just because our every utterance is so saturated with it that it forms the significance of what we say and hear" (John Dewey, "Context and Thought," in John *Dewey: The Later Works, 1925–1953, vol. 6, 1931–1932*, ed. Jo Ann Boydston. [Carbondale: Southern Illinois University Press, 1985], 4).

critical theory An offspring of twentieth-century Marxism, critical theory is principally concerned with addressing issues of control, justice, power, and privilege. The philosophy's founders were German intellectuals of the Frankfurt School who flourished in the twentieth century between World War I and World War II. These theorists adopted the name "critical theory"—in part—to underscore their commitment to assessing and remedying social inequalities. There may also be a more practical reason for the adoption and popularization of the term. Members of the Frankfurt School were in exile in the United States during much of the era of Nazi Germany (1933–1945). Use of the term "critical theory" served to obscure the Marxist roots of the philosophy to American audiences, who shared a national culture that was and is notoriously inhospitable to Marxism, communism, and most varieties of socialism. Not unexpectedly, the critical theory research philosophy holds a particularly strong position in European and non-Western intellectual circles, where Marxist thought has been more a part of the intellectual mainstream.

cultural pragmatism A philosophy that builds upon classical pragmatism and holds, as does its intellectual progenitor, that "truth" is subject to construction in ongoing processes within cultural and other human communities. Cultural pragmatists hold that the true test of any theory resides in analyzed experience. It understands that everyday truths tend to be culture specific, but it is open to the possibility of constructing larger truths that transcend cultural and geographical boundaries. Cultural pragmatists value past experience but hold that "truths" are always more or less provisional and must be continually tested in a variety of contexts. Since cultural pragmatists deem the future "workability" of a theory to be more important than its historical source, they are open to seeing philosophical competitors—such as critical theory, feminism, and even revealed religion—as both potential collaborators and valuable repositories of human experience. As such, philosophical competitors are all capable of producing theories for testing in a variety of contexts.

culture A complex system of symbols and their interpretations that helps members of a society, including a national society, structure their experience and categorize their natural and social worlds.

custom A behavior or belief supported by a culture.

Ex corde Ecclesiae A 1990 document issued by Pope John Paul II outlining his vision for Catholic higher education. The document asserts that "the president and a majority of faculty members and trustees of a college should be Catholic, and that the local bishop has local authority in deciding whether an institution has the right to call itself Catholic" (Beth McMurtrie, "Vatican Backs Catholic-College Rules That Spur Fears over Academic Freedom," *Chronicle of Higher Education* 46, no. 41 [June 16, 2000]: A18).

faculty rewards system The contemporary "system" or, more appropriately, "systems" through which faculty in colleges and universities are promoted and tenured. In America's major research universities, where teaching and service are prized far less than research, the dominant system relies heavily on the publication of articles in peer-reviewed journals, the writing of scholarly monographs, and the analysis of "citation counts," or the number of times a faculty member's published work has been cited by other writers in selected publications. The current arrangements, controlled largely by faculty, evolved as the *solution* to the *problem* represented by the administrator-driven "old boys' system" for hiring and promotion that flourished prior to the mid-twentieth century. Of late, the present system has been criticized for emphasizing the quantity of publications over their quality, and for the production of research and publications often deemed irrelevant outside of limited scholarly networks.

fallacy of public expectations The idea that only the unjustifiable intransigence of university and college faculty prevents the production of useful research.

fallacy of the academic lens The erroneous assumption that a faculty member who follows academic norms for "good" research will inevitably produce findings useful to practitioners in the worlds outside of the university.

feminism A philosophy that puts issues related to gender and gender discrimination at the heart of its analysis. In part, feminism arose in reaction to cultural and intellectual traditions that identified "human" with "male" and neglected women's contributions and issues.

globalization A process that harnesses the dynamics of multinational corporations to new telecommunications infrastructures. Although the term first developed in describing new business environments, it is now evolving to deal with such realities as transnational cultures, religions, intellectual standards, and so on, in particular, as such realities are affected by both technology and market forces.

hegemony Often termed "cultural hegemony." Hegemony exists where a particular class controls financial, military, and other resources and, more fundamentally, dominates the religions, schools, and other cultural "tools" that guide people in understanding their world and their place in it.

incommensurability The perceived inability of humans to communicate effectively with one another because of a lack of common standards for meaning and other shared cultural foundations.

inerrancy The belief that the Christian *Holy Bible* is literally true, both in its revelation of dogma and in its historical accuracy. By extension, "inerrancy" can apply to a belief that the revealed scriptures of another religion have the same freedom from error.

intellectual predestination The erroneous assumption that the views of other theorists, due to a presumed knowledge of either their secular philosophy or their religious faith, are knowable in advance of working with such scholars in a particular context.

interlanguage As used in this work, an interlanguage is a negotiated, evolving, mutually acceptable repertoire of common understandings about the world or aspects of the world viewed as important by humans seeking to communicate in a given context. Currently, the interlanguage known as "International Standard English," evolving independently of British, Australian, or American language rules, is becoming essential to a great deal of international trade and cross-cultural exchange.

intracultural reciprocity The changing, context-specific perceptions of mutual worth by participants in geographical, organizational, social, and other arenas, as well as the willingness of arena participants to act on the basis of such perceptions.

lens A way of looking at the world. Typically, lenses are provided by local or national cultures. However, additional lenses may be acquired through life experience or adoption of a research philosophy. As with the eye's optic lens or prescription lenses in a pair of glasses, a research lens highlights some aspects of the world while making other features more difficult to see. Use of a cultural or theoretical lens, for example, can lead a researcher to focus on the operation of certain factors, such as the status of women or the role of elites, even as it obscures the actions of what may be equally important variables, such as a society's commitment to democracy or the impact on a culture of religious belief. Awareness of both the benefits and the limitations of individual philosophical lenses often leads cultural pragmatists to employ several such perspectives in formulating and solving research problems.

mandatum The formal authentication that a theologian teaches "authentic Catholic doctrine." A *mandatum* is issued to a faculty theologian at a Catholic institution of higher education by the bishop of the diocese in which the school is located.

metaparadigm A paradigm or way of looking at the world so large and embracing that it really is a broad, fundamental worldview that can contain a number of subordinate paradigms. At the risk of oversimplification, it can be asserted that traditionalism, postmodernism, and modernism are the three most influential metaparadigms in the contemporary world.

metaphysics A branch of philosophy that attempts to describe the whole of reality, including truths that transcend, or rise above, observable reality, through the use of human reason. A metaphysical philosophical stance may be open to divine revelation and may exclude analyzed experience and replicable experiment. At times, metaphysics may be difficult to distinguish from theology.

model An incomplete, simplified version of some aspect of reality, used by people to solve problems.

modernism At its most fundamental, a "Western" metaparadigm or worldview that privileges the ability of humans to create or discover knowledge. Historians often trace the development of modernism to the influence of the Protestant Reformation and the European Enlightenment, since both movements were seen as providing an intellectual "space" within which alternative religious and secular interpretations of the roles and capabilities of humanity could be developed. In their development through this centuries-long struggle with traditional (generally theological) worldviews, some variants of modernism came to reject defining humanity's history as part of a divine plan for ordering the world. As with all metaphilosophies, modernism contains a wide spectrum of viewpoints. At its most extreme, it embodies the belief that certain "truths," both in science and society, will be seen as "objectively" valid in all contexts and at all times.

norm A rule that guides behavior within a given society and its culture(s). According to Robert K. Merton, norms vary in their impact since they "may *prescribe* behavior or *proscribe* it; they may only indicate what behavior is *preferred* or simply permitted" (Robert K. Merton, *Social Research and the Practicing Professions,* ed. Aaron Rosenblatt and Thomas F. Gieryn [Cambridge, MA: ABT Books, 1982], 75).

paradigm A mental construct or way of looking at the world that, initially, is supplied to an individual by a culture and, subsequently, may be affirmed, transformed, or replaced by the intellectual currents within a profession or academic discipline. A research paradigm such as critical theory or pragmatism can be envisioned as being part of a metaparadigm such as traditionalism, modernism, or postmodernism.

positivism Possibly the most extreme example of modernist thought. In the early to mid-twentieth century, positivists could and did hold that nothing could be true that could not be verified through experience or observation.

postmodernism In its most straightforward variants, this metaphilosophy holds that the pursuit of "objective" truth—the central component of modernism, one of postmodernism's rival metaphilosophies—is an effort doomed to failure. Postmodernists see modernism's privileging of "objectivity" as an illusion, hold that reality is socially constructed, and deem that differences in such factors as culture, gender, and class inevitably compound difficulties in effective communication. In turn, this makes impossible the development of universal rules to describe the world or attain "truth." Whatever small "truths" exist, in the postmodern perspective, exist only through agreement among the members of a given community.

pragmatism (classical) Although the origin of the term was credited by William James to his friend Charles Sanders Peirce, "classical pragmatism" is most associated with James himself, Jane Addams, and, most prominently, John Dewey. At the risk of oversimplification, classical pragmatism may be defined as a philosophy grounded in the ongoing analysis and testing of the results of human experience. For pragmatists, the reliability of "human" truth is contingent upon growth in human understanding. Consequently, since time is expected to provide more experience for analysis, it is expected that today's theories will be replaced by tomorrow's more effective successors. Although Dewey would consider experience drawn from religious understandings to be unacceptable for such analysis, James would apply essentially the same analytical rules to religious experience as he would to experience in other areas of human interest and effort. *Cultural pragmatism*, a more inclusive, twenty-first-century successor to classical pragmatism, follows James in recognizing the intellectual limitations that result when religious knowledge is excluded as a source of useful understanding that can be subjected to analysis and testing. *See* **cultural pragmatism**; **prophetic pragmatism**

predestination In religion, the view that God has determined in advance which individuals will be saved and which individuals will be damned. *See* **intellectual predestination**

prophetic pragmatism A philosophy grounded in the view of philosophy as both social criticism and a source of ideas for reform. Initially formulated by the philosopher Cornel West, particularly in his *American Evasion of Philosophy: A Genealogy of Pragmatism* (Madison: University of Wisconsin Press, 1989), prophetic pragmatism is a philosophy that relies on the understanding that human beings are formed in the context of specific historical conditions ("historical consciousness"). It also explicitly draws for inspiration on such intellectual resources as critical theory; Christian theology, especially in its African American Protestant variant; and classical pragmatism, albeit less on the concepts of John Dewey and more on the religiously friendly formulations of William James. See "Prophetic Pragmatism: Cultural Criticism and Political Engagement" in West's *American Evasion of Philosophy* for a more in-depth assertion of the philosophy's components.

psychoanalysis An approach to understanding, initially formulated by Sigmund Freud in the nineteenth century, that seeks "truth" through a concentration on analyzing the subjective or emotional elements in individual and group lives.

rule A mental model for solving problems. *Condition-action* rules, which are encoded in our mental processes, have the form "*if* such-and-such, *then* so-and-so." At the individual level, such rules are derived from both experiences and formal instruction. Rules are often associated in clusters and function more as suggestions than as commands. They are relatively slow to change and seem to be modified to the least extent necessary to address new situations. New rules, such as those learned in traditional or electronic classrooms or in the course of professional practice, are in competition with an individual's already-existing rules. As rule clusters, they tend to be activated simultaneously to provide a provisional *model* of a given situation. They are in constant competition with one another to predict what will come next and what, if anything, ought to be done about it.

Further, in the competition to become active, such rules "bid" for opportunities to "post their messages." See John H. Holland, Keith J. Holyoak, Richard E. Nisbett, and Paul R. Thagard, *Induction: Processes of Inference, Learning, and Discovery* (Cambridge, MA: MIT Press, 1987).

scientific method In the late nineteenth century and much of the twentieth century, the scientific method was seen as being concerned with systematic experimentation and analysis, replication of research results, and the development of theories (1) to explain what happened and (2) to predict future occurrences. However, by 1964, the research theorist Abraham Kaplan had refused to define "scientific method," on the grounds that "if a definition of 'scientific method' is specific enough to be of some use in methodology, it is not sufficiently general to embrace all the procedures that scientists may eventually come to find useful." Kaplan also cited, with approval, the assertions of "historians and philosophers of science" that there is "no such thing as *the* scientific method" as being "a public service" (Abraham Kaplan, *The Conduct of Inquiry: Methodology for Behavioral Science* [San Francisco: Chandler, 1964], 27).

society "A loose, handy term of reference to the group of people who live in and carry a culture" (Robert S. Lynd, *Knowledge for What? The Place of Social Science in American Culture* [Princeton, NJ: Princeton University Press, 1948], 152–53).

theory A supposition that explains or seeks to explain something. (See Loraine Blaxter, Christina Hughes, and Malcolm Tight, *How to Research* [Buckingham, UK: Open University Press, 1996], 185.) In the complex and varying arenas that constitute human cultures, *good theory* advances understanding. But understanding derived from theory is just one source of awareness among many. Outside the university, competitors to faculty-generated theory, such as models fashioned from common sense, religious beliefs, explicit knowledge learned in school, and tacit knowledge discovered on the job, all vie to provide explanations of what is happening in the world. *Better* or *useful theory* contributes to effectiveness, generally through facilitating prediction. Effective prediction involves specifying a context, such as a culture, nation, neighborhood, profession, or institution, within which whatever is envisioned by the theory developer will or will not take place.

traditional paradigm The worldview that a culture's customs, often including religious revelations, determine what is or is not acceptable knowledge. Although a premodern culture's understandings of its acceptable knowledge can and do evolve over time, the convention is often to view such changes as elaborations on long-standing or eternally valid truths. Variations of the traditional paradigm may hold that God, however defined, provides humanity with revealed knowledge for understanding the natural and supernatural worlds. Such knowledge is usually contained in works of sacred scriptures that are elaborated through the accepted traditions of faith communities. Normally, revealed knowledge is not subject to testing through experimentation and experience. Traditional, specifically theological paradigms dominated the European Middle Ages and retain a significant influence in the United States and other Western nations, even as they may play a preeminent role in, for example, much of the Middle East, parts of Africa, and significant parts of Asia.

Works Cited

Alinsky, Saul D. *Rules for Radicals: A Practical Primer for Realistic Radicals.* New York: Vintage, 1971.

Alvarez, Lizette. "After Months of Rancor, Speaker Names a Catholic Priest as House Chaplain." *New York Times*, March 24, 2000.

American Library Association, Committee on Accreditation. *Accreditation under the 1992 Standards for Accreditation of Master's Programs in Library and Information Studies: An Overview.* Chicago: Office for Accreditation, American Library Association, 1994.

———. *Standards for Accreditation of Master's Programs in Library and Information Studies.* Chicago: Office for Accreditation, American Library Association, 1992.

Anderson, Charles W. *Prescribing the Life of the Mind: An Essay on the Purpose of the University, the Aims of Liberal Education, the Competence of Citizens, and the Cultivation of Practical Reason.* Madison: University of Wisconsin Press, 1993.

Anees, Munawar Ahmad, and Merryl Wyn Davies. "Islamic Science: Current Thinking and Future Directions." In *The Revenge of Athena: Science, Exploitation, and the Third World*, ed. Ziauddin Sardar, 249–60. London: Mansell, 1988.

Angeles, Peter A. *The HarperCollins Dictionary of Philosophy.* 2d ed. New York: HarperCollins, 1992.

Appleby, Joyce, Lynn Hunt, and Margaret Jacob. *Telling the Truth about History.* New York: Norton, 1994.

Argyris, Chris. "Tacit Knowledge and Management." In *Tacit Knowledge in Professional Practice: Researcher and Practitioner Perspectives*, ed. Robert J. Sternberg and Joseph A. Horvath. Mahwah, NJ: Lawrence Erlbaum Associates, 1999.

Austin, Arthur. *The Empire Strikes Back: Outsiders and the Struggle over Legal Education*. New York: New York University Press, 1998.

Bagnall, Roger S. *Report of the Review Committee for the School of Library Service*. New York: Columbia University, 1990.

Barzun, Jacques. *A Stroll with William James*. Chicago: University of Chicago Press, 1983.

Bates, Marcia. J. "The Invisible Substrate of Information Science." *Journal of the American Society for Information Science* 50, no. 12 (October 1999): 1043–50.

Bauman, Zygmunt. *Legislators and Interpreters: On Modernity, Post-Modernity, and Intellectuals*. Ithaca, NY: Cornell University Press, 1987.

Becher, Tony. *Academic Tribes and Territories: Intellectual Enquiry and the Cultures of Disciplines*. Buckingham, UK: Society for Research into Higher Education/Open University Press, 1989.

Beckwith, Harry. *Selling the Invisible: A Field Guide to Modern Marketing*. New York: Warner, 1997.

Berger, Peter L. "Globalization and Religion." *Hedgehog Review* 4, no. 2 (Summer 2002): 7–20.

Berry, John N., III. "LIS Recruiting: Does It Make the Grade?" *Library Journal*, May 1, 2003, 5. Available at http://libraryjournal.reviewsnews.com/index.asp?layout=artiiclePrint&articleID=CA292594 (accessed June 2, 2003).

———. "We Must Have *Library* Education." *Library Journal*, February 15, 1998, 82.

Blaxter, Loraine, Christina Hughes, and Malcolm Tight. *How to Research*. Buckingham, UK: Open University Press, 1996.

Blumberg, Roger B. "Ex Libris." *The Sciences* 35 (September/October 1995): 16–19.

Blumenstyk, Goldie. "Companies' Graduate Programs Challenge Colleges of Education: For-Profit Institutions Find a New Market—Schoolteachers." *Chronicle of Higher Education* 50, no. 2 (September 5, 2003). Available at http://chronicle.com/weekly/v50/i02/02a03001/htm (accessed December 30, 2003).

———. "Financial Outlook 2004: For-Profit Colleges: Growth at Home and Abroad." *Chronicle of Higher Education* 50, no. 17 (December 19, 2003). Available at http://chroicle.com/weekly/v50/i17/17a01201.htm (accessed December 30, 2003).

Boas, George. Preface to Arthur O. Lovejoy, *The Thirteen Pragmatisms and Other Essays*. Baltimore: Johns Hopkins University Press, 1963.

Booth, Wayne C. "The Idea of a University—as Seen by a Rhetorician." In *The Vocation of a Teacher: Rhetorical Occasions, 1967–1988*. Chicago: University of Chicago Press, 1988.

Botstein, Leon. "Some Thoughts on Curriculum and Change." In *Rethinking Liberal Education*, ed. Nicholas H. Farnham and Adam Yarmolinsky, 51–61. New York: Oxford University Press, 1996.

Bourne, Randolph. "Twilight of Idols." In *The Radical Will: Selected Writings, 1911–1918*. Berkeley: University of California Press, 1992.

Boyer, Ernest L. *Scholarship Reconsidered: Priorities of the Professoriate*. Princeton, NJ: Carnegie Foundation for the Advancement of Teaching, 1990.

Breslin, Meg McSherry. "Trend toward Temporary Faculty Worries U. of I.— Officials Fear School's Reputation Could Suffer." *Chicago Tribune*, April 9, 2000.

Broderick, Dorothy M. "Turning Library into a Dirty Word: A Rant." *Library Journal*, July 1997, 42–43.

Budd, John M. "The Library, Praxis, and Symbolic Power." *Library Quarterly* 73, no. 1 (2003): 19–32.

Butler, Pierce. *An Introduction to Library Science*. Chicago: University of Chicago Press, 1933.

Calhoun, Craig. "Social Theory and the Public Sphere." In Turner, Bryan S., ed., *The Blackwell Companion to Social Theory*, 429–70. Oxford: Blackwell, 1996.

Campbell, James. *Understanding John Dewey: Nature and Cooperative Intelligence*. Chicago: Open Court, 1995.

Carlson, Thomas. "James and the Kantian Tradition." In *The Cambridge Companion to William James*, ed. Ruth Anna Putnam, 363–83. Cambridge: Cambridge University Press, 1997.

Casanova, José. "An Interview with José Casanova." By Krishan Kumar and Ekaterina Makarova. *Hedgehog Review* 4, no. 2 (Summer 2002): 91–108.

Christian, Sue Ellen. "When Culture, Medicine Don't Quite Cooperate." *Chicago Tribune*, May 7, 2000.

Clark, Burton R. *The Academic Life: Small Worlds, Different Worlds*. Princeton, NJ: Carnegie Foundation for the Advancement of Teaching, 1987.

Clark, Burton R., ed. *The Academic Profession: National, Disciplinary, and Institutional Settings*. Berkeley and Los Angeles: University of California Press, 1987.

Cohen, Arthur M., and Florence B. Brawer. *The American Community College*. 3d ed. San Francisco: Jossey-Bass, 1996.

Cole, Jonathan R. "Balancing Acts: Dilemmas of Choice Facing Research Universities." *Daedalus* 122, no. 4 (Fall 1993): 1–36.

———. *Report of the Provost on the School of Library Service at Columbia*. New York: Columbia University, 1990.

Collins, H. M. "Tacit Knowledge and Scientific Networks." In *Science in Context: Readings in the Sociology of Science*, ed. Barry Barnes and David Edge, 44–64. Cambridge, MA: MIT Press, 1982.

Corcoran, Mary, Lynn Dagar, and Anthea Stratigos. "The Changing Roles of Information Professionals: Excerpts from an Outsell, Inc., Study." *Online*, March/April 2000, 28–34.

Coughlin, Caroline, and Pamela Snelson. "Searching for Research in ACRL Papers." *Journal of Academic Librarianship* 9, no. 1 (1983): 21–26.

Cox, Richard J. "Testing the Spirit of the Information Age." *Journal of Information Ethics* 10, no. 2 (Fall 2001): 51–66.

Crainer, Stuart, and Des Dearlove. *Gravy Training: Inside the Business of Business Schools*. San Francisco: Jossey-Bass, 1999.

Cronin, Blaise. "Cutting the Gordian Knot." *Information Processing and Management* 31, no. 6 (1995): 897–902.

———. "The Dean's List: The Dreaded 'L' Word." *Library Journal*, March 15, 2001, 58.

Crowley, Bill. "Building Useful Theory: Tacit Knowledge, Practitioner Reports, and the Culture of LIS Inquiry." *Journal of Education for Library and Information Science* 40, no. 4 (Fall 1999): 282–95.

———. "The Control and Direction of Professional Education." *Journal of the American Society for Information Science* 50 (October 1999): 1127–35.

———. [William A. Crowley Jr.] "Deviance, Moral Voices, and Group Bound-aries: Labeling Perspective and the Occupational Folklore of Night School Education." Master's thesis, Ohio State University, 1991. EDRS, ED333150, microfiche.

———. "The Dilemma of the Librarian in Canadian Higher Education." *Cana-dian Journal of Information and Library Science* 22, no. 1 (April 1997): 1–18.

———. [William A. Crowley Jr.] "A Draft Research Model of the Research University Library: Exploring the Scholar–Librarian Partnership of Jaroslav Pelikan in *The Idea of the University: A Reexamination*." PhD diss., Ohio University, 1995.

———. "Dumping the 'Library.'" *Library Journal*, July 1998, 48–49.

———. "The Suicide of the Public Librarian." *Library Journal*, April 15, 2003, 48–49.

———. "Tacit Knowledge, Tacit Ignorance, and the Future of Academic Librarianship." *College and Research Libraries* 62, no. 6 (November 2001): 565–84.

Crowley, Bill, and Deborah Ginsberg. "Intracultural Reciprocity, Information Ethics, and the Survival of Librarianship in the Twenty-First Century." In *Ethics and Electronic Information: A Festschrift for Stephen Almagno*, ed. Barbara Rockenbach and Tom Mendina, 94–107. Jefferson, NC: McFarland, 2003.

Cuban, Larry. *How Scholars Trumped Teachers: Change without Reform in University Curriculum, Teaching, and Research, 1890–1990*. New York: Teachers College Press, 1999.

Cuvillier, Armand. "Preface to the French Edition of 1955." In Emile Durkheim, *Pragmatism and Sociology*. Trans. J. C. Whitehouse. Ed. John B. Allcock. Cambridge: Cambridge University Press, 1983.

Dalton, Peter, Glen Mynott, and Michael Shoolbred. "Barriers to Career Development within the LIS Profession." *Library Review* 49, no. 6 (2000): 271–76.

Dan-Cohen, Meir. "Listeners and Eavesdroppers: Substantive Legal Theory and Its Audience," *University of Colorado Law Review* (1992): 569–94.

Dewey. John. *Art as Experience*. 1934. Reprint. New York: Capricorn Books, 1958.

———. "A Common Faith." In *John Dewey: The Later Works, 1925–1953, vol. 9, 1933–1934*, ed. Jo Ann Boydston. Carbondale: Southern Illinois University Press, 1989.

———. "Context and Thought." In *John Dewey: The Later Works, 1925–1953, vol. 9, 1931–1932*, ed. Jo Ann Boydston. Carbondale: Southern Illinois University Press, 1985.

———. *Logic: The Theory of Inquiry*. In *John Dewey: The Later Works, 1925–1953, vol. 12, 1938*, ed. Jo Ann Boydston. Carbondale: Southern Illinois University Press, 1986.

Diesing, Paul. *How Does Social Science Work? Reflections on Practice*. Pittsburgh: University of Pittsburgh Press, 1991.

Douglas, Gretchen V. "Professor Librarian: A Model of the Teaching Librarian of the Future." *Computers in Libraries* 19, no. 10 (November/December 1999).

Douglas, Mary. *How Institutions Think*. Syracuse, NY: Syracuse University Press, 1986.

Douglas, William O. Introduction to *Jane Addams: A Centennial Reader*. New York: Macmillan, 1960.

Doyle, Robert P. "Islamic Resources for Libraries." *ILA Reporter* 20, no. 6 (December 2002), 4–6.

Dreistadt, Roy. "An Analysis of the Use of Analogies and Metaphors in Science." *Journal of Psychology* 68, first half (January 1968): 97–116.

Dubin, Robert. *Theory Building*. Rev. ed. New York: Free Press, 1978.

Duran, Jane. "The Intersection of Pragmatism and Feminism." *Hypatia* 8, no. 2 (Spring 1993): 159–71.

Durkheim, Emile. *Pragmatism and Sociology*. Trans. J. C. Whitehouse, ed. John B. Allcock. Cambridge: Cambridge University Press, 1983.

Dyson, Lillie Seward. "Improving Reference Services: A Maryland Training Program Brings Positive Results." *Public Libraries* 31 (September/October 1992): 284–89.

"Earned Degrees Conferred, 2000–2001." *Chronicle of Higher Education* 50, no. 1 (August 29, 2003): 19.

Eliot, Charles W. "The New Education." *Atlantic Monthly* 23 (1869): 203–20, 358–67.

Elshtain, Jean Bethke. "Jane Addams and the Social Claim." *Public Interest* 145 (Fall 2002): 82–92.

Farrell, Elizabeth R. "Phoenix's Unusual Way of Crafting Courses: The For-Profit Giant Uses a Systematic Grid and a Guy Named 'Joe' to Set Curriculum."

Chronicle of Higher Education 49, no. 23 (February 14, 2003). Available at http://chronicle.com/weekly/v49/i23/23a01001.htm (accessed December 30, 2003).

Fessler, Vera. "Consulting Products and Library Processes." *Library Hi Tech* 8, no. 2 (1991): 107–8. Part of "Library Automation Consultants: Current Realities and Issues," a forum edited by Edwin M. Cortez.

Fidel, Raya. "The Case Study Method: A Case Study." In J. D. Glazier and R. R. Powell, eds., *Qualitative Research in Information Management* 37–50. Englewood, CO: Libraries Unlimited, 1992. Reprinted from *Library and Information Science Research* 6 (1984): 273–88.

Figler, Howard. "Succeeding in the Nonacademic Job Market." In English Showalter et al., *The MLA Guide to the Job Search: A Handbook for Departments and for PhDs and PhD Candidates in English and Foreign Languages*, 75–101. New York: Modern Language Association of America, 1996.

Fine, Sara. "Reference and Resources: The Human Side." *Journal of Academic Librarianship* 21, no. 1 (1995): 17–20.

Fischer, Steven Roger. *A History of Language*. London: Reaktion, 1999.

Gallagher, H. M. "Dr. Osborn's 1941 'The Crisis in Cataloging': A Shift in Thought toward American Pragmatism." *Cataloging and Classification Quarterly* 12, nos. 3/4 (1991): 3–33.

Gers, Ralph, and Lillie J. Seward. "Improving Reference Performance: Results of a Statewide Study." *Library Journal* 110 (November 1, 1985): 32–35.

Gerth, H. H., and C. Wright Mills. "Introduction: The Man and His Work." In *From Max Weber: Essays in Sociology*, trans. and ed. H. H. Gerth and C. Wright Mills, 3–74. New York: Oxford University Press, 1946.

Glaser, Barney G., and Anselm L. Strauss. *The Discovery of Grounded Theory: Strategies for Qualitative Research*. New York: Aldine de Gruyter, 1967.

Glassick, Charles E., Mary Taylor Huber, and Gene I. Maeroff. *Scholarship Assessed: Evaluation of the Professoriate*. San Francisco: Jossey-Bass, 1997.

Glazier, Jack D., and Ronald R. Powell, eds. *Qualitative Research in Information Management*. Englewood, CO: Libraries Unlimited, 1992.

Goranzon, Bo, and Magnus Florin, eds. *Skill and Education: Reflection and Experience*. London: Springer-Verlag, 1992.

Gorman, Michael. *Our Enduring Values: Librarianship in the Twenty-First Century*. Chicago: American Library Association, 2002.

———. "A Profession That Looks Like America." *SRRT Newsletter*, December 2003, 2.

Graff, Gerald. "Introduction: Public Intellectual and the Future of Graduate Education." *Minnesota Review*, nos. 50–51 (Spring and Fall 1998): 161–63.

Gramsci, Antonio. *Selections from the Prison Notebooks of Antonio Gramsci*. Ed. and trans. Quintin Hoare and Geoffrey Nowell Smith. New York: International, 1971.

Grant, E. B., and M. J. Gregory, "Tacit Knowledge, the Life Cycle, and International Manufacturing Transfer." *Technology Analysis and Strategic Management* 9, no. 2 (1997): 149–61.

Grenz, Stanley J. *A Primer on Postmodernism*. Grand Rapids, MI: Eerdmans, 1996.

Gulbenkian Commission on the Restructuring of the Social Sciences. *Opening the Social Sciences: Report of the Gulbenkian Commission on the Restructuring of the Social Sciences*. Stanford, CA: Stanford University Press, 1996.

Haack, Susan. "The Best Man for the Job May Be a Woman." *Partisan Review* 65, no. 2 (1998): 214–20.

———. "Concern for Truth: What It Means, Why It Matters." *Annals of the New York Academy of Science* 775 (1996): 57–63.

———. "Puzzling Out Science." *Academic Questions* 8, no. 2 (Spring 1995): 20–31.

Halpern, Sydney Ann. "Professional Schools in the American University." In *The Academic Profession: National, Disciplinary, and Institutional Settings*, ed. Burton R. Clark, 304–30. Berkeley: University of California Press, 1987.

Hannigan, Jane Anne. "A Feminist Standpoint for Library and Information Science Education." *Journal of Education for Library and Information Science* 36, no. 4 (Fall 1994): 297–319.

Hansen, Olaf. "Introduction: Affinity and Ambivalence." In *Randolph Bourne: The Radical Will: Selected Writings, 1911–1918*, ed. Olaf Hansen, 18–62. 1977. Reprint. Berkeley: University of California Press, 1992.

Hardy, Cynthia: *The Politics of Collegiality: Retrenchment Strategies in Canadian Universities*. Montreal: McGill-Queen's University Press, 1996.

Harris, Michael H. "The Dialectic of Defeat: Antimonies in Research in Library and Information Science." *Library Trends* 34 (Winter 1986): 515–31.

Harris, Michael H., and Masaru Itoga. "Becoming Critical: For a Theory of Purpose and Necessity in American Librarianship." In Charles R. McClure and Peter Hernon, eds., *Library and Information Science Research: Perspectives and Strategies for Improvement*. (Norwood, NJ: Ablex, 1991), 347–57.

Harris, Roma M. *Librarianship: The Erosion of a Woman's Profession*. Norwood, NJ: Ablex, 1992.

Haskins, Charles Homer. *The Rise of the Universities*. New York: Henry Holt, 1923.

Hausknecht, Murray. "At First Glance: The Role of the Intellectual." *Dissent* 44, no. 2 (Spring 1986): 131–32, 160.

Hennen, Thomas J. "Great American Public Libraries: The 2003 HAPLR Rankings." *American Libraries*, October 2003, 44–48.

Heresniak, E. J. "Adventures in Cyberspace: The Business of Education—A Higher Calling? For Higher Profits, Maybe." *Across the Board*, November/December 2002, 61–62.

Hernon, Peter. "Research in Library and Information Science: Reflections on the Journal Literature." *Journal of Academic Librarianship* 35, no. 4 (July 1999).

Hewitt. Joe A. "The Role of the Library Administrator in Improving LIS Research." In Charles R. McClure and Peter Hernon, eds., *Library and Information Science Research: Perspectives and Strategies for Improvement* (Norwood, NJ: Ablex, 1991), 163–78.

Holland, John H., Keith J. Holyoak, Richard E. Nisbett, and Paul R. Thagard. *Induction: Processes of Inference, Learning, and Discovery*. Cambridge, MA: MIT Press, 1987.

Hollis, Martin. *The Philosophy of Social Science: An Introduction*. Cambridge: Cambridge University Press, 1994.

Holmes, Christine. "The Dirty Little Secret." *Alum News* (CSU School of Library and Information Science, San Jose State University), Fall 2003, 7.

Hook, Sidney. *Philosophy and Public Policy*. Carbondale: Southern Illinois University Press, 1980.

Horvath, Joseph A., George B. Forsythe, Richard C. Bullis, Patrick J. Sweeney, Wendy M. Williams, Jeffrey A McNally, John A. Wattendorf, and Robert J. Sternberg. "Experience, Knowledge, and Military Leadership." In *Tacit Knowledge in Professional Practice: Researcher and Practitioner Perspectives*, ed. Robert J. Sternberg and Joseph A. Horvath, 39–57. Mahwah, NJ: Lawrence Erlbaum Associates, 1999.

Horvath, Joseph A., George B. Forsythe, Patrick J. Sweeney, Jeffrey A. McNally, John Wattendorf, Wendy M. Williams, and Robert J. Sternberg. *Tacit Knowledge in Military Leadership: Evidence from Officer Interviews*. Technical Report 1018. Alexandria, VA: U.S. Army Research Institute for the Behavioral and Social Sciences, 1994.

House Committee on Science and Technology, Task Force on Science Policy. *Research Policies for the Social and Behavioral Sciences*. Report prepared by the Library of Congress Congressional Research Service, 99th Cong., 2d sess., 1986, *Science Policy Study Background Report No. 6*.

Houser, L., and Alvin M. Schrader. *The Search for a Scientific Profession: Library Science Education in the U.S. and Canada*. Metuchen, NJ: Scarecrow Press, 1978.

Huberman, Michael. "How Well Does Educational Research Really Travel?" *Educational Researcher* 16, no. 1 (January/February 1987): 5–13.

Intner, Shelia S. "From the Editor's Desk: Ah, Yes, the Old Practice vs. Theory Debate." *Technicalities* 15, no. 10 (October 1995): 1–3.

"Introduction: Pragmatism—What's the Use?" *Hedgehog Review* 3, no. 3 (Fall 2001): 5–8.

James, William. "Absolutism and Empiricism." In *Essays in Radical Empiricism*, 266–79. 1912. Reprint. Lincoln: University of Nebraska Press, 1996.

———. "The Ph.D. Octopus." In *Memories and Studies*. 1911. Reprint. New York: Greenwood, 1968. Article first published in the *Harvard Monthly*, March 1903.

———. *"Pragmatism" and "The Meaning of Truth."* 1907. Reprint. Cambridge, MA: Harvard University Press, 1975.

———. *The Varieties of Religious Experience*. 1902. Reprint. Middlesex, UK: Penguin, 1982.

———. "The Will to Believe." In *The Writings of William James: A Comprehensive Edition*, ed. John J. McDermott, 717–35. Chicago: University of Chicago Press, 1977.

———. "A World of Pure Experience." In *Essays in Radical Empiricism*, 39–91. 1912. Reprint. Lincoln: University of Nebraska Press, 1996.

Janik, Allan. "Why Is Wittgenstein Important?" In *Skill and Education: Reflection and Experience*, ed. Bo Goranzon and Magnus Florin, 33–40. London: Springer-Verlag, 1992.

Jarvis, Peter. *The Practitioner-Researcher: Developing Theory from Practice*. San Francisco: Jossey-Bass, 1999.

Jenkins, Philip. "Bringing the Loathsome to Light." *Chronicle of Higher Education* 48, no. 25 (March 1, 2002). Available at http://chronicle.com/weekly/v48/i25/25b01601.htm (accessed April 4, 2002).

Jost, Kenneth. "Libraries and the Internet." *CQ Researcher* 11, no. 21 (June 1, 2001): 465–68.

Kaplan, Abraham. *The Conduct of Inquiry: Methodology for Behavioral Science*. San Francisco: Chandler, 1964.

———. *The New World of Philosophy*. New York: Random House, 1961.

Keller, George. "Academic Duty: The Role of the Intellectual." *ASHE Newsletter* 16, no. 2 (Winter 2002): 3.

Kerr, Clark. *The Uses of the University*. 4th ed. Cambridge, MA: Harvard University Press, 1995.

Kertzer, David I. *Ritual, Politics, and Power*. New Haven, CT: Yale University Press, 1988.

Kloppenberg, James T. "Pragmatism: An Old Name for Some New Ways of Thinking?" *Journal of American History* 83, no. 1 (June 1996): 100–138.

Knorr, Karen D. "Producing and Reproducing Knowledge: Descriptive or Constructive? Towards a Model of Research Production." *Social Science Information* 16, no. 6 (1977): 669–96.

Koenig, Michael E. D. "Buttering the Toast Evenly: Library School Closings at Columbia and Chicago Are Tragic, but They Don't Have to Signal a Trend." *American Libraries,* September 1990, 723–26.

Konvitz, Milton R. Introduction to *John Dewey: The Later Works, 1925–1953, vol. 9, 1933–1934*, ed. Jo Ann Boydston, xi–xxxii. Carbondale: Southern Illinois University Press, 1989.

Kronman, Anthony T. *The Lost Lawyer: Failing Ideals of the Legal Profession.* Cambridge, MA: Belknap Press/Harvard University Press, 1993.

Kuhn, Thomas S. "Logic of Discovery or Psychology of Research?" In *Criticism and the Growth of Knowledge,* ed. Imre Lakatos and Alan Musgrave, 1–23. Cambridge: Cambridge University Press, 1970.

———. *The Structure of Scientific Revolutions.* 2d ed., enl. Chicago: University of Chicago Press, 1970.

Landrum, Joe, and Dorothy White. "Intellectual Freedom in Public Libraries." *Louisiana Libraries* 62 no. 2 (Fall 2001): 15–16.

Laurence, David. "From the Editor." *ADE Bulletin,* no. 107 (Spring 1994): 1–5.

Levett, John. "A Critical Nexus: The Link between Research and Practice." In *Public Librarianship: A Critical Nexus: Proceedings of the Public Library Research Forum, Monash University, 8 April 1994,* ed. B. J. McMullin and Radha Rasmussen, 1–6. Melbourne, Australia: Ancora Press, 1995.

Light, Richard J., Judith D. Singer, and John B. Willett. *By Design: Planning Research on Higher Education.* Cambridge, MA: Harvard University Press, 1990.

Lipset, Seymour Martin. *American Exceptionalism: A Double-Edged Sword.* New York: Norton, 1996.

Lovejoy, Arthur O. *The Thirteen Pragmatisms and Other Essays.* Baltimore: Johns Hopkins University Press, 1963.

Lovell, Terry. "Feminist Social Theory." In Turner, Bryan S., ed., *The Blackwell Companion to Social Theory,* 307–39. Oxford: Blackwell, 1996.

Lucas, Christopher J. *American Higher Education: A History.* New York: St. Martin's, 1994.

Lynd, Robert S. *Knowledge for What? The Place of Social Science in American Culture.* Princeton, NJ: Princeton University Press, 1948.

Lyotard, Jean-Francois. *The Postmodern Condition: A Report on Knowledge.* Trans. Geoff Bennington and Brian Massumi. 1979. Reprint. Minneapolis: University of Minnesota Press, 1984.

MacIntyre, Alasdair. *Whose Justice? Which Rationality?* Notre Dame, IN: University of Notre Dame Press, 1988.

Mahowald, Mary B. "What Classical American Philosophers Missed: Jane Addams, Critical Pragmatism, and Cultural Feminism." *Journal of Value Inquiry* 31, no. 1 (March 1997): 39–54.

Marsden, George M. "Theology and the University: Newman's Idea and Current Realities." In John Henry Newman, *The Idea of a University,* ed. Frank M. Turner, 302–17. New Haven, CT: Yale University Press, 1996.

Martin, Robert S. "Returning to the Center: Libraries, Knowledge, and Education." Address to the annual meeting of the Colorado Library Association, October 29, 2001. Available at http://www.imls.gov/scripts/text.cgi?/whatsnew/current/sp102901.htm (accessed April 24, 2003).

Marty, Martin E., with Jonathan Moore. *Education, Religion, and the Common Good: Advancing a Distinctly American Conversation about Religion's Role in Our Shared Life*. San Francisco: Jossey-Bass, 2000.

Maryland State Department of Education, Division of Library Development and Services. *1994 Maryland Statewide Reference Survey: Statewide Objectives, Facts, and Figures*. Baltimore: Division of Library Development and Services, 1995. Leaflet.

———. *1994 Statewide Reference Survey: Overall Conclusions*. Baltimore: Division of Library Development and Services, n.d. Leaflet.

[Master, Melissa.] "A Sharper Look." *Across the Board* 40, no. 6 (November/December 2003). Available at http://newfirstsearch.oclc.org/images/WSPL/wsppdfl/HTML/04816/QRGWD/TF6.HTM (accessed January 12, 2004).

McCarthy, Timothy G. *The Catholic Tradition: Before and after Vatican II, 1878–1993*. Chicago: Loyola University Press, 1994.

McClure, Charles R. "Increasing the Usefulness of Research for Library Managers: Propositions, Issues, and Strategies." *Library Trends* 38, no. 2 (Fall 1989): 280–94.

McClure, Charles R., and Ann Bishop. "The Status of Research in Library/Information Science: Guarded Optimism." *College and Research Libraries* 50, no. 2 (March 1989): 127–43.

McClure, Charles R., and Peter Hernon, eds. *Library and Information Science Research: Perspectives and Strategies for Improvement*. Norwood, NJ: Ablex, 1991.

McMurtrie, Beth. "Accreditors Revamp Policies to Stress Student Learning: Agencies Say They Are Responding to Years of Complaints about Regulations and Paperwork." *Chronicle of Higher Education* 46, no. 44 (July 7, 2000): A29–A31.

———. "Silence, Not Confrontation, over the 'Mandatum.'" *Chronicle of Higher Education* 48, no. 40 (June 14, 2002): A10–A11.

———. "Vatican Backs Catholic-College Rules That Spur Fears over Academic Freedom." *Chronicle of Higher Education* 46, no. 41 (June 16, 2000): A18.

Mellon, Constance Ann. *Naturalist Inquiry for Library Science: Methods and Applications for Research, Evaluation, and Teaching*. New York: Greenwood, 1990.

Menand, Louis, ed. *Pragmatism: A Reader*. New York: Vintage, 1997.

Merton, Robert K. *Social Research and the Practicing Professions*. Ed. Aaron Rosenblatt and Thomas F. Gieryn. Cambridge, MA: ABT Books, 1982.

———. *Social Theory and Social Structure*. Enl. ed. New York: Free Press, 1968.

———. "The Unanticipated Consequences of Purposive Social Action." *American Sociological Review* 1 (1936): 894–904.

Meyer, Samuel, ed. *Dewey and Russell: An Exchange*. New York: Philosophical Library, n.d.

Mill, John Stuart. "Introduction: An Appraisal of Volume I of *Democracy in America*, Published in the London (and Westminster) Review in 1835 on the Occasion of the First Appearance of the English Translation." In Alexis de Tocqueville, *Democracy in America*, vol. 1. New York: Schocken Books, 1961.

———. "Introduction: An Appraisal of Volume II of *Democracy in America*, Published in the *Edinburgh Review* in 1840 on the Occasion of the First Appearance of the English Translation." In Alexis de Tocqueville, *Democracy in America*, vol. 2. New York: Schocken Books, 1961.

Miller, D. W. "In the Nation's Battle against Drug Abuse, Scholars Have More Insight Than Influence." *Chronicle of Higher Education* 46, no. 33 (April 21, 2000): A19–A22.

———. "Measuring the Role of 'the Faith Factor' in Social Change." *Chronicle of Higher Education* 46, no. 14 (November 26, 1999): A21–A22.

Mitroff, Ian I. "The Myth of Objectivity; or, Why Science Needs a New Psychology of Science." *Management Science: Application* 18 (1972): B613–B618.

Molotch, Harvey. "Going Out." *Sociological Forum* 9 (1994): 221–39.

Moore, Deirdre. "Consultancy: A Career Option for Professional Librarians." *Argus* 34, no. 3 (September/December 1995).

Myers, Gerald E. *William James: His Life and Thought*. New Haven, CT: Yale University Press, 1986.

Nash, Dennison. "The Ethnologist as Stranger: An Essay in the Sociology of Knowledge." *Southwestern Journal of Anthropology* 19 (1963): 149–67.

Neustadt, Richard E., and Ernest R. May. *Thinking in Time: The Uses of History for Decision-Makers*. New York: Free Press, 1986.

Newman, John Henry. *The Idea of a University*. 1873. Reprint. Notre Dame, IN: University of Notre Dame Press, 1982.

———. *The Idea of a University*. Ed. Frank N. Turner. New Haven, CT: Yale University Press, 1996 (published in various editions and formats since 1852).

O'Connor, Daniel, and J. Philip Mulvaney. "LIS Faculty Research and Expectations of the Academic Culture versus the Needs of the Practitioner." *Journal of Education for Library and Information Science* 37 (Fall 1996): 306–16.

Ohio Board of Regents. "Board of Regents Recommends Temporary Limits on Doctoral Program Enrollments." Press release January 13, 1995, at http://www.regents.state.oh.us/newsitems/news5.html (accessed January 11, 2000).

———. "Board Resolution 1/13/95—Ohio Board of Regents—Agenda Item 8." At http:www.regents.state.oh.us/newitems/news4.html (accessed January 11, 2000).

———. "Regents' Actions." Press release, July 17, 1998. Available at http://www.regents.state.oh.us/bdmeet/jul98/nr071798.html (accessed January 11, 2000).

———. "Regents Approve Restructured Doctoral Programs in Educational Administration and English." Press release, April 11, 1997. Available at http://www.regents.state.oh.us/newsitems.news153html (accessed January 11, 2000).

———. *Report of the Commission on Graduate Education: July 17, 1998.*

———. *Report of the Regents' Advisory Committee on Faculty Workload Standards and Guidelines: February 18, 1994.* Available at http://summit.bor.ohio.gov.plandocs.workload.html (accessed March 24, 1999).

Olsen, Florence. "Phoenix Rises: The University's Online Program Attracts Students, Profits, and Praise." *Chronicle of Higher Education* 49, no. 10 (November 1, 2002). Available at http://chronicle.com/weekly/v49/i10/10a02901.htm (accessed December 30, 2003).

Olson, Hope A. "The Feminist and the Emperor's New Clothes: Feminist Deconstruction as a Critical Methodology for Library and Information Studies." *Library and Information Science Research* 19, no. 2 (1997): 181–98.

O'Neill, Ann L. "Library Education in the West." *Colorado Libraries*, Summer 2003. Available at http://vnweb.hwwilsonweb.com/hww/results/results_single.jhtml?nn=9 (accessed November 11, 2003). First delivered by O'Neill, the director of the ALA Office of Accreditation, as remarks to the Colorado Association of Libraries annual conference in October 2002.

Owen, Whitney J. "In Defense of the Least Publishable Unit." *Chronicle of Higher Education* (February 13, 2004): C1, C4.

Owens, Robert G. "Methodological Rigor in Naturalistic Inquiry: Some Issues and Answers." *Educational Administration Quarterly* 18 (Spring 1982): 1–21.

Pawley, Christine. "Hegemony's Handmaid? The Library and Information Studies Curriculum from a Class Perspective." *Library Quarterly* 68, no. 2 (April 1998): 123–44.

Peirce, Charles Sanders. "How to Make Our Ideas Clear." 1878. In *Pragmatism: A Reader*, ed. Louis Menand, 26–48. New York: Vintage, 1997.

Pelikan, Jaroslav. *The Idea of the University: A Reexamination.* New Haven, CT: Yale University Press, 1992.

Peters, F. E. *Judaism, Christianity, and Islam: The Classical Texts and Their Interpretation.* Princeton, NJ: Princeton University Press, 1990.

Pierce, Sydney J. "Dead Germans and the Theory of Librarianship." *American Libraries*, September 1992, 641–43.

Platt, Jennifer. "Evidence and Proof in Documentary Research 1: Some Specific Problems of Documentary Research." *Sociological Review* 29, no. 1 (1981): 31–52.

Polansky, Norman A. "There Is Nothing So Practical as a Good Theory." *Child Welfare* 65 (January/February 1986): 3–15.

Polanyi, Michael. *The Tacit Dimension*. Garden City, NY: Doubleday Anchor, 1967.

Polkinghorne, John. *Belief in God in an Age of Science*. New Haven, CT: Yale University Press, 1998.

———. *Quarks, Chaos, and Christianity: Questions to Science and Religion*. New York: Crossroad, 1994.

———. *Science and Theology: An Introduction*. Minneapolis: Fortress Press, 1998.

Porterfield, Amanda. *The Transformation of American Religion: The Story of a Late Twentieth-Century Awakening*. Oxford: Oxford University Press, 2001.

Postel, Danny. "Sidney Hook, an Intellectual Street Fighter, Reconsidered." *Chronicle of Higher Education* 49, no. 11 (November 8, 2001): A19.

Prado, C. G. *The Limits of Pragmatism*. Atlantic Highlands, NJ: Humanities Press International, 1987.

Prasad, Pushkala, and Paula J. Caproni. "Critical Theory in the Management Classroom: Engaging Power, Ideology, and Praxis." *Journal of Management Education* 21, no. 3 (August 1997): 284–91.

Putnam, Robert D. *Bowling Alone: The Collapse and Revival of American Community*. New York: Simon and Schuster/Touchstone: 2000.

Quinn, Philip L. "Philosophy of Religion." In *The Cambridge Dictionary of Philosophy*, ed. Robert Audi, 607–11. Cambridge: Cambridge University Press, 1995.

Ratcliffe, John W. "Notions of Validity in Qualitative Research Methodology." *Knowledge: Creation, Diffusion, Utilization* 5 (1983): 147–67.

"Reading Assignments: Can We Persuade Students They Matter?" *Teaching Professor*, February 2003, 3.

Redding, W. Charles. Foreword to Sue DeWine, *The Consultant's Craft: Improving Organizational Communication*, xxiii–xxvii. New York: St. Martin's, 1994.

Reis, Richard M. "When Faculty Consulting Helps—and When It Hurts—Your Career." *Chronicle of Higher Education*, "Career Network Catalyst," October 22, 1999, http://chronicle.com.jobs/99/10/99102202c.htm (accessed June 22, 2000).

Riedner, Rachel, and Noreen O'Connor, eds. "Activism and the Academy." *Minnesota Review*, nos. 50–51 (Spring and Fall 1998).

Riggs, Donald E. "Writing for the LIS Profession: Introductory Comments and Questions." In *How to Get Published in LIS Journals: A Practical Guide*, ed. Lisa Janicke Hinchliffe and Jennifer Dorner, 2. San Diego, CA: Elsevier Library Connect, 2003.

Robbins, Jan C. "Social Functions of Scientific Communication." *IEEE Transactions on Professional Communication* PC-16 (September 1973): 131–35, 181.

Rogers, Everett M. *Diffusion of Innovations*. 5th ed. New York: Free Press, 2003.

Roof, Wade Clark. *Spiritual Marketplace: Baby Boomers and the Remaking of American Religion*. Princeton, NJ: Princeton University Press, 1999.

Rorty, Richard. "Philosophy and the Future." In *Rorty and Pragmatism: The Philosopher Responds to His Critics*, ed. Herman J. Saatkamp Jr., 197–205. Nashville, TN: Vanderbilt University Press, 1995.

Rosenau, Pauline Marie. *Post-Modernism and the Social Sciences: Insights, Inroads, and Intrusions*. Princeton, NJ: Princeton University Press, 1992.

Rubin, Herbert J., and Irene S. Rubin. *Qualitative Interviewing: The Art of Hearing Data*. Thousand Oaks, CA: Sage, 1995.

Rubin, Richard E. *Foundations of Library and Information Science*. Updated version. New York: Neal-Schuman, 2000.

Rudolph, Frederick. *The American College and University: A History*. 1962. Reprint. Athens: University of Georgia Press, 1990.

———. *Curriculum: A History of the American Undergraduate Course of Study since 1636*. San Francisco: Jossey-Bass, 1977.

Russell, Bertrand. *A History of Western Philosophy*. New York: Simon and Schuster, 1945.

Ryle, Gilbert. *The Concept of Mind*. 1949. Reprint. London: Hutchinson, 1958.

Sachedina, Abdulaziz. "Political Islam and the Hegemony of Globalization: A Response to Peter Berger." *Hedgehog Review* 4, no. 2 (Summer 2002): 21–29.

Sannwald, William. "Understanding Organizational Culture." *Library Administration and Management* 14, no. 1 (Winter 2002): 8–14. Available at http://vnweb.hwwilsonweb.com/hww/results/results_single.jhtml?nn=17 (accessed January 7, 2002).

Schleihagen, Barbara. "Intellectual Freedom and Libraries: German Perspectives." *IFLA Journal* 28, no. 4 (2002): 185–89.

Schon, Donald A. *Educating the Reflective Practitioner*. San Francisco: Jossey-Bass, 1987.

Schutz, Alfred. "The Stranger: An Essay in Social Psychology." In *Collected Papers II: Social Theory*, ed. A. Brodersen, 91–105. The Hague: Martinus Nijhoff, 1964.

Scott, Robert A., and Arnold R. Shore. *Why Sociology Does Not Apply: A Study of the Use of Sociology in Public Policy*. New York: Elsevier, 1979.

Searing, Susan E. "Women's Studies for a 'Women's' Profession: Theory and Practice in Library Science." In *The Knowledge Explosion: Generations of Feminist Scholarship*, ed. Cheris Kramarae and Dale Spender, 225–34. New York: Teachers College Press, 1992.

Sexton, Mark. "Why a Consultant?" *Scholarly Publishing* 20, no. 2 (January 1989): 89–92.

Shalin, Dmitri N. "Critical Theory and the Pragmatist Challenge." *American Journal of Sociology* 98, no. 2 (September 1992): 237–79.

———. "Modernity, Postmodernism, and Pragmatist Inquiry: An Introduction."
Symbolic Interaction 16, no. 4 (Winter 1993): 303–32.

Shearer, Kenneth. "The Impact of Research on Librarianship." *Journal of Education for Librarianship* 20, no. 2 (1979): 114–28.

Sherkat, Darren E., and Christopher G. Ellison. "Recent Developments and Current Controversies in the Sociology of Religion." *Annual Review of Sociology* 25 (1999): 363–94.

Shils, Edward. "Social Science as Public Opinion." In *The Calling of Sociology and Other Essays on the Pursuit of Learning*. Chicago: University of Chicago Press, 1980.

Shusterman, Richard. "The Perils of Making Philosophy a Lingua Americana." *Chronicle of Higher Education* 46, no. 49 (August 11, 2000): B4–B5.

Silver, Linda R. "Up for Discussion: Judging Judaica." *School Library Journal,* January 1, 2002. Available at http://slj.reviewsnews.com/index.asp?layout= articlePrintandarticleID=CA188165 (accessed July 5, 2003).

Simmel, Georg. "The Stranger." In *The Sociology of Georg Simmel,* ed. Kurt H. Wolff, 402–4. Glencoe, IL: Free Press, 1950.

Simon, Herbert A. *Administrative Behavior: A Study of Decision-Making Processes in Administrative Organizations.* 4th ed. New York: Free Press, 1997.

Singer, Benjamin D. "The Criterial Crisis of the Academic World." *Sociological Inquiry* 50 (1989): 127–43.

Slaughter, Sheila, and Larry L. Leslie. *Academic Capitalism: Politics, Policies, and the Entrepreneurial University.* Baltimore: Johns Hopkins University Press, 1997.

Smart, Barry. "Postmodern Social Theory." In Turner, Bryan S., ed., *The Blackwell Companion to Social Theory*, 396–428. Oxford: Blackwell, 1996.

Smith, Anthony, and Frank Webster. "Changing Ideas of the University." In *The Postmodern University? Contested Visions of Higher Education in Society*, ed. Anthony Smith and Frank Webster, 1–14. Buckingham, UK: Society for Research into Higher Education/Open University Press, 1997.

Smolin, Lee. *The Life of the Cosmos.* New York: Oxford University Press, 1997.

Snelson, Pamela, and S. Anita Talar. "Content Analysis of ACRL Conference Papers." *College and Research Libraries* 52 (1991): 466–72.

Sparanese, Ann. "Activist Librarianship." *Progressive Librarian* 22 (Summer 2003). Available at http://www.libr.org/PL/22_Sparanese.html (accessed January 15, 2004).

Spivey, Mark A. "Feminist Scholarship: Implications for Information Management and Research." *Journal of Academic Librarianship* 21, no. 3 (May 1995): 159–66.

Steffen, Nicolle O. "Challenging Times: Challenges to Materials in Colorado Public Libraries." *Colorado Libraries* 28, no. 3 (Fall 2002): 9–12.

Stephan, Sandy, Ralph Gers, Lillie Seward, Nancy Bolin, and Jim Partridge. "Reference Breakthrough in Maryland." *Public Libraries* 27 (Winter 1988): 202–3.

Sternberg, Robert J., Richard K. Wagner, Wendy M. Williams, and Joseph A. Horvath. "Testing Common Sense." *American Psychologist* 50 (1995): 912–27.

Stieg, Margaret. "The Closing of Library Schools: Darwinism at the University." *Library Quarterly* 61, no. 3 (July 1991): 266–72. Included as part of the issue section "Perspectives on the Elimination of Graduate Programs in Library and Information Studies: A Symposium."

Strauss, Anselm L. *Qualitative Analysis for Social Scientists.* Cambridge: Cambridge University Press, 1987.

Swanson, Don R. Introduction to *The Intellectual Foundations of Library Education: The Twenty-Ninth Annual Conference of the Graduate Library School, July 6–8, 1964*, ed. Don R. Swanson, 1–6. Chicago: University of Chicago Press, 1965.

Swartz, Louis H. "Implicit Knowledge (Tacit Knowing), Connoisseurship, and the Common Law Tradition." Paper presented at the faculty workshop of the University at Buffalo School of Law, Buffalo, NY, April 11, 1997.

Tabboni, Simonetta. "The Stranger and Modernity: From Equality of Rights to Recognition of Difference." *Thesis Eleven* 43 (1995): 17–27.

Tempte, Thomas. "The Practical Intellect and Master-Apprenticeship: Some Reflections on Cross-Contacts between Theory and Practice." Trans. Angela E. Andegren. In *Skill, Technology, and Enlightenment: On Practical Philosophy*, ed. Bo Goranzon, 11–17 (London: Springer-Verlag, 1995).

Tepper, Michele. "Doctor Outsider." *Minnesota Review*, nos. 50–51 (Spring/Fall 1988): 257–62.

Terenzini, Patrick. T. "Presidential Address: Rediscovering Roots: Public Policy and Higher Education Research." *Review of Higher Education* 20, no. 1 (1995), 5–13.

Therborn, Goran. "Critical Theory and the Legacy of Twentieth-Century Marxism." In Turner, Bryan S., *The Blackwell Companion to Social Theory*, 53–82. Oxford: Blackwell, 1996.

Thorpe, Catherine. "School of Library Service to Close—Trustees: School to Be Phased Out in Two Years." *Columbia Summer Spectator*, June 6, 1990.

Tinder, Glenn. "Review Essay: At the End of Pragmatism." Review of *The Promise of Pragmatism: Modernism and the Crisis of Knowledge*, by John Patrick Diggins. *First Things* 56 (October 1995): 43–46.

Toulmin, Stephen. "On from 'The Two Cultures.'" In *Skill and Education: Reflection and Experience*, ed. Bo Goranzon and Magnus Florin, 249–58. London: Springer-Verlag, 1992.

Turner, Bryan S. "The Nature of the Social." In Bryan S. Turner, ed., *The Blackwell Companion to Social Theory*, 303–6. Oxford: Blackwell, 1996.

Turner, Bryan S., ed. *The Blackwell Companion to Social Theory*. Oxford: Blackwell, 1996.

Underhill, Paco. *Why We Buy: The Science of Shopping*. New York: Simon and Schuster, 1999.

Van House, Nancy A. "Assessing the Quality and Impact of LIS Research." In Charles R. McClure and Peter Hernon, eds., *Library and Information Science Research: Perspectives and Strategies for Improvement* (Norwood, NJ: Ablex, 1991), 85–100.

Van House, Nancy A., and Thomas A. Childers. "The Use of Public Library Roles for Effectiveness Evaluation." *Library and Information Science Research* 16 (1994): 41–58.

Van Maanen, John. "Golden Passports: Managerial Socialization and Graduate Education." *Review of Higher Education* 6 (Summer 1983): 435–55.

——. "Reclaiming Qualitative Methods for Organizational Research: A Preface." *Administrative Science Quarterly* 24, no. 4 (December 1979): 520–26.

Veysey, Laurence R. *The Emergence of the American University*. Chicago: University of Chicago Press, 1965.

Waples, Douglas. "The Graduate Library School at Chicago." *Library Quarterly* 1 (1931): 26–36.

Warner, R. Stephen. "Approaching Religious Diversity: Barriers, Byways, and Beginnings." *Sociology of Religion* 59, no. 3 (Fall 1998): 193–215.

"The Way We Live Now Poll: Spirituality." *New York Times Magazine*, May 7, 2000, 84.

Weber, Max. "Science as a Vocation." In *From Max Weber: Essays in Sociology*, trans. and ed. H. H. Gerth and C. Wright Mills. New York: Oxford University Press, 1946.

Weiner, Stephen S. "Shipyards in the Desert." *Review of Higher Education* 10, no. 2 (Winter 1986): 159–64.

Wentz, Richard E. "The Merits of Professors Emeriti." *Chronicle of Higher Education* 48, no. 13 (December 14, 2001): B5.

Wessells, Mike. "Faith at the Front Desk: Spirituality and Patron Service." *American Libraries*, May 2003, 42–43.

West, Cornel. *The American Evasion of Philosophy: A Genealogy of Pragmatism*. Madison: University of Wisconsin Press, 1989.

West, Edwin G. *Higher Education in Canada: An Analysis*. Vancouver, BC: Fraser Institute, 1988.

Whitehead, Alfred North. *The Aims of Education and Other Essays*. New York: Free Press, 1929.

Whitson, Bill. "From the President: Do We Have a Future?" *CARL Newsletter*, September 1995, 1–2. Available at http://www.carl.acrl.org/Archives/NewsletterArchive/1995/news95-9pres.html.

Wiegand, Wayne A. "Misreading LIS Education." *Library Journal*, June 15, 1997, 36–38.

Williams, Malcolm, and Tim May. *Introduction to the Philosophy of Social Research*. London: University College London Press, 1996.

Williamson, C. C. "The Place of Research in Library Service." *Library Quarterly* 1, no. 1 (January 1931): 1–17.

Wilshire, Bruce. "The Breathtaking Intimacy of the Material World: William James's Last Thoughts." In *The Cambridge Companion to William James*, ed. Ruth Anna Putnam, 103–24. Cambridge: Cambridge University Press, 1997.

Wilson, Patrick. *Second-Hand Knowledge: An Inquiry into Cognitive Authority*. Westport, CT: Greenwood, 1983.

Wilson, Robin. "Supreme Court Says Ohio Can Bypass Collective Bargaining in Push to Raise Faculty Workloads." *Chronicle of Higher Education*. "Today's News," March 23, 1999, http://chronicle.com/daily/99/03/99032301n.htm (accessed March 24, 1999).

Winter, Michael. "Garlic, Vodka, and the Politics of Gender: Anti-Intellectualism in American Librarianship." *Progressive Librarian* 14 (Spring 1998). Available at http://www.libr.org/PL/14_Winter.html (accessed January 15, 2004).

Young, Robert B. *No Neutral Ground: Standing By the Values We Prize in Higher Education*. San Francisco: Jossey-Bass, 1997.

Zweizig, Douglas L. "The Secret Science: The Role of Consulting and LIS Research." In Charles R. McClure and Peter Hernon, eds., *Library and Information Science Research: Perspectives and Strategies for Improvement* (Norwood, NJ: Ablex, 1991), 202–13.

Index

academic librarians, research and, 151

academic mores and useful theory, 148

academic practitioners, 16, 129, 147; faculty-centered useful theory, 148; off-campus oriented useful theory, 148

academic world, fragmentation of, 5

Addams, Jane, vi, 60; Hull House, 60

Alinsky, Saul D.: faculty versus practitioners, 146–47; *Rules for Radicals: A Practical Primer for Realistic Radicals*, 146

American culture, maxims for understanding, 15–16, 24–25

American Library Association–accredited programs: role of expert judgment in accreditation process, 102; varying terminology for describing, 25–26

Americanization, defined, 201

analogy, use of, 35

analyses, self-reflective, 41

analytic philosophy. *See* logical empiricism

Argyris, Chris, and theories of action, 39

Aristotle, 95

Association for Library and Information Science Education (ALISE), 159

Association of College and Research Libraries (ACRL), misleading analyses of papers presented at conferences, 101–2

Barthes, Roland, 67

Berger, Peter, on modernity, secularization, and American religiosity, 185

Berry, John N., III: fielding reactions to "The Suicide of the Public Librarian," 119–23; on "information," 25; on practice versus theory, 164

"Beth," 1

"Blame the customer mentality" and lack of practitioner use of faculty research, 85

Booth, Wayne C., on fragmentation of academic world, 6, 10